New World,
New Roles

**Recent Titles in
Contributions in Women's Studies**

NEW WORLD, NEW ROLES

A Documentary History of Women in Pre-Industrial America

SYLVIA R. FREY
AND
MARIAN J. MORTON

CONTRIBUTIONS IN WOMEN'S STUDIES, NUMBER 65

GREENWOOD PRESS
NEW YORK · WESTPORT, CONNECTICUT · LONDON

Library of Congress Cataloging-in-Publication Data

Frey, Sylvia R., 1935–
New world, new roles.

(Contributions in women's studies, ISSN 0147–104X ; no. 65)
Bibliography: p.
Includes index.
1. Women—United States—History—17th century.
2. Women—United States—History—18th century.
3. Women—United States—Social conditions.
4. Family—United States—History—17th century.
5. Family—United States—History—18th century.
I. Morton, Marian J., 1937–   . II. Title.
III. Series.
HQ1416.F74   1986   305.4'0973   85–27159
ISBN 0–313–24896–6 (lib. bdg. : alk. paper)

Library of Congress Catalog Card Number: 85–27159
ISBN: 0–313–24896–6
ISSN: 0147-104X

First published in 1986

Greenwood Press, Inc.
88 Post Road West, Westport, Connecticut 06881

Printed in the United States of America

The paper used in this book complies with the Permanent Paper Standard issued by the National Information Standards Organization (Z39.48–1984).

10 9 8 7 6 5 4 3 2 1

To Carol Ruth Berkin

CONTENTS

ACKNOWLEDGMENTS

This book began as a homework assignment in the summer of 1980 at an institute in women's history, sponsored by the National Endowment for the Humanities and administered by the Woodrow Wilson Foundation. We would like to thank first both of those generous institutions and our teachers at the institute, Carol R. Berkin, Linda K. Kerber, Lois W. Banner, and Sara Evans, and our colleagues, Fane Downs, Michael D'Innocenzo, and Peter H. Jaynes.

In the ensuing five years, as we got the book ready for publication, we incurred many more debts. We owe thanks to the staffs of the following: the Western Reserve Historical Society, the Maryland Hall of Records, the Library of Congress, the Caroliniana Library, the South Carolina State Archives, and the South Carolina Historical Society.

Thanks also go to professional colleagues for suggestions and advice and to students who were our unwitting audiences.

We are much indebted to John Carroll University for generous financial support in the preparation of the manuscript and to the John Carroll University faculty secretaries, Margie P. Wasdovich and Gina Arcoria, for skill and tolerance beyond the call of duty.

INTRODUCTION

New World, New Roles is a book principally, although not exclusively, about women. Its cast of characters includes the "huswife" and the midwife, the spinster and the widow, the servant and the slave. Although men are not central to our story, the book also is about the fathers and husbands, the ministers and magistrates, the artisans and soldiers who struggled to survive the hardships of life in early America on the bleak New England shores, the fertile fields of the middle colonies, and the estuarine marches of the southern lowlands. Our purpose in compiling and editing this book is to remind readers that American history has been made by women as well as men.

Although part of the same past, women experienced it differently from men in significant ways. Most men and women lived within families, essential to the survival of both the individual and the social order, but the family hierarchy, inherited from the Old World, was patriarchal; women were, moreover, constrained by their reproductive capabilities, their lives limited and shortened by long years of childbearing and childraising. Both men and women worked hard, especially in the early years of settlement, but women's work was done almost exclusively within the home and brought increasingly fewer economic rewards. Men and women worshiped together in churches where, however, only men could be spiritual leaders and decision makers. Men and women were subject to the same legal codes, but these man-made laws, like theology, institutionalized and reinforced the secondary position women held within the family, the economy, and the church. We have accordingly organized our material around these four interrelated themes—the family, religion, work, and the law, which seem best to encompass although by no means delimit women's lives.

We have also focused less upon the familiar public events of the early centuries of the American past—exploration, the development of political institutions, warfare among European nations and against Indians—and more upon the institutions and circumstances that impinged directly upon the private lives of American women and men: family laws and customs, religious teachings and practices, childbirthing and childrearing, household management, and control of family property.

Consequently, the traditional periodization of these years is less appropriate. For example, because women were almost totally excluded from the political world, the ratification of the Constitution in 1788 and the creation of the new American nation had little immediate relevance for them. The changes in women's lives, which only begin to be evident after the American Revolution, were due less to decisions made in Philadelphia by the Founding Fathers than to the growth of cities with shops and factories, the opening of the western territories, and the proliferation of Protestant and non-Protestant churches. This book, therefore, brings the stories of American women into the early years of the nineteenth century, setting the stage for the more dramatic changes of the later decades.

The book also brings together a wide variety of documents in order to illustrate the social, economic, legal, and political realities of women's lives in early America. We have chosen primary sources because they help the student to develop a more intimate sense of the past. Without the intermediary historian to filter and interpret the materials, the reader can enter the past directly and touch in a uniquely personal way the lives of ordinary as well as extraordinary Americans. We have elected to use these primary sources also because of their special value in developing analytical skills. As they work with documents ranging from cookbooks to court records, students can learn to appreciate the uses and limitations of various kinds of data. At the same time they become familiar with the basic materials from which the professional historian reconstructs the past, allowing them to gain useful insights into the interpretative function of history.

Primary sources offer a special challenge for students of women's history. Hampered by their lack of education and leisure time and rendered less visible by the private nature of their lives, even fewer women than men have left records about themselves. The historian of women, therefore, must often rely on public records left by men, necessitating a more imaginative and critical approach to these documents in order to ferret out the female realities which are peripheral to male interests or distorted by the gender of their authors.

And yet these primary sources—statutes and court proceedings, fiction and private correspondence, sermons and conversion literature, journals, diaries, wills, and inventories—also demonstrate that the opportunities for studying and writing women's history are as readily available to the fledgling student as to the serious scholar. In all these and in the published writings of public officials such as Governor John Winthrop or of the great Puritan divines like Cotton Mather, women can be discovered in the full range of human activities that American society allowed: as wives and whores, saints and sinners, workers and idlers, paupers and ladies.

Some historians have looked to just such sources when in recent years they began to put women at the center of their historical inquiries. The result has been a growing body of literature that depicts women in an astonishing variety of roles: as wives and mothers in John Demos's *A Little Commonwealth*; as heretics in Lyle Koehler's *A Search for Power*; as litigants in Nancy Cott's "Divorce and the Changing Status of Women in Eighteenth-Century Massachusetts" and in "Eighteenth-Century Family and Social Life Revealed in Massachusetts Divorce Records"; as political activists in Linda Kerber's *Women of the Republic* and Mary Beth Norton's *Liberty's Daughters*; as religious dissenters in Mary Maples Dunn's "Saints and Sisters: Congregational and Quaker Women in the Early Colonial Period," as widows in Alexander Keyssar's "Widowhood in Eighteenth-Century Massachusetts," as murderers in Ann Jones' *Women Who Kill*. As these titles and the list of suggested readings appended indicates, extensive work has already been done in the field of women's history.

Although the research is impressive, many questions remain unanswered: What did "love" mean to early Americans? Did husbands and wives "love" one another? What can we infer about sexual norms or sexual behavior from the many incidents of adultery and bastardy? How difficult was it to cook a meal or keep a house tidy? How hard was it for women to earn a living outside the home? What did their religious experiences mean to women? Why did they join churches in such large numbers? How equitable were the colonial courts? Did they protect or stifle women's legal rights? How important to women was the lack of political opportunities? What difference did the American Revolution make to women? How were the lives of white and black women different? How were they the same? In what ways did the female experience change from the seventeenth century to the early nineteenth century?

When answered, these questions should tell us a good deal about the dramatic moments in history that had important consequences for the future. They should also tell us something about the routine of life in a society which, though culturally distinct from our own, still tends to influence the habits and conventions of the present. The answers should, in short, present another scene in the rich panorama of life that written history continually unrolls for us.

I WOMEN AND THE FAMILY IN THE SEVENTEENTH CENTURY

The first Englishmen who immigrated to America planted colonies that stretched along the Atlantic coast from Maine to South Carolina. The earliest settlement was made at Jamestown, Virginia in 1607. Despite hard times, by 1642 the population had reached 8,000 and settlement had pushed northward toward the Potomac River. In 1634 a group of English Catholics founded St. Mary's, just north of the Virginia colony. While the Chesapeake settlements struggled to survive the epidemics of typhoid, dysentery, and salt poisoning that were the cause of high mortality in the saltwater environments of the lower estuaries, a group of religious dissenters called Pilgrims established a small agricultural community at Plymouth, just north of Cape Cod Bay on the bleak Massachusetts shore. Beginning in 1635, groups of Massachusetts settlers, joined later by Puritans from England, migrated in a southwesterly direction into the fertile valley of the Connecticut River. While the English were settling Virginia and New England, the Dutch were planting small outposts on the present site of Albany and along the Hudson River. The Dutch exploited the area for furs for a half century before groups of Swedes, New Haven Puritans, and Quakers flooded into the region, attracted by promises of cheap land, religious freedom, and democratic government. Promotional campaigns also attracted settlers to the "fruitful and pleasant" land south of Virginia. Although it was, as one settler put it, "in the very chops of the Spanish," by the end of the seventeenth century, nearly 3,000 persons had settled around Albemarle Sound in the northern part of Carolina and some 5,000 others had fanned out from Charleston in the South. Throughout the century, until the planting of the last English colony of Georgia in 1733, the influx of immigrants continued, with small infusions of non-

English stock, including some 6,000 French Huguenots, 1,500 Jews, and a sprinkling of German Quakers and Pietists.

Refugees from a world just beginning to move away from feudalism, the seventeenth-century migrants brought to the new world a set of cultural and social forms characteristic of the European societies they had left. Settling in ethnic and religious enclaves strung like beads along the coast, they tried to re-create the most important institutions to which life in the old world had accustomed them: the family, the church, the state. As the population grew due to prolific natural increase and inward migration, as the fringe of settlement expanded slowly westward, as social organizations grew and matured, the original forms underwent change, developing eventually their own distinctive features. When and how quickly this transformation occurred has been a subject of interest to historians, particularly those who are concerned with the colonial roots of the modern family.

Most research in early American family history agrees as to the centrality of family life. Throughout the seventeenth century the family was the basic social and economic unit of the colonial social order. Both Puritans and Anglicans looked to the family to carry out a number of vital functions. Together with the church and the network of community relations, the family was expected to help stabilize the social order. It was responsible for the proper moral upbringing of children and for the training of family members in social as well as religious obligations. As the basic institution of social welfare, the family was supposed to care for dependent members at home, without disrupting either their lives or society.

With respect to the structure of the family and interpersonal relations, historical opinion begins to diverge sharply. A first line of debate centers on the persistence of patriarchalism in America. The growing interest in sex roles touched off by the women's movement in the 1960s produced a second line of debate over the status of women in society and within the family. One school of thought represented by the work of Mary P. Ryan has advanced the thesis of the colonial period as a "golden age" for women. In a general survey published in 1975, Ryan argued that the new world environment destroyed the old patriarchal and hierarchic family structure and raised in its place the prototypical modern family, in which women, because of their economic importance, enjoyed a position of relative equality.

A second school of thought, represented by Philip Greven and John Demos among others, argues for the persistence of patriarchalism and the hierarchical patterns of family life. Recent findings by demographic historians have clarified matters somewhat by uncovering striking regional differences in family life. Although all of the English colonies attempted to re-create traditional procedures and norms where marriage and family life were concerned, alterations in the forms of marriage and in family relationships were the inevitable result of migration and demographic change. In the southern colonies and in New York, where the Anglican church was established, marriage was viewed as a sacrament ordained by God for the purpose of procreation. In New England, the Puritans, carrying forth the ideas of the Protestant Reformation, looked on marriage as an ordinance of God but not as a sacrament. They made it, therefore, a civil contract, performed before a civil magistrate. In the Puritan colonies the procedure for a valid marriage was regularized and consisted of the espousal, publication of banns at three successive public meetings, the marriage ceremony, and sexual intercourse. Because of primitive conditions and a shortage of clergy in the Chesapeake, the marriage procedure there often consisted of the espousal followed directly by sexual consummation, with all intermediate steps being eliminated.

Differing demographic experience was also a cause of other apparent differences in family life. Because of the high death rate in the Chesapeake most marriages were of brief duration, with the surviving partner remarrying almost immediately. Longer life expectancy in New England meant that few people married more than once. Types of family also varied according to region, race, and class. In the Chesapeake a high mortality rate produced greater reliance on kinship networks, while in New England the nuclear family prevailed. Whereas in New England the most common households averaged four to six persons, typically including both parents, children, a young servant or on occasion a widowed mother, in the Chesapeake households tended to be more complex, including half-brothers, step-brothers, or stepsisters, with the father-figure or mother-figure frequently being a relative or a new spouse.

Exactly how these demographic differences affected family relationships in general and the status of women in particular continues to spark scholarly interest. A recent study of New England women by Lyle Koehler maintains that Calvinists in male-dominated Massachusetts rigidly enforced the patriarchal creed, keeping their wives in "servile subjection." By contrast, important work by Lois Green Carr and Lorena Walsh shows that demographic conditions peculiar to the Chesapeake significantly improved the status of women within the family and in society, at least until equalization of the sex ratio after 1700 cost them their earlier advantages. The institutionalization of black slavery, which formed the basis of the patriarchy in the South, confirmed the subordinate status of southern women.

Although the strength of the patriarchy rested on slaves, blacks did not completely assimilate the norms and values of white society. A growing body of literature on the origins of Afro-American society reveals that demographic conditions before 1740 prevented blacks from developing their own social institutions and culture. Once the demographic composition changed, however, slaves quickly developed a cohesive family life, combining some aspects of white family life with which they were in daily contact and elements of the African societies from which they were derived. The native peoples of eastern America had, of course, their own distinct familial values and practices. Although practice varied considerably from the Plains and Pueblo peoples to that of the tribes of the northeast, similar views on sexual conduct and on childbearing were fairly common among all the tribes.

PATTERNS OF MARRIAGE

During the course of the seventeenth century, thousands of individuals and families left the old world for the new. When the first European settlers arrived in the American wilderness, they were met by the tribal peoples of eastern America, including the Creeks of the lower South, the Powhatan confederacy in Virginia, and the Iroquois and the Hurons of New York and lower Ontario. Despite linguistic differences and certain cultural and social variations, the eastern tribes formed a culturally homogeneous unit. They were predominantly farming people whose basic unit of social membership was the exogamous clan. With only a few exceptions, the tribes were matrilineal. Shortly after the arrival of the first European settlers, the first blacks were introduced into Virginia from a Dutch vessel. Later in the 1640s, black men and women were imported into New England, thus developing the racial heterogenity that continues to characterize America to the present.

Differences in the racial and ethnic makeup of the new world inhabitants and in demographic conditions inevitably produced diversity in domestic values and practices. Whatever the differences, the importance of the family to communal stability quickly led the European settlers to adopt rules designed to establish the well-ordered family according to local norms and values. Although slavery was not institutionalized until the 1660s, perceptions of racial difference, particularly in the southern colonies, led to the enactment of laws that established black slavery and created an elaborate set of rules to regulate relations between the races.

Courtship and Marriage Customs

A Relation of Maryland, 1635[1]

Almost all Europeans who came in contact with the Indian peoples of eastern America were struck by the differences in sexual and marriage customs among Indian tribes. The Christian condemnation of premarital and extramarital sex led many of them to censure what they regarded as the Indian's sexual promiscuity. In some cases, Christian moralizing produced such biased reporting that the accounts are of limited value to historians. The writer of the unsigned report below, however, managed to avoid platitudes and stereotypes. In a straightforward account of conditions in Maryland in 1634, he wrote this interesting description of betrothal procedures and marriage rituals among the native population of colonial Maryland.

The women serve their husbands, make their bread, dress their meat, such as they kill in hunting, or get by fishing; and if they have more wives than one, as some of them have (but that is not general) then the best beloved wife performs all the offices of the house, and they take great content therein. The women also (beside the household business) used to make mats, which serve to cover their houses, and for beds; they also make baskets, some of rushes, other of silk-grass, which are very handsome.

The women remain with their parents until they have husbands, and if the parents be dead, then with some other of their friends. If the husband die, he leaves all that he has to his wife, except his bow and arrows, and some beads (which they usually bury with them) and she is to keep the children until the sons come to be men, and then they live where they please, for all men's houses are free unto them; and the daughters until they have husbands. The manner of their marriages is thus; he that would have a wife, treats with the father, or if he be dead, with the friend that take[s] care of her whom he desires to have to wife, and agrees with him for a quantity of beads, or some such other thing which is accepted among them; which he is to give for her, and must be payed on the day of their marriage; and then the day being appointed, all the friends of both parts meet at the man's house that is to have the wife, and each one brings a present of meat, and the woman that is to be married also brings her present: when all the company is all come, the man he sits at the upper end of the house, and the woman's friends lead her up, and place her by him, then all the company sits down upon mats, on the ground (as their manner is) and the woman rises and serves dinner, first to her husband, then to all the company. The rest of the day they spend in singing and dancing (which is not unpleasant) at night the company leaves them, and commonly they live very peaceably and lovingly together; yet it falls out sometimes, that a man puts away one wife and takes another: then she and her children return to her friends again. They are generally very obedient to their husbands, and you shall seldom hear a woman speak in the presence of her husband, except when he asks her some question.

A Common-Law Marriage, 1665[2]

Whereas most immigrants to New England arrived within a decade, immigration to Virginia and Maryland continued through most of the seventeenth century. While the New England population tended to cluster in small towns and villages, settlers in the Chesapeake spread out along tidal river banks on isolated farms. Although procedures were more or less regularized, at least to the extent that a license was supposed to be required for marriage, a shortage of ministers in the sparsely settled Chesapeake led to much more informal arrangements, as the common-law marriage of Gils Tomkinson and Elizabeth Smaldrige, described below, suggests. Such common-law marriages were, according to legal historians, apparently unique to America.

Thomas Gibson constable accuses a woman living at Gils Tomkinsons to be illegitimately got with child but the said Gils Tomkinson affirms in open court that she is and was before the getting of her with child his lawful wife and confesses himself the father of the child she now goes with and here in open court alleges that his marriage was as good as possible it could be made by the Protestants he being one because that before that time and ever since there has not been a Protestant minister in the province and that to matrimony is only necessary the parties consent and publication thereof before a lawful churchman and for their consents it is apparent and for the worlds satisfaction they here publish themselves man and wife til death them do part.

A Marriage Festival, 1686[3]

Few records of wedding celebrations in the Chesapeake exist until after 1700. The description of the festivities following the ceremony which united a young indentured servant from Abbeville, France and a prominent young Virginia woman suggests, however, that when conditions permitted, affluent families staged elaborate celebrations, which often lasted one or two days. The sober French Huguenot from Provence, Durand de Dauphiné, who left the following account, was clearly astonished at the immoderation of the wedding guests. With the growth after 1700 of a native population and the subsequent development of kinship networks, such celebrations became common, at least among the middle and upper classes of Chesapeake society.

A few days after returning to my room [I was visited by] a good French boy from Abbeville in Picardy, who, having finished his service, had become a Lieutenant and thereby saved some money. He was about to be married two leagues away from my lodgings and as he had been to see me before, he came to invite me to his wedding. He had become a Protestant and was marrying a good girl of a very decent family. On his wedding-day, then, he sent two of his father-in-law's negroes for me in a boat, and I went by water. The Indians [Durand uses the term "Indians" to refer to colonists born in America] make a great festival of a wedding. There were at least a hundred guests, many of social standing, and handsome, well-dressed ladies. Although it was November, we ate under the trees. The day was perfect. We were twenty-four at the first table. They served us so copiously with meats of all kinds that I am sure there would have been enough for a regiment of five hundred soldiers, even entirely made up of men from Languedoc, Provence, or Dauphiné. The Indians eat almost no bread, seldom drink during meals; but they did nothing afterwards, for the rest of the day and all night, but drink, smoke, sing and dance. They had no wine; they drank beer, cider, and punch, a mixture prepared in a large bowl. They put in three jugs of beer, three jugs of brandy, three pounds of sugar, some nutmegs and cinnamon, mix these well together and when the sugar has melted they drink it, and while making away with the first, they prepare another bowl of it. As for me, I drank beer only, cider makes me ill and I do not care for sugar. It is the custom to take only one meal upon such occasions, at two o'clock in the afternoon. They do not provide beds for the men; those available are for the women and girls, so that about midnight, after much carousing, when some were already lying on the floor, I fell asleep in a chair close by the fire. The master of the house saw me and took me to the room of the women and girls, where four or five cots had been arranged, also feather beds. Collecting all the blankets, he laid me a bed on the floor, saying he would not put it in the hall for fear the drunken fellows would fall over me and keep me from sleeping. They caroused all night long and when it was day I got up. I did not see one who could stand straight. A little later the bridegroom arose, gave me a good breakfast, and had me taken back to my lodgings by his slave.

Marriage and the Community

*Law against Unlawful Implied Contracts
of Marriage, 1624*[4]

Over the course of the seventeenth century an estimated 130,000 to 150,000 immigrants arrived in the Chesapeake to settle. Studies by demographic historians show that for every female there were six males who left English cities and ports such as Bristol or London for Virginia and Maryland. Most were single men from agricultural backgrounds or from the semiskilled or unskilled occupations. The leaders of the Virginia Company, which planted the first colony, quickly realized that if the colony was to succeed, stable family life must be promoted. Consequently, beginning in 1619 the Company sent over young women to be wives. Although the gender ratio improved, for most of the seventeenth century the supply of women was not sufficient to meet the demand. The pressures of the sex ratio produced characteristics peculiar to family life in the Chesapeake. Settlers, for example, tended to marry later and to produce smaller families than in New England, where the demographic experience was different. Probate records analyzed by one scholar suggest that perhaps more than one quarter of the male settlers in southern Maryland died unmarried. By contrast, the competition for wives made it possible for virtually every woman to marry if she desired. Some women apparently took advantage of the ratio to become engaged to several men at once, leading the Virginia assembly to prohibit the practice in 1624.

Whereas to the great contempt of the majesty of God and ill example to others, certain women within this colony have of late contrary to the laws ecclesiastical of the Realm of England contracted themselves to two several men at one time, whereby much trouble does grow between parties: and the Governor and Council of State, thereby much disquieted: to prevent the like offense in others hereafter, it is by the Governor and Council ordered in court, that every Minister give notice in his church to his parishoners, that what man or woman soever shall hereafter use any word or speech tending to contract of marriage unto two several persons at one time (though not precise and legal, yet so as may entangle and breed scruple in their consciences) shall for such their offense undergo either corporal punishment (as whipping etc.) or other punishment by fire, or otherwise, according to the quality of the person so offending. Given at James City this 24th of June 1624.

Massachusetts Marriage Acts, 1639–1679[5]

By contrast to the Chesapeake where early settlers were predominantly young, single males, immigrants to the Puritan colonies of New England included larger numbers of women and children. Because New Englanders were less afflicted by the epidemics of typhoid, dysentery, fevers, and fluxes that ravaged settlers in the Chesapeake, they enjoyed longer life spans and raised more children. Living in highly structured religious communities instead of on isolated farms as did the settlers in the Chesapeake, New Englanders were more easily able to preserve community values and to maintain traditional family structures. The Massachusetts marriage acts which follow below suggest how this was accomplished. They also reveal how family life, religion, and law intersected at important points as well as the degree to which parental, and especially paternal authority influenced marriage decisions.

It is ordered by this court and authority thereof; that no man shall strike his wife, nor any woman her husband, on penalty of such fine not exceeding ten pounds for one offense, or such corporal punishment as the County Court shall determine.

2. For prevention of all unlawful marriages;

It is ordered, that henceforth no person shall be joined in marriage, before the intention of the parties proceeding therein, has been three times published, at some time of public lecture or town-meeting, in both the towns where the parties or either of them do ordinarily reside, or be set up in writing upon some post of their meeting house door in public view, there to stand so as it may easily be read, by the space of fourteen days. [1639]

3. And whereas God has committed the care and power into the hands of

parents for the disposing their children in marriage, so that it is against rule to seek to draw away the affections of young maidens, under pretense of purpose of marriage, before their parents have given way and allowance in that respect; and whereas it is a common practise in divers places, for young men irregularly and disorderly to watch all advantages for their evil purposes, to insinuate into the affection of young maidens, by coming to them in places and seasons unknown to their parents for such ends, whereby much evil has grown among us, to the dishonor of God, and damage of parties; for prevention whereof for time to come;

It is further ordered, that whatsoever person from henceforth, shall endeavor directly or indirectly, to draw away the affection of any maid in this jurisdiction, under pretense of marriage, before he has obtained liberty and allowance from her parents or governors (or in absence of such) of the nearest magistrate, he shall forfeit for the first offense five pounds, for the second toward the party ten pounds, and be bound to forbare any further attempt and proceedings in that unlawful design, without or against the allowance aforesaid; and for the third offense upon information or complaint by such parents or governors to any magistrate, giving bond to prosecute the party, he shall be committed to prison, and upon hearing and conviction by the next court, shall be adjudged to continue in prison, until the Court of Assistants shall see cause to release him. [1647]

4. Whereas divers persons, both men and women, living within this jurisdiction, whose wives and husbands are in England, or elsewhere, by means whereof, they live under great temptations here, and some of them committing lewdness and filthiness here among us, others make love to women and attempt marriage, and some have attained it, and some of them live under suspicion of uncleanness, and all to the great dishonor of God, reproach of Religion, Common-wealth and Churches;

It is therefore ordered by this Court and Authority thereof, for the prevention of all such future evils, that all such married persons as aforesaid, shall repair to their said relations by the first opportunity of shipping, upon the pain or penalty of twenty pounds, except they can show just cause to the contrary to the next County Court or Court of Assistants, after they are summoned by the Constable there to appear, who are hereby required so to do, upon pain of twenty shillings for every such default wittingly made;

Provided this order do not extend to such as are come over to make way for their families, or are in a transient way, only for traffic or merchandize for some small time. [1647]

5. As the ordinance of marriage is honorable among all, so should it be accordingly solemnized;

It is therefore ordered by this Court and Authority thereof; that no person whatsoever in this jurisdiction, shall join any persons together in marriage, but the magistrate, or such other as the General Court, or Court of Assistants shall authorize in such place, where no magistrate is near.

Nor shall join themselves in marriage, but before some magistrate or person authorized as aforesaid.

Nor shall any magistrate or other person authorized as aforesaid, join any persons together in marriage, or suffer them to join together in marriage in their presence, before the parties to be married have been published according to law. [1646]

In answer to the question; whether it be lawful for a man that has buried his first wife, to marry with her that was his first wife's natural sister? The court resolves it on the negative. [1679]

Records of the Third Haven Monthly Meeting of Friends, 1680[6]

The pervasive influence of religion in marriage and family noted in the Puritan communities of New England was equally strong in the Quaker settlements of the middle colonies and elsewhere. Within the Society of Friends, as the Quakers were more properly known, the meeting structure not only controlled church membership, discipline, and policy, but was also responsible for protecting the institution of marriage. Because marriage "out of Union" was strictly forbidden, a couple like William Dixon and Elizabeth Christerson who wanted to marry had to prove their "cleerness"; that is, to produce proof that they were both single and were members of the meeting. The Third Haven Meetings' scrutiny of the couple's financial situation was due to the fact that the Widow Christerson was "neere altering her condition by marriage," which under the laws of coverture meant that effective control of her first husband's estate would pass to her new husband, William Dixon.

At our man meeting at John Pitts the 14th of the 3rd month 1680 William Dixon and Elizabeth Christerson appeared before the meeting and declared the intentions of coming together as husband and wife it being the second time of their laying it before the meeting inquiry being made by Stephen Keddy and Bryon Omealia who were appointed by the meeting to inquire into William Dixon's cleerness. Likewise Sarah Edmondson and Mary Sockwell being made choice of by the womens meeting to inquire concerning Elizabeth Christersons being cleer and upon inquiry of the meeting the aforesaid friends informs the meeting that they find nothing to the contrary but that they are cleer. The meeting having nothing against their coming together but for the truths sake and their sakes did make inquiry of Elizabeth, whether her former husband's will were performed or not and whether she had or would set out anything for her children and she not being in a capacity to answer without further advice the meeting appointed William Berry John Edmondson William Southebee and John Pitts with the executors Thomas Taylor and William Sharpe to meet the next 3rd day at the widow's house to proof the will and to see that it may be answered and to settle the estate as near as may be agreeable to the same and if it should so happen that any of the aforesaid friends should not be there then the rest that meet have power from the meeting to make choice of others in their stead and friends give an account to our next mans meeting at Howell Powells—after which time things being cleered, the meeting has allowed of their in marriage according to the order of truth they appointing a time for that end and making it public.

Miscegenation, 1630, 1640, 1664[7]

Until roughly 1740 a combination of factors, including cultural differences among the blacks brought to America, death and disease on the middle passage, the small size of slave units, an unfavorable sex ratio, and the trauma of enslavement, made it extremely difficult for blacks to establish stable family life. One of the most serious impediments both to slave morality and to family stability was the white man's lust for black women. Although slavery was not institutionalized until the 1660s, perceptions of racial difference, particularly in the southern colonies, quickly led to adoption of the view that miscegenation was illegal, leading, as in Virginia, to harsh punishment for transgressors. By 1664, the colony of Maryland had adopted a law prohibiting racial miscegenation; South Carolina, with probably 60 percent of its population black, did so in 1717.

MISCEGENATION, 1630, 1640

17 September 1630. Hugh Davis to be soundly whipped, before an Assembly of Negroes and others for abusing himself to the dishonor of God and shame of Christians, by defiling his body in lying with a negro; which fault he is to acknowledge next Sabbath day.

1640. Robert Sweet to do penance in church according to laws of England, for getting a negro woman with child and the woman whipped.

An Act concerning Negroes and Other Slaves, 1664[8]

Be it enacted by the Right Honorable the Lord Proprietary by the advice and consent of the upper and lower house of this present General Assembly that all Negroes or other slaves already within the Province and all Negroes and other slaves to be hereafter imported into the Province shall serve Durante Vita and all children born of any Negro or other slave shall be slaves as their fathers were for the term of their lives and forasmuch as divers freeborn English women forgetfull of their free condition and to the disgrace of our nation do intermarry with Negro slaves by which also divers suits may arise touching the issue of such women and a great damage does befall the Masters of such Negroes for prevention whereof for deterring such freeborn women from such shameful matches be it further enacted by the authority advice and consent aforesaid that whatsoever freeborn woman shall intermarry with any slave from and after the last day of this present Assembly shall serve the master of such slave during the life of her husband and that all the issue of such freeborn women so married shall be slaves as their fathers were and be it further enacted that all the issues of English or other freeborn women that have already married Negroes shall serve the Masters of their parents til they be thirty years of age and no longer.

CONJUGAL RELATIONS

Although conditions in the New World would inevitably produce some modifications, the men and women who immigrated to America in the seventeenth century brought with them familiar notions respecting family arrangements and patterns of behavior. The patriarchal family structure that prevailed in Elizabethan and Stuart England was quickly established in the American colonies. In most respects attitudes toward women and their roles within the family remained traditional, differing little from those of contemporary Europeans. In the deeply religious environment of the seventeenth century, early Americans justified patriarchy by reference to the Bible. Popular assumptions regarding man's superiority, both in the home and in the community, found support in the Biblical account of creation, which defined woman's primary role as "helpmeet" to man. Nature, which endowed woman with passive characteristics and equipped her for childbearing, determined her second and even more basic function: motherhood.

Prescriptive literature, such as sermons and tracts, are important in helping us to understand the ideals of marriage and the family as well as the religious and social values that informed those ideals. They do not necessarily tell us how marriages actually worked on a day-to-day basis. Unfortunately, the paucity of personal documents, such as diaries, memoirs, and letters, makes it impossible to examine in any detail the intimacies of domestic life. Whether marriages were more or less happy in colonial America than in other periods is thus a matter of speculation. Extant records of life by educated white families, most of them from New England, suggest strong emotional ties between spouses. Court records, on the other hand, reveal that marital discord was a common feature of colonial family life.

Family Structure

Cotton Mather's Ornaments for the Daughters of Zion, *1692*[9]

The subordinate status of women within the family, which was decreed by law and custom, found powerful support from the church. Sermons and religious tracts as well as handbooks, such as Cotton Mather's *Ornaments for the Daughters of Zion*, were extremely important in shaping colonial role definitions and in setting behavioral standards. The fact that *Ornaments* went through three editions—1682, 1694, and 1741—testifies to its popularity. Addressed to women, it describes those virtues, both spiritual and temporal, that were considered most desirable in a wife.

I. As for her love to her husband, I may say, 'Tis even strong as death, many waters cannot quench it, neither can the floods drown it. She can like Sarah, Rebeckah, Rachel, freely leave all the friends in the world for his company; and she looks upon that charge of God unto his ministers, teach the young women to love their husbands, as no less profitable, than highly reasonable. When she reads that Prince Edward in his wars against the Turks, being stabbed with a poisoned knife, his princess did suck the poison out of his wounds with her own royal mouth; she finds in her own heart a principle disposing her to show her own husband as great a love....

II. But her love to her husband, will also admit, yea, and produce the fear of, a cautious diligence never to displease him. 'Twas this which the apostle Peter meant when he recommends unto the women, a chaste conversation coupled with fear; and Paul, when he requires of the woman, to reverence her husband. While she looks upon him as her guide, by the constitution of God, she will not scruple with Sarah to call him her lord; and though she does not fear his blows, yet she does fear his frowns, being loath in any way to grieve him, or cause an head-ache in the family by offending him.... In every lawful thing she submits her will and sense to his, where she cannot with calm reasons convince him of inexpediences; and instead of grudging or captious contradiction, she acts as if there were but one mind in two bodies. If her Abraham gives order, make ready quickly three measures of meal, or the like, 'tis as quickly done; if her Jacob say to her, I must have you go with me, she most readily yields unto him. If his unreasonable humours happen to be such, that she must give some diversion to them, she remembers that rule, in her tongue is the law of kindness; 'tis by the kindness, the sweetness, the goodness of her expressions that she gives law unto him....

IV. But she is for plenty as well as peace in her household; and by her thriftiness makes an effectual and sufficient reply unto her husband, when he does ask her, as he must, whether he shall thrive or no? She is a Deborah, that is, a bee for her diligence and industry in her hive. As on the one side she will have none in her house to want, so on the other side, she will have all of them to work; or as the Holy Spirit of God expresses it, she looks well to the ways of her household, and eats not the bread of idleness....

V. And this thriftiness is accompanied by such fidelity to her husband, as that she will not give a lodging to the least stragling or wandering thought of disloyalty in his bed; lest by her parlying with wicked thoughts, the devil should insensibly decoy her to the deeds which God will judge. She is a dove, that will sooner die than leave her mate; and her husband is to her, the covering of her eyes, at such a rate, that she sees a desirableness in him, which she will not allow herself to behold or suppose in any other; neither will she look upon another.... She accounts adultery to be as the law of Moses adjudged it, a capital crime; and if the Egyptians of old cut off the nose of the adulteress, or if the Athenians tore her to pieces with wild horses, rather had she undergo the pain of such things than commit the crime. . . .

VI. But her fidelity is no where more signalized, than in her sollicitude for the eternal salvation of her husband. O how unwilling she is that the precious and immortal soul of her poor husband, should go from her arms, to make his bed among the dragons of the wilderness forever. . . . Truly, tho' a woman may not speak in the church, yet she may humbly repeat unto her husband at home what the minister spoke in the church, that may be pertinent to his condition. Thus every Paul may have women that labour with him in the gospel. Vast opportunities are those that a woman has to bring over her husband unto real and serious Godliness. And a good woman will use those opportunities.

William Secker, A Wedding Ring Fit for the Finger, *1658*[10]

Despite the patriarchal emphasis, in Puritan theology the accent was on love and instruction rather than on fear and dominance. The excerpts below, taken from a sermon delivered by Reverend William Secker at a wedding in Edmonton, Massachusetts in 1658, show how Puritan divines used the major rituals of local life to shape domestic ideals. In this case the Reverend Secker employs familiar metaphors to describe the husband's authority in detail.

If thou wouldst have thy wife's reverence, let her have thy respect. To force a fear from this relation, is that which neither befits the husband's authority to enjoin, nor the wife's duty to perform. A wife must not be sharply driven, but sweetly drawn. Compassion may bend her, but compulsion will break her. Husband and wife should act toward each other with consent, not by constraint. Four things in which the husband is to be a helpmeet to the wife:

1. In his protecting her from injuries. It's well observed by one, that the rib of which woman was made, was taken from under the man's arm. As the use of the arm is to keep off blows from the body, so the office of the husband is to ward off blows from the wife. The wife is the husband's treasury, and the husband should be the wife's armoury. In darkness he should be her sun for direction, in danger he should be her shield for protection.

2. In his providing for her necessities. The husband must communicate maintenance to the wife, as the head conveys influence to the members. Thou must not be a drone, and she a drudge. A man in a married estate is like a chamberlain in an inn, there's knocking for him in every room. Many persons in this condition waste the estate in luxury, which should support their wives necessity. They have neither the faith of a Christian, nor the love of a husband. It's a sad spectacle to see a virgin sold with her own money unto slavery, when services are better than marriages. The one receives wages, whilst the other buys their fetters.

3. In his covering of her infirmities. Who would trample upon a jewel because it is fallen in the dirt? Or throw away a heap of wheat for a little chafe? Or despise a golden wedge because it retains some dross? These roses have their

prickles. Now husbands should spread a mantle of charity over their wives infirmities. They be ill birds that defile their own nests. It is a great deal better you fast, than feast upon their railings. Some husbands are never well longer than they are holding their fingers in their wives sores. Such are like crows, that fatten upon carrion. Do not put out the candle because of the snuff. If the gold be good, allow it grains. Husband and wife should provoke one another to love, and they should love one another notwithstanding of provocation. Take heed of poisoning those springs from whence the streams of your pleasure flows.

4. By his delighting in her society. A wife takes sanctuary, not only in her husband's house, but in his heart. The tree of love should grow up in the family, as the tree of life grew up in the garden. They that marry where they affect not, will affect where they marry not. Two joined together without love, are but two ty'd together to make one another miserable.

Personal Relations

Anne Bradstreet's "Another," n.d.[11]

In the seventeenth century, romantic love was not regarded as a necessary prerequisite for marriage. Married couples were, however, expected to learn to love one another. Sexual intercourse was viewed as a proper expression of that love and therefore indispensable to a successful marriage. Although it is not a complete poetic statement about a love relationship, the sexual character of marriage is hinted at in Anne Bradstreet's "Another" ("As loving Hind"). Addressed to her husband Simon, it's imagery displays an unabashedly sensual attitude.

> As loving Hind that (Hartless) wants her Deer,
> Scuds through the woods and Fern with harkning ear,
> Perplext, in every bush and nook doth pry,
> Her dearest Deer, might answer eye to eye;
> So doth my anxious soul, which now doth miss,
> A dearer Dear (far dearer Heart) than this.
> Still wait with doubts, and hopes and failing eye,
> His voice to hear, or person to discry.
> Or as the pensive Dove doth all alone
> (On withered bough) most uncommonly bemoan
> The absence of her love, and loving Mate,
> Whose loss hath made her so unfortunate;
> Ev'n thus doe I, with many a deep sad groan
> Bewail my turtle true, who now is gone,
> His presence and his safe return, still wooes,
> With thousand doleful sighs and mournful Cooes.
> Or as the loving Mullet, that true Fish,
> Her fellow lost, nor love nor life do wish,

> But launches on that shore, there for to dye,
> Where she her captive husband doth espy.
> Mine being gone, I lead a joyless life,
> I have a loving phere, yet seem no wife:
> But worst of all, to him can't steer my course,
> I here, he there, alas, both kept by forces:
> Return my dear, my joy, my only love,
> Unto thy Hinde, thy Mullet and thy Dove,
> Who neither joyes in pasture, house nor streams,
> The substance gone, O me, these are but dreams.
> Together at one Tree, oh let us brouze,
> And like two Turtles roost within one house,
> And like the Mullets in one River glide,
> Let's still remain but one, till death divide.
> > Thy loving Love and Dearest Dear,
> > At home, abroad, and every where.

An Act against Adultery and Polygamy, 1647[12]

Because of the importance of the family to the community, disruptions in domestic harmony were considered to be of sufficient interest to warrant interference by the community. Despite regional differences in the patterns of family life, it is clear that illicit sexual activity, particularly adultery, was a common source of marital conflict. Colonial Americans accepted sexual relations as an expression of love, central to their family-centered ideals. They insisted, however, that intercourse be limited to married couples and used harsh secular weapons to punish promiscuity and sexual deviance. It is interesting to note that the following Massachusetts act defined adultery in terms of sexual relations between a man, either married or single, and a married woman, which suggests the operation of a double standard of sexual morality.

Whereas the violation of the marriage covenant is highly provoking to God, and destructive to families,

Sect. 1. Be it therefore enacted by the governor, council and representatives, in general court assembled, and by the authority of the same, that if any man be found in bed with another man's wife, the man and woman so offending, being thereof convicted, shall be severely whipped, not exceeding thirty stripes, unless it appear upon trial, that one party was surprised and did not consent, which shall abate the punishment as to such party.

And if any man shall commit adultery, the man and woman that shall be convicted of such crime before their majesties justices of assize and general gaol delivery shall be set upon the gallows by the space of an hour, with a rope about their neck, and the other end cast over the gallows, and in the way from thence to the common gaol shall be severely whipped, not exceeding forty stripes each; also every person and persons so offending shall for ever after wear a capital A of two inches long, and proportionable bigness, cut out of cloth of a contrary color to their clothes, and sewed upon their upper garments, on the outside of their arm, or on their back, in open view; and if any person or persons, having been convicted and sentenced for such offense, shall at any time be found without their letter so worn, during their abode in this province, they shall by warrant from a justice of the peace be forthwith apprehended and ordered to be publicly whipped, not exceeding fifteen stripes.

Grace Miller v. Richard Miller, 1672[13]

Unless domestic conflicts grew violent or were sufficiently serious to attract the attention of authorities, marital problems were not made public. Cases that came before colonial courts, however, suggest that quarreling, desertion, and abusive treatment created severe tension in many marriages. There is, moreover, ample evidence in the courts' handling of marital problems to suggest that the norms colonial communities wished to protect were everywhere the same: regular and exclusive cohabitation, normal and exclusive sexual union, and a harmonious relationship.

Upon the complaint of Grace Miller wife unto Richard Miller for several abusive speeches and behaviors toward his wife per great provocations and by throwing of her over board out of a canoe and calling of her whore diverse times, whereby she is deeply provoked, pulling off her clothes and stripping of her naked, threatening to pull her child out of her body, &c.

For preventing whereof for time to come it is hereby ordered that the said Richard Miller shall and does stand bound in a bond of good behavior toward all persons especially toward his wife Grace Miller unto the next County Court holden for this county [interlined: and to take necessary care for her maintenance as a husband ought to do]. The said Richard Miller owns himself to be in drink, fined for his delinquency therein three shillings, four pence, for swearing ten shillings, fees 2 shillings.

And whereas it appears that Grace Miller has given too much cause of suspicion of neglect of her family and want of industry therein, with other imprudent carriages which may administer jealousies to her husband, we do therefore order for the time to come that the said Grace shall for the time hereafter be more careful to avoid all appearances of offense toward her husband and attend the care and occasions of her husband and family with more carefullness and diligence.

MOTHERS AND CHILDREN

In early America, child-bearing and child-rearing practices varied widely according to cultural and ethnic background. Except for the Quakers, the devout of most religious sects accepted the Biblical explanation of childbirth as the curse of Eve. By using her seductive powers to lure the innocent Adam from the Garden of Eden, Eve introduced sin into the world. Only through the pain of childbearing could that sin be redeemed. Such a Biblical philosophy was well-suited to conditions in the New World, which favored large families. Unlike their European counterparts, who often delayed marriage until their late twenties or remained single, the first generation of American immigrants married relatively young, the median age being the mid-twenties for women, the late twenties for men. Regional demographic differences, however, affected family size and structure as well as population growth. A life expectancy for women in New England of about sixty-three years meant an average of twenty child-bearing years. With only *coitus interruptus* or primitive methods of birth control, such as the sponge, to curtail pregnancy, the average woman could expect to bear seven to nine children, born at intervals of roughly two years. An unbalanced ratio of men to women as well as a shorter life expectancy (about forty-five years) in the disease-ridden Chesapeake limited the growth of family size in Maryland and Virginia.

Through their analyses of vital records, demographic historians have been able to develop more precise information about family size and structure in early America. Although their task is made more difficult by the absence of extensive records, during the last twenty years historians of the family have begun to study child-rearing practices in an effort to understand more about the emotional life of the family. The lack of personal records such as diaries or letters makes it difficult to know anything about child-rearing practices in the Chesapeake. Conceivably the maternal nursing bond created strong emotional attachments between mother and child; more likely infant mortality and a short life expectancy militated against the development of the affectionate family until the eighteenth century, when demographic conditions changed dramatically. In New England and the middle colonies, the overriding influence of Protestantism, particularly the notion of infant depravity, apparently produced authoritarian child-rearing practices. Rooted in the doctrine of original sin, the idea of infant depravity taught that at birth the child was possessed of a mature nature; headstrong and inexperienced, the young had therefore a special propensity for evil, making each child a potential criminal. The parents' responsibility in raising their young was to control the natural proclivity to evil. Although few sources survive to describe precisely how this was accomplished, the aim was to instill discipline by breaking the will of the child, usually within the first year of life. Restrictions upon their food and eating habits, strict regulation of their dress, and close supervision of their daily lives were intended to create affectionate, submissive, and obedient Quaker and Puritan children.

Childbearing

John Oliver, A Present to be Given to Teeming American Women by Their Husbands and Friends, *1694*[14]

Better nutrition and a healthier environment reduced the hazards of childbearing in the New World. Still, one out of every thirty births resulted in the death of the mother. Because pregnant women were particularly susceptible to malarial infections, the risks of maternal death were considerably higher in the Chesapeake than elsewhere. Contemporary tracts, such as John Oliver's *A Present to be Given to Teeming American Women by Their Husbands and Friends,* depicted the hazards of childbirth as divinely ordained and urged lying-in women to submit patiently to the dangers as a means of achieving personal redemption. The term "teeming" was commonly used in colonial America to describe the uninterrupted cycle of conception, birth, nursing, weening, conception.

... Women in this condition should be very careful of their bodies while they are with child, and very careful of providing all possible helps and conveniences against the lying in. But all these may prove miserable comforters, they may perchance need no other linen shortly but a *winding sheet* and have no other chamber but a *grave*, no neighbors but *worms*; and if they be delivered while yet they retain such unwillingness to prepare for death (as we say of all other deliverances granted to the ungodly) they are delivered not in favor, and with God's curse, not with his blessing, and are in all likelihood reserved to the greater condemnation when their sin is ripened. Whereas they would seek the Lord while he may be found, if they would mind diligently the one thing necessary, if they would speedily go to Christ for refuge, then they are safe; for whether they live or die their souls cannot miscarry.

Anne Bradstreet, "Before the Birth of One of Her Children," n.d.[15]

Most colonial women probably did not need to be reminded of the dangers of childbirth. Although the risks were less in New England, gynecologic problems, difficult parturitions, and primitive medical care could lead to complications that endangered the health and even the life of the lying-in woman. Recognizing the possibility of a premature death in childbirth, and the possibility of an abusive stepmother raising her children, Anne Bradstreet addressed this poignant verse to her husband Simon.

All things within this fading world hath end,
Adversity doth still our joyes attend;
No types so strong, no friends so clear and sweet,
But with deaths parting blow is sure to meet,
The Sentence past is most irrevocable,
a common thing, yet so inevitable;
How soon, my Dear, death may my steps attend,
How soon't may be thy Lot to lose thy friend,
We both are ignorant, yet love bids me
These farewell lines to recommend to thee,
That when that knots unty'd that made us one,
I may seem thine, who in effect am none.
And if I see not half my dayes that's due,
What nature would, God grant to yours and you;
The many faults that well you know I have,
Let be interr'd in my oblivious grave;
If any worth or virtue were in me,
Let that live freshly in thy memory.
And when thou feel'st no grief, as I no harms,
Yet love thy dead, who long lay in thine arms:
And when thy loss shall be repaid with gains
Look to my little babes my dear remains.
And if thou love thyself, or love'st me
These O protect from step Dames injury.
And if chance to thine eyes shall bring this verse,
With some sad sighs honour my present Herse;
And kiss this paper for thy loves dear sake,
Who with salt tears this last Farewel did take.

Chirurgions, Midwives, Physicians, 1649[16]

Childbearing in colonial America was exclusively a female communal experience. In preparing for her day of delivery, the typical colonial woman called upon female family members and friends and a midwife to help her through the ordeal. Until the professionalization of medicine in the nineteenth century, midwifery was totally monopolized by women, some of whom were trained by apprenticeship in Europe, others only by personal experience or by presiding at births. Although licensing oaths were required in England, they were not required in the American colonies until 1716, when the Common Council of New York City prescribed an oath for midwives. In the interim only Massachusetts and New York attempted to regulate the medical care of pregnant women. While the Massachusetts act of 1649, shown below, imposed no test of skills, it did prevent untrained midwives from using obstetrical procedures that might endanger the life or damage the reproductive capacities of the mother.

Forasmuch as the law of God allows no man to impair the life, or limbs of any person, but in a judicial way;

It is therefore ordered, that no person or persons whatsoever, employed at any time about the bodies of men, women or children, for preservation of life or health; as Chirurgions, Midwives, Physicians or others, presume to exercise, or put forth any act contrary to the known approved rules of art, in each mystery and occupation, nor exercise any force, violence or cruelty upon, or toward the body of any, whether young or old, (no not in the most difficult and desperate cases) without the advice and consent of such as are skillful in the same art, (if such may be had) or at least of some of the wisest and gravest then present, and consent of the patient or patients if they be *mentis compotes*, much less contrary to such advice and consent; upon such severe punishment as the nature of the fact may deserve, which law nevertheless, is not intended to discourage any from all lawful use of their skill, but rather to encourage and direct them in the right use thereof, and inhibit and restrain the presumptuous arrogancy of such as through presidence of their own skill, or any other sinister respects, dare boldly attempt to exercise any violence upon or toward the bodies of young or old, one or other, to the prejudice or hazard of the life or limb of man, woman or child.

Fr. Gabriel Sagard, The Long Journey to the Country of the Hurons, *1632*[17]

Among the most extensive records of Indian culture are the accounts left by Christian missionaries. During his years among the Hurons, Fr. Gabriel Sagard, a member of the Recollects, or reformed Franciscans, was able to observe Indian customs first hand. Although Father Sagard was generally a careful observer, he did not associate prolonged lactation with the limited size of Indian families, but erroneously attributed it instead to Indian female promiscuity. His brief description of Indian child-bearing practices provides an interesting basis of comparison with European customs. While Indian culture was not monolithic, some of the practices observed by Fr. Sagard among the Hurons—the use, for example, of the cradleboard to flatten the heads of infants—were also common among the Indians of the upper South.

In spite of the women giving themselves free play with others than their husbands and the husbands with others than their wives, it is a fact that they all are very fond of their children, in obedience to that law of caring for them which nature has implanted in the hearts of all animals. Now what makes them love their children, however vicious and wanting in respect, more than is the case here is that they are the support of their parents in old age, either helping them to a living or else defending them from their enemies, and nature preserves unimpaired its authority over them in this respect. Wherefore what they most desire is to have many children, to be so much the stronger and assured of support in the time of their old age. And yet the women are not so prolific as they are here, perhaps as much on account of their lubricity as from choosing so many men. . . .

The ancient German women were praised by Tacitus because each fed her children at her own breast and would have been unwilling that any other than herself should give them milk. Our savage women also nourish their children with milk from their own breasts, and since they do not know the use or suitability of pap they give them the very same meat that they take themselves, after chewing it well, and so by degrees they bring them up. If the mother happens to die before the child is weaned the father takes water in which Indian corn has been thoroughly boiled and fills his mouth with it, then putting the child's mouth against his own makes it take and swallow the liquid, and this is to make up for the lack of the breast and of pap; just so I saw it done by the husband of the woman savage whom we baptized. The women use the same method in feeding the puppies of their bitches, but I found this very displeasing and nasty, to put their mouth in this way to the puppies' muzzles, which are often not too clean.

During the day they swathe their children upon a little wooden board, on which sometimes there is a rest or small bit of wood bent into a semi-circle under the feet, and they stand it up on the floor of the lodge, unless they carry the child with them when they go out, with this board on their back fastened to a belt, which is supported on the forehead; or they take them out of their swaddling clothes and carry them wrapped up in their dress above the girdle in front, or behind their back almost straight up, the child's head outside, looking from side to side over the shoulders of the woman who carries it.

When the child is swaddled on this board, which is usually decked out with little paintings and strings of wampum beads, they leave an opening in front of its private parts through which it makes water, and if the child is a girl they arrange a leaf of Indian corn upside down which serves to carry the water outside without the child being soiled with its water; and instead of napkins, for they have none, they put under it the beautifully soft down of a kind of reed on which it lies quite comfortably, and they clean it with the same down. At night they put it to bed quite naked between the father and the mother, without any accident happening, or very seldom. In other tribes I have seen them, in order to put the child to sleep, lay it in its wrappings on a skin which is hung up, tied by the four corners to the wooden supports and poles of the lodge, like the reed hammocks of sailors under the ship's deck, and when they want to rock the child they have only from time to time to give a push to the skin thus suspended.

The Cimbri used to put their new-born children into the snow to harden them to suffering, and our savages do no less; for not only do they leave them naked in the lodge, but the children, even when rather big, roll, run about, and play in the snow and during the greatest heat of summer [naked], without receiving any harm, as I have seen in many instances, wondering that these tender little bodies could endure such great cold and such great heat, according to the weather and the season, without being disordered by them. And hence it is that they become so inured to pain and toil that when they have grown up and are old and white-haired they remain always strong and vigorous, and feel hardly any discomfort or indisposition. Even the women with child are so strong that they give birth by themselves, and for the most part do not lie up. I have seen some of them come in from the woods, laden with a big bundle of wood, and give birth to a child as soon as they arrive; then immediately they are on their feet at their ordinary employment.

Since the children of such marriages cannot be vouched for as legitimate, this custom prevails among them, as well as in many other parts of the West Indies, that the children do not succeed to their father's property; but the fathers constitute the children of their own sisters their successors and heirs, since they are sure that these are of their blood and parentage. Nevertheless they love their children dearly, in spite of the doubt that they are really their own, and of the fact that they are for the most part very naughty children, paying them little respect, and hardly more obedience; for unhappily in these lands the young have no respect for the old, nor are children obedient to their parents, and moreover there is no punishment for any fault. For this reason everybody lives in complete freedom and does what he thinks fit; and parents, for failure to punish their children, are often compelled to suffer wrong-doing at their hands, sometimes being beaten and flouted to their face. This is conduct too shocking and smacks of nothing less than the brute beast. Bad example, and bad bringing up, without punishment or correction, are the causes of all this lack of decency.

Childrearing

Cotton Mather, Ornaments for the Daughters of Zion, *1692*[18]

Although child care was generally regarded as a joint duty, in practice early childhood was the peculiar responsibility of the mother. Maternal nursing provided the first opportunity to establish a relationship between mother and child. Extant evidence suggests that the typical colonial woman breast-fed her own children, which seems also to have served as a contraceptive. After a difficult parturition, or if for some reason the mother was unable to nurse her child, a wet-nurse was hired by families who could afford the expense. Seventeenth-century writers of family tracts strongly condemned the practice, however. Arguing from the Bible and daily experience, they asserted the mother's crucial responsibility to breast-feed her baby as the best way to express her love and protect it from disease.

Her care for the bodies of her children, shows itself in her nursing of them herself, if God have made her able for it, and it [is] easy for her. She is not a dame that shall scorn to nourish in the world, the children whom she has already nourished in her womb: if like Sarah she be a lady, yet she counts it not below her to be a nurse. If God have granted her bottles of milk on her breast, she thinks that her children have a claim unto them. It shall not be her niceness, but her necessity and calamity, if she do not suckle her own off-spring; and she will not from sloth and pride, be so unnatural as to give cause for that exclamation, the sea monsters draw out the breast they give suck to their young ones; but the daughter of my people is become cruel, like the ostrich in the wilderness, who is hardened against her young ones, as though they were not hers. Now having nursed her young ones, 'tis her next care that they be well provided, as with such conveniences as belong to their present state, so with such callings and portions as may hereafter make them serviceable in their generation; and when they are grown marriageable, her discretion and her tenderness is yet more eminently seen in her matching of them.

William Secker, A Wedding Ring Fit for the Finger, *1658*[19]

According to Puritan theology the redemptive power of childbearing inclined women toward godliness. As a champion of religion within the family, the mother was responsible for shaping the character and piety of the children, at least during their early years before childrearing became a more specifically gender-related enterprise. Sermon literature, such as William Secker's *A Wedding Ring Fit for the Finger*, regularly reminded mothers of their crucial role in nurturing and discipline. Personal records that survive from the seventeenth century testify to the lasting influence of pious mothers on their children.

A spouse should be more careful of her children's breeding than she should be fearful of her children's bearing. Take heed lest these flowers grow in the devil's garden. Though you bring them out in corruption, yet do not bring them up to damnation. Those are not mothers, but monsters, while they should be teaching their children in the way of heaven with their lips, are leading them the way to hell with their lives. Good education is the best livery you can leave them dying. You let out your cares to make them great. Oh! Lift up your prayers to make them good. That before you die from them, you may see Christ live in them. While these twigs are green and tender, they should be bowed toward God. Children and servants are in a family, as passengers are in a boat. Husband and wife are as a pair of oars, to row them to their desired heaven. Let these small pieces of timber be hewed and squared for the caelestical building.

Acts respecting Children and Youth, 1671[20]

Parental authority also conferred responsibility for the preservation and promotion of communal values. Knowledge, the Puritans believed, was necessary to enable persons to learn God's will, which was revealed in history and the Scriptures. It was also important to help citizens to understand and obey the laws. Although the Massachusetts General Court passed a law in 1647 requiring every town of 100 families to set up a grammar school, for most of the seventeenth century the primary responsibility for teaching reading and writing fell on the family or on literate women of the community who established "dame schools."

Concern that some families were neglecting their duties led to the passage of this law in 1671, which reiterates the function of the family in the process of acculturation.

Sect. 1. Forasmuch as the good education of children is of singular behoof and benefit to any commonwealth, and whereas many parents and masters are too indulgent and negligent of their duty in that kind:

It is ordered that the selectmen of every town, in the several precincts and quarters where they dwell, shall have a vigilant eye over their brethren and neighbors, to see first that none of them shall suffer so much barbarism in any of their families, as not to endeavor to teach, by themselves or others, their children and apprentices, so much learning, as may enable them perfectly to read the English tongue, and knowledge of the capital laws: upon penalty of twenty shillings for each neglect therein.

Also that all masters of families do once a week (at the least) catechise their children and servants in the grounds and principles of religion; and if they be unable to do so much, that then at the least they procure such children and apprentices to learn some short orthodox catechism without book, that they may be able to answer unto the questions that shall be propounded to them out of such catechism, by their parents or masters, or any of the selectmen when they shall call them to trial, of what they have learned in that kind.

And farther that all parents and masters do breed and bring up their children and apprentices in some honest lawful calling, labour or employment, either in husbandry or some other trade, profitable for themselves and the commonwealth, if they will not or cannot train them up in learning, to fit them for higher employments.

And if any of the selectmen after admonition by them given to such masters of families, shall find them still negligent of their duty in the particulars aforementioned, whereby children and servants become rude, stubborn and unruly: the said selectmen with the help of two magistrates, or the next county court for that shire, shall take such children or apprentices from them, and place them with some masters for years, (boys till they come to twenty-one, and girls eighteen years of age complete) which will more strictly look unto, and force them to submit unto government, according to the rules of this order, if by fair means and former instructions they will not be drawn into it.

Charles County Court Records, 1694[21]

A shorter life expectancy, the low density of settlement, and the dispersal of the population resulted in less emphasis on education in the Chesapeake. Children who received an academic education were generally taught within the home; education consisted of learning to read in the Bible. Widows, like Elizabeth Williams, frequently bound out their sons as a means of preparing them to earn a living. The stipulation in the "putting out" agreement that Mrs. Williams's sons be taught to read was increasingly common by the end of the seventeenth century. As this example illustrates, the apprenticeship system served to train the young and organize the work force; as one scholar has observed, it also functioned as a kind of welfare institution and at times as a substitute for adoption.

Mr. Henry Hawkins produced these ensuing notes here in court. These are to satisfy the court that I am very willing that Mr. Hawkins should have my boy Edward until he shall arrive at one and twenty years of age, he being three years of age and one month, the said boy is to learn to read as witness my hand the 7th day of November 1694.

> [her mark]
> Elizabeth Williams

Therefore it is ordered that the said Edward Williams the son of the said Elizabeth Williams [be] sent [to] the said Henry Hawkins and Elizabeth his wife until he arrive to the age of twenty one years, they learning or causing the said Edward to be taught to read.

Mr. John Hawkins produced the ensuing notes here in court. These are to satisfy the court that I am very willing John Hawkins should have my boy William until he comes to the age of one and twenty years of age, he being ten years of age the last day of October past, provided John Hawkins puts him to school til he can read in the Bible as witness my hand November 7 1692.

> [her mark]
> Elizabeth Williams

Therefore it is ordered that the said William Williams the son of the said Elizabeth Williams [be] sent to said John Hawkins until he has arrived to the age of twenty one years as provided the said John Hawkins puts the said William Williams to school to learn to read in the Bible.

WIDOWHOOD

As a result of the high mortality and high fertility that characterized early American society, old age was comparatively rare, particularly in the Chesapeake where demographic disruptions were the most extreme. The few men and women who survived to old age were therefore believed to enjoy God's special favor and were treated with special deference. Respect for age was, moreover, reinforced by religious precepts and, in New England, by strong paternal controls over the supply of land, which created powerful ties of economic dependency and had important implications for father-son relationships and on patterns of family ties and kinship connections. Even when the family patriarch died, full financial independence did not necessarily follow, since in the seventeenth century surviving children had primary responsibility for providing for the widowed mother. By contrast, early parental death in the Chesapeake apparently resulted both in earlier autonomy for sons and greater prominence for widows.

Cotton Mather's Ornaments for the Daughters
of Zion, *1692*[22]

By the late seventeenth century, longevity for men began to decline
while that of women remained more or less constant. For that reason
and because men were almost always older than the women they married, a disproportionately high percentage of all marriages ended with
the death of the husband. Cotton Mather's address to women recognizes
that fact and attempts to define a proper role for widows, who were increasingly visible in seventeenth-century communities everywhere.

The vast numbers of poor widows in every neighborhood, make it very suspicious that our virtuous mother may at some time or other taste the sad, sour,
tearful cup of widowhood. If this be the portion of her cup, we must suppose
that she gives her husband a decent burial; that is, as on the one side, a funeral
that shall not be below his figure, so on the other side, a funeral that shall
not be above her estate.... Conceiving our virtuous woman to have her widows
vail upon her, we may behold her demeaning herself as a most virtuous person
in it.

I. Her grief on the death of her husband is great, and yet wise, and as wisely
great as greatly wise. Her mourning is more like a still rain, than a loud storm;
and instead of bellowing passions, which usually moulder away into a total
and the coldest forgetfulness, faster than the corpse of the husband in the
grave; she has a silent but a lasting sorrow; and yet that sorrow moderated
by a filial submission to the hand of that glorious God, before whom she opens
not her mouth any more than humbly to say, Lord thou did it....

II. It is now her main study and solace to have an interest in that promise,
Isai. 54.5. THY MAKER IS THY HUSBAND. And therefore like her whom
the apostle calls a widow indeed, she trusts in God, and continues in suppli-
cations and prayers night and day. She considers herself as now more than
ever belonging to the family of God, with a persuasion that he will certainly
and faithfully provide for her.... Moreover, if she be capable of it, she will now
more abound in all the exercises of charity toward her needy neighbors; whether
she have the name of Alice or no, yet according to the signification of it, she'll
be noble: and she will be an Helena, or an Eleanor, which is to say, as much
as pitiful: her visits, her bounties, and her succours to the poor are now increased rather than abated, with her new leisure for them; and if she be a
person of quality, she becomes yet more excellent for this quality....

III. She reckons that she must now be father as well as mother to the orphans
with whom she is left entrusted; and their father's beloved image on them,
does farther augment, yea, double her care concerning them. While her husband was alive she still acted as deputy husband, for the maintaining of all
good orders in the house, when he was out of the way. And now her husband
is deceased, she thinks that upon the setting of the sun, the moon is to govern;
and there shall not be one prayer the less performed, or one fault the more

indulged among her poor lambs, because he is gone. The kindred of her expired husband are also still welcome and grateful to her, upon this account....

IV. She is not forward and hasty now to take the liberty which the scripture does give unto younger widows; that is to marry. While she has one eye weeping for her departed husband, she has not the other eye open to see who comes next; nor will she think an Ephesian matron a fit copy for her. She counts it no hard law, which even the ancient pagans kept with great severity, that no widow should marry within ten or twelve months after the death of her husband: and she wonders that any Christians ordinarily can marry sooner. If she had a good husband, his memory has been so embalmed with her, that she cannot presently make room in her affections for another. If she had a bad husband, the cross felt so heavy, that she will be slow to be sure that it [has] been renewed upon her. But if after a convenient stay she do marry, it shall be, only in the Lord; unto a man that shall be neither heritical in his principles, nor exorbitant in his practices, and unto one that may be proper for her. Wherefore also if she be very old, she will not without special causes marry one that is very young; suspecting that such a pretended lover may court *hers* more than *her*; and that if there be too much (as perhaps a score of year) inequality of age, it may otherwise prove as temptatious, as it looks indecent....

V. When she is matched unto a second husband, whom she will never twit with any reflections and uncomely rememberances of her first; she is more than ordinarily solicitous to be a good mother-in-law, if she must be one at all; and so do her part, for the removing of the imputations which mothers-in-law have generally labored under. She knows that the way for her to have the blessing of heaven upon her children, is for her to make herself a blessing to his; and unkindness to the motherless little birds which now call her their Dam, will certainly be repaid by the just revenges of God. She is therefore so far from the partiality of that mother-in-law, who when her own child hurt a child of her husband's by throwing of a stone, whipped the child that felt the stone, for standing in the way of the child that flung it; that she makes no observable difference between his children and hers; unless it be this, that she corrects hers herself and refers his to him....

A True Inventory, 1638[23]

The death of the husband meant not only the loss of labor but of the legally recognized head of the household. Basic legal provisions for the care of widows was firmly established in the American colonies and specifications for their support, such as reserved space in the family house or water and barn rights, were often written into the husband's will. Such arrangements served to protect middle- and upper-class women from indigency and the community from responsibility for their upkeep. In poorer families, or for widowed women with no living children, however, life could be far more precarious, especially in the Chesapeake, where dispersed patterns of settlement often effectively isolated the widow from her family and friends. For these women, as the inventory of Widow Road's household goods poignantly reveals, widow-hood meant poverty.

Item	pounds tobacco
13 old napkins	030
a very mean bed with indifferent white rug	060
1 very ragged sheet	010
2 Bandes	025
2 caps	020
frying pans	016
3 old dublettes	020
1 old coat	025
2 small pewter dishes	030
1 old pewter pissepot	008
2 old porringers	004
1 old candlestick	006
1 pewter drinking cup	102
1 pewter cup	006
1 small salt seller	004
1 old spoon and aquavita bottle	005
3 old coils	012
3 old crose clothes	003
1 coil	002
4 old neck clothes	010
3 ragged waistcoats	006
1 iron pot and 1 iron kettle	100
2 ragged torn mats	000
2 empty cases	004
1 old brush	002
1 old case for smoothing iron	004
1 old small trunk	000
1 pillow bare	006
Total sum	430 [sic] pounds tobacco

Minutes, Third Haven Monthly Meeting, 1679, 1684[24]

In colonial America the burden of support for destitute widows without families fell upon some community institution. In the Quaker colonies the meeting structure carried out this responsibility. The Friends had separate meetings for men and women. Held in private homes, they were generally known by the locality where they met. Ordinarily the women's meetings were concerned with enforcing proper conduct for female Friends and with providing aid to the needy, although they sometimes sent representatives to the men's meetings. The men's monthly meetings were business meetings, which took up problems such as overseeing the administration of estates of deceased members and, as the minutes of the Third Haven Monthly Meeting suggest, took responsibility for the care of widows and orphans.

At our Man's Meeting at Harrell Powells, May, 4, 1679
The women's meeting signifying to this meeting that there is a real necessity for visiting the widow Parrott did for the effecting of the same request the assistance of this meeting to which the meeting readily assented and in order for the performance of the same requests William Berry and William Southbee to assist them and to give an answer to the next man's meeting.

At our Monthly Man's Meeting at Thomas Taylors the 8 June 1679
William Berry and William Southbee did according to the request of the last man's meeting visit the widow Parrott and Clement Sales and the service they had for the Lord and his truth in that particular visit had good acceptance and friends left them in a good sense of the love of God so that it is hoped wherein there had been a remissness it may be amended.

At our Monthly Meeting at our meeting house at the head of Third Haven Creek, November 17, 1684
Mary Swift widow laying her poverty before the meeting and that she had great need of a bed this meeting considering her condition has ordered John Edmondson or Emanuel Jenkinson to buy one and give their answer at the next meeting.

NOTES

1. Clayton Coleman Hall, ed., *Narratives of Early Maryland, 1633–1684* (New York, 1910), pp. 85–86.

2. William Browne et al., eds., *Archives of Maryland* (Baltimore, 1883–1912), LIII, p. 599.

3. Durand of Dauphiné, *A Huguenot Exile in Virginia; or, Voyages of a Frenchman Exiled for His Religion, 1686*, intro. and notes by Gilbert Chinard (New York, 1934), pp. 137–39.

4. Susan M. Kingsbury, ed., *Records of the Virginia Company of London*, 4 vols. (Washington, D.C., 1906–1935), IV, p. 487.

5. William H. Whitmore, ed., *The Colonial Laws of Massachusetts Reprinted from the Edition of 1672* (Boston, 1890), pp. 101–2.

6. "Extracts from the Records of Third Haven Monthly Meeting of Friends, Easton, Talbot County, Maryland, 1680," *Pennsylvania Magazine of History and Biography*, XVII (No. 1, 1893), pp. 88–92.

7. William W. Hening, *The Statutes-at-Large, Being a Collection of all the Laws of Virginia (1619–1792)*, 13 vols. (Philadelphia, New York, 1823), I, pp. 146 and 552.

8. Browne et al., eds., *Archives of Maryland*, I, pp. 533–34.

9. Cotton Mather, *Ornaments for the Daughters of Zion* (Delmar, N.Y., 1978), pp. 86–97. Reprinted with permission of Scholars Facsimiles and Reprints.

10. William Secker, *A Wedding Ring Fit for the Finger* (Boston, 1750), pp. 19–21.

11. Joseph R. McElrath, Jr. and Allan P. Robb, eds., *The Complete Works of Anne Bradstreet* (Boston, 1981), pp. 182–83. Reprinted with permission of Twayne Publishers, a division of G. K. Hall, Boston.

12. *The Charters and General Laws of the Colony and Province of Massachusetts Bay* (Boston, 1814), pp. 277–78.

13. Maine Historical Society, *Maine Province and Court Records* (Portland, 1931), II, p. 460. Reprinted with permission of the Maine Historical Society.

14. John Oliver, *A Present to be Given to Teeming Women by Their Husbands and Friends* (Boston, 1694).

15. McElrath and Robb, eds., *The Complete Works of Anne Bradstreet*, pp. 179–80. Reprinted with permission of Twayne Publishers, a division of G. K. Hall, Boston.

16. Whitmore, ed., *The Colonial Laws of Massachusetts*, p. 28.

17. Fr. Gabriel Sagard, *The Long Journey to the Country of the Hurons*, George M. Wrong, ed. (Toronto, 1939), pp. 127–31. Reprinted with permission of the Champlain Society.

18. Mather, *Ornaments for the Daughters of Zion*, pp. 205–6.

19. Secker, *A Wedding Ring Fit for the Finger*, p. 17.

20. *Charters and General Laws of the Colony of Massachusetts Bay*, pp. 73–74.

21. Charles County Court Records, S #1 (1692–1694), p. 402, Maryland Hall of Records, Annapolis, Maryland. Reprinted with permission of the Maryland Hall of Records.

22. Mather, *Ornaments for the Daughters of Zion*, pp. 110–15.

23. Susie M. Ames, ed., *County Court Records of Accomack—Northampton, Virginia 1630–1640* (Washington, D.C., 1954), p. 123. Reprinted with permission of the American Historical Association.

24. Minutes, Third Haven Monthly Meetings, 1676–1746, Maryland Hall of Records, Annapolis, Maryland. Reprinted with permission from the Maryland Hall of Records.

BIBLIOGRAPHY

Axtell, James, ed. *The Indian Peoples of Eastern America: A Documentary History of the Sexes.* New York, 1981.

Carr, Lois Green and Lorena S. Walsh. "The Planter's Wife: The Experience of White Women in Seventeenth Century Maryland." *William and Mary Quarterly*, 3d ser., 34 (1977): 542–71.

Demos, John. *A Little Commonwealth: Family Life in Plymouth Colony.* New York, 1970.

Frost, J. William. *The Quaker Family in Colonial America: A Portrait of the Society of Friends.* Ithica, N.Y., 1973.

Greven, Philip, Jr. *Four Generations: Population, Land and Family in Colonial Andover, Massachusetts.* New York, 1970.

———. *The Protestant Temperament: Patterns of Child-Rearing, Religious Experience and the Self in Early America.* New York, 1977.

Koehler, Lyle. *A Search for Power: The "Weaker Sex" in Seventeenth-Century New England.* Urbana, Chicago, London, 1980.

Kulikoff, Allan. "The Beginnings of the Afro-American Family in Maryland," in Aubrey C. Land et al., eds., *Law, Society, and Politics in Early Maryland*. Baltimore, 1977, 171–96.

Menard, Russell. "The Maryland Slave Population, 1658–1730: A Demographic Profile of Blacks in Four Counties." *William and Mary Quarterly*, 3d. ser., 32 (1975): 29–54.

Morgan, Edmund. *The Puritan Family: Religion and Domestic Relations in Seventeenth-Century New England*. Rev. ed. New York, 1966.

Rutman, Darrett B. and Anita H. Rutman. "Of Agues and Fevers: Malaria in the Early Chesapeake." *William and Mary Quarterly*, 3d Ser., 33 (1976): 31–60.

——. " 'Now-Wives and Sons-in-Law': Parental Death in a Seventeenth-Century Virginia County." In Thad W. Tate and David L. Ammerman, eds., *The Chesapeake in the Seventeenth Century, Essays on Anglo-American Society*. Chapel Hill, North Carolina, 1979, 153–82.

Ryan, Mary P. *Womanhood in America from Colonial Times to the Present*. New York, 1975.

Walsh, Lorena S. " 'Till Death Us Do Part': Marriage and Family in Seventeenth-Century Maryland." In Tate and Ammerman, eds., *The Chesapeake in the Seventeenth Century*. 126–52.

Ulrich, Laurel T. *Good Wives: Images and Reality in the Lives of Women in Northern New England, 1650–1750*. New York, 1982.

Wolf, Stephanie Grauman. *Urban Village: Population, Community and Family Structure in Germantown, Pennsylvania, 1683–1800*. Princeton, N.J., 1976.

2 WOMEN AND WORK IN THE SEVENTEENTH CENTURY

Nobody came to the New World to get poor. The limited opportunities created by a land shortage and a rigid class structure and the economic dislocations created by inflation, growing commercialization, and nascent industrialization, were perhaps the primary economic reasons that emigrants left Europe. They were encouraged by the enthusiastic promoters of colonization who described the New World's fertile soil, abundant rivers, and verdant forests, and promised settlers lives of plenty and leisure. Most of these pamphleteers never visited the New World, and those earliest planters or settlers who had believed the promotional literature were often sadly disappointed. The continent did provide bountifully, but work, not leisure, was the key to unlocking its wealth.

This wealth lay in the abundant lands, and the first planters made their livings as farmers. Some colonies—for example, Virginia and Plymouth colonies—began with communal land holdings, but private property, hedged by legal restrictions imposed by local or imperial governments, quickly became the rule.

Farms varied in size from small holdings in the New England towns to large plantations in the Chesapeake colonies. Most of the earliest colonists were subsistence farmers, producing enough for household use and selling or bartering the small surplus for whatever items could not be made on the farm and within the household. Yet almost from the beginning of settlement, commercial agriculture also existed, whether it was the tobacco culture of the Chesapeake or the New England efforts to trade fish, lumber, livestock, and grain to the West Indies.

The predominantly agricultural economy dictated that almost all men, and almost all women and children as well, must work. Only the very wealthy were exempt from labor. A woman's work, if she were white and free, was done within her family's household. Since it was within this household that the necessities of life were produced, her role was essential to the survival and well-being of her family and of the community. Her husband worked nearby in the fields or house.

Some historians, like Gerda Lerner, building upon the early work of Alice Clark, have maintained that women's economic significance and relatively undifferentiated work place brought self-esteem and prestige within the family and the community. Mary Ryan, for example, uses the term "Adam's Rib" to suggest women's crucial, although supporting, role. Mary Beth Norton, on the other hand, has countered this "myth of the golden age" by pointing out that although women produced wealth, men controlled it, and further, that women's economic roles were far more limited and limiting than men's. It is possible also to argue that the assignment to women of the physically arduous drudgery of housework suggests an underlying belief in women's inferiority, reflected in and reinforced by her second-class position within the family, church, and state, and that economic contributions did not automatically confer political power or prestige.

Occasionally, out of necessity or ingenuity, women worked outside of the family household. Yet even this work was often delimited by family responsibilities and social constraints. Hampered as well by laws that denied married women property rights, these women seldom met with success. Their resulting poverty and dependence were both cause and effect of their secondary position.

European observers often viewed the labor of Indian women more sympathetically than they did women's work within their own culture. The apparent absence of the expected sexual division of labor was further proof that Indians were not civilized by European standards.

A significant portion of the colonial population, male and female, was unfree: white indentured servants or black slaves. White and black servitude filled the ever-present need for workers in a primitive, labor-intensive agrarian economy. Indentured servants were white Europeans who contracted to serve a master for a specified length of time—usually four to seven years—in return for passage to the New World, clothing and shelter, perhaps the acquisition of a skill, and a piece of property or a small sum of money at the end of their term of service. The first Africans arrived as servants, but because of racial prejudice and the need for a stable labor force, perpetual and hereditary servitude for blacks became institutionalized in law and custom by the 1660s in both northern and southern colonies. Fewer gender distinctions existed between the work of male and female servants and slaves.

FREE WOMEN

The work done by free women in their households indicates a division of labor according to gender, women generally being responsible for the house and adjacent yard and men for work in the fields or nearby town. Indeed, that division made more imperative the importation of women into Virginia to become wives of the men, who apparently could not take care of their own domestic needs even though they had brought male servants with them. "Huswifery," therefore, was highly valued, and a good housewife was highly praised, if not paid. Her work, without domestic technology, was never-ending and physically demanding, even with the help of children, servants, and perhaps her husband. She raised and prepared food, made family clothing, medicine, soap, candles, and other household items, and cared for her several offspring.

A few enterprising women supported themselves outside of the household economy, but only with the greatest difficulty. Outside jobs were few and unremunerative in an agricultural economy, especially when women were granted less land than men, denying them an equal chance at economic success since land was the primary source of wealth. More often than men, therefore, women became paupers, dependent upon public charity.

Work Within the Family Context

Starving Time in Virginia, 1609–1610[1]

Almost all of the first settlers in Jamestown, Virginia were male, many of them gentlemen—second or third sons of the English aristocracy who came to the New World to acquire wealth as quickly and with as little effort as possible. Lacking both skills and the motivation to labor, these men quickly found themselves in desperate straits, such as the "starving time" described in this document, after the departure of John Smith ended his rigorous discipline. Mortality rates for both men and women in these early years were staggeringly high; the woman described here suffered an unusual fate indeed.

Now we all found the loss of Captain [John] Smith, yea his greatest maligners could now curse his loss. As for corn, provision, and contribution from the savages, we had nothing but mortal wounds, with clubs and arrows. As for our hogs, hens, goats, sheep, horse, or what lived, our commanders, officers, and savages daily consumed them. Some small proportions sometimes we tasted, till all was devoured. Then swords, arms, pieces, or anything, we traded with the savages whose cruel fingers were so often embrewed in our blood, that what by their cruelties, our Governors' indiscretion, and the loss of our ships, of five hundred [settlers] in six months after Captain Smith's departure, there remained not past sixty men, women, and children, most miserable and poor creatures. And those were preserved for the most part by roots, herbs, acorns, walnuts, berries, now and then a little fish.

Nay, so great was our famine, that a savage we slew and buried, the poorer sort took him up again and ate him, and so did diverse one another boiled and stewed with roots and herbs. And one amongst the rest did kill his wife, powdered [salted] her, and had eaten part of her before it was known, for which he was executed, as he well deserved. Now whether she was better roasted, boiled or carbonadoed [grilled], I know not, but of such a dish as powdered wife I never heard of.

The Virginia Company Sends Wives, 1621[2]

By 1618 the dreams of easy wealth had vanished, and Virginia company officials had begun to plan for a permanent colony based upon private property and families. In 1619 a first shipment of ninety "young maids" arrived in the colony; they were to provide male settlers with domestic services and goods, children, and the basis of a stable social order. The 1621 letter below reveals the company's reasons for importing women but does not tell us why these women, who were not indentured servants, might have chosen to come to this dreary wilderness.

A LETTER TO THE GOVERNOR AND COUNCIL IN VIRGINIA, 1621

We send you in this ship one widow and eleven maids for wives for the people in Virginia. There hath been especial care had in the choice of them, for there hath not any one of them been received but upon good commendations, as by a note herewith sent you may perceive. We pray you all therefore that at their first landing they may be housed, lodged, and provided for of diet till they be married, for such was the haste of sending them away, as that straitened with time, we had no means to put provisions aboard, which defect shall be supplied by the magazine ship. And in case they cannot be presently married, we desire they may be put to several householders that have wives till they can be provided of husbands. There are near fifty more which are shortly to come, are sent by our most honorable Lord and Treasurer, the Earl of Southampton and certain worthy gentlemen who taking into their consideration, that the plantation can never flourish till families be planted, and the respect of wives and children fix the people on the soil, therefore have given this fair beginning. For the reimbursing of whose charges, it is ordered that every man that marries them give 120 £ weight of the best leaf tobacco for each of them, and in case any of them die, that proportion must be advanced to make it up upon those that survive.

Edward Taylor on "Huswifery"[3]

The use by the Puritan poet and minister Edward Taylor (1642?–1729) of domestic imagery in this graceful poem suggests the centrality of huswifery in his imagination. This use also suggests that Taylor was familiar with the artifacts of seventeenth-century housekeeping, which was to be expected when men and women inhabited the same work and living space. Would Taylor's wife have described her spinning wheel in these terms?

Huswifery

Make me, O Lord, thy spinning wheel complete.
    Thy holy word my distaff make for me.
Make mine affections thy swift flyers neat.
    And make my soul thy holy spool to be.
My conversation make to be thy reel
And reel the yarn thereon spun of thy wheel.
Make me thy loom then; knit therein this twine;
    And make thy holy spirit, Lord, wind quills.
Then weave the web thyself. The yarn is fine.
    Thine ordinances make my fulling mills.
Then dye the same in heavenly colors choice,
    All pinked with varnished flowers of paradise.
Then clothe therewith mine understanding, will,
    Affections, judgement, conscience, memory,
My words, and actions, that their shine may fill
    My ways with glory and thee glorify.
Then mine apparel shall display before ye
That I am clothed in holy robes for glory.

Plymouth Colony Wills and Inventories, 1653[4]

By learning what colonial housewives had to work with, we can partially re-create their work lives and living standards. It is particularly useful to note the variety of household utensils listed in these wills. The reader, however, must try to imagine what the utensils were used for, and by whom, and what the housekeeping tasks actually were like. Both of the deceased men (few women left wills) were clearly of the gentry class, but the number and kinds of their possessions differ, indicating differences in socioeconomic status even within this small colony.

REV. JOHN LOTHROP'S WILL AND INVENTORY

The last will and testament of Mr. John Lothrop, Pastor of the Church of Christ at Barnstable, August 1, 1653.

First, I will and bequeath unto my wife the house wherein I now dwell with the furniture thereof and the ground belonging thereunto with the marsh land that lyeth on the east besides Randevou Creek, and also my ground in the common field;

To my son Thomas, my eldest son, I will and bequeath the house I first lived in in Barnstable with the ground belonging thereunto and the marsh joining to the lower end thereof which butts and bounds upon the Creek northward with this condition that he, my said son Thomas, is to give to my son John in England and to my son Benjamin here in the Bay each of them a good cow of five pound;

My daughter Jane and my daughter Barbara have had their portions already.

To the rest of my children, both mine and my wife's, my will is that every of them shall have a cow.

THIS 8TH OF DECEMBER, 1653

A true inventory of the cattle and goods of Mr. John Lothrop, pastor of the Church of Christ at Barnstable, late deceased:

	£	s	d
Imprimis six cows valued at	26	00	00
It 3 two yearlings	07	10	00
It 2 calves	01	00	00
It 5 pigs	00	15	00
It his wearing apparel of all sorts	13	09	00
It a bedstead with bed and furniture	05	10	00
It a bed and furniture	02	00	00
It sheets, napkins, with other linen	02	16	00
It 5 chests with a cupboard and hangings	00	14	00
It table, chairs, and cushions	01	00	00
It tubs and other wooden lumber	01	11	00
It tin and earthen ware	00	07	06
It 4 brass kettles with other brass	02	00	00
It one iron pot kettle hangers with other iron	00	14	00
It one musket	00	10	00
It his books	05	00	00
It for other small things omitted	00	05	00
The total sum is	65	121	06

JOHN BARKER'S INVENTORY

A true and just inventory of the estate chattels and goods of John Barker of Marshfield, deceased, being apprised by Kanelme Winslow, Joseph Beedle, Edmond Hincksman, and John Bourne, of the same town.

Taken the 17th of December 1652 and exhibited to the General Court held at Plymouth the sixth of June, 1653, on the oath of Anna Barker, widow.

	£	s	d
Imprimis one cassock and breeches of cloth	01	05	00
It the wearing apparel that he died in	00	05	00
It 3 handkerchiefs, a cap, and a band	00	02	00
It one powder horn and a small dial	00	01	06
It a musket sword and belt and bandeliers	01	04	00
It a feather bed and bolster, 4 pillows and 2 coverlets	03	00	00
It a straw bed and blanket	00	04	00
It 3 chests, a box, and a cradle	00	10	00
It 2 iron pots and one iron kettle and a pothook and hangers	01	08	00
It 3 brass kettles and a skillet	00	16	00
It 2 pewter dishes, 2 pint pots, a little basin and porringers and 3 spoons	00	05	00
It 8 trays, 6 trenchers, 2 dishes, a little pail	00	09	00
It 5 tubs and a hogshead	00	06	00
It 2 old Bibles and other books	00	03	00
It an old scythe and an old hatchet, 2 axes, 2 wedges, a smoothing iron, and old iron things	00	12	00
It a looking glass	00	02	00
It a thwart saw	00	03	00
It a yard and a quarter of cotton cloth	00	06	00
It a cart and wheels and a plow and share, two chains and a yoke	01	08	00
It 5 bushels of Indian corn	00	15	00
It a spinning wheel	00	01	06
It hemp and hempseed	00	13	00
It eight loads of hay	02	00	00
We do judge the wheat and barley in the straw that is unthreshed in the barn at the price of	07	00	00
It one yoke of oxen at	13	10	00
It 2 cows	10	00	00
It one cow, 2 heifers, one steer at 4 £ a head	16	00	00
It an heifer of year and vantage	02	05	00
It two calves	02	00	00
It 2 swine	01	04	00
It one cow	04	10	00
It for the table and form	00	01	06
It we do price all his lands and meadows and houses and all appurtenances thereunto	60	00	00
It for householdments belonging to his estate	00	01	06
	124	169	24

Women as Independent Landholders, New Haven Colony,
1643[5]

Few women chose to try to make a living on the land by themselves, as these partial records show. Most women married or lived within familial households with male heads such as fathers, brothers, or sons. When widowhood or other misfortune necessitated a woman's living alone, unequal allocation of town lands by the town fathers made her position more difficult. This inequity is indicated in the annual property taxes listed here. How have the women listed here probably acquired their property? What do the tax payments indicate about the distribution of property and wealth in this community?

Names of the planters	Rates yearly paid for land		
	£	s	d
Mr. Theophilus Eaton	10	13	00
Mr. Samuel Eaton	2	19	00
Mrs. Eaton	00	12	00
David Yale	01	12	06
Will Touttle	02	01	06
Ezekial Cheevers	00	05	11
Captain Turner	03	06	06
Richard Pery	01	02	08
Richard Malbon	02	05	06
Thomas Nash	00	18	02
John Benham	00	12	04
Thomas Kimberley	00	11	02
John Chapman	01	04	00
Mathew Gilbert	02	05	00
Jasper Craine	01	15	01
An elder	02	01	00
George Lamberton	03	19	00
Will Wilks	00	13	06
Thomas Jeffrey	00	13	06
Robert Ceely	00	18	05
Nicholas Elcey	00	05	01
John Budd	02	00	06
Richard Hull	00	07	04
William Preston	00	17	09
Benjamin Fenne	00	08	07
Will Jeanes	00	18	00
John Brockett	00	02	06
Roger Allen	00	04	03
Mr. Hickocks	03	19	00
Stephen Goodyear	09	19	02

Names of the planters	Rates yearly paid for land		
	£	s	d
Jeremy Whitnell	00	06	06
Samuel Bayley	00	19	00
Thomas Buckingham	00	10	02
Richard Miles	00	19	00
Thomas Welch	01	19	00
Nathaniel Axtell	01	16	07
Henry Stonell	01	02	06
Will Fowler	03	06	06
Peter Preden	02	01	00
James Preden	00	05	02
Edmond Tapp	03	06	06
Widow Baldwin	03	03	06
An elder	0	0	0
Richard Platt	01	00	00
Zackariah Whitman	02	19	00
Thomas Osborne	01	10	00
Henry Rudderforde	00	10	00
Thomas Trobridge	02	02	06
Widow Potter	00	05	01
John Potter	00	07	09
Samuel Whitehead	00	06	06
John Clark	01	11	00
Luke Atkinson	00	09	06
Arthur Halbidge	00	07	04

Work Outside the Family Context

A Woman Merchant, New Haven Colony, 1645[6]

Some women did carry on profitable enterprises outside the family setting. The cloth that Mrs. Stolion traded for cows in the following dispute, though, was made in her own household, which is presumably where she planned to use the cows. Complex business ventures such as hers involved not only the ability to produce goods for sale but to drive a shrewd bargain which rested upon barter rather than currency. The colonial laws that were supposed to restrain excessive profit making landed Mrs. Stolion in court.

Captain Turner informed the court that Mrs. Stolion had complained to sundry persons that he made a bargain with her for cloth for which she accepted cows, but was disappointed to her great damage, and therefore, he desired she might show what cause he had given her so to do.

Mrs. Stolion pleaded that the captain came to her house to buy some cloth, chose a piece of 20 shillings a yard, and said he would have six yards of it, and Mrs. Stolion should have a cow, and both agreed to have her prized [appraised] by some indifferent men. The captain said also that he had need of more cloth and commodities to the value of 12 pounds and told her she should have two cows, and she said when her son came home, he went to the captain, chose two cows, and when he came home, he told her the captain would come the next day and speak with her, but came not according to his promise, and though she sent to him, yet he came not.

The captain said he did really intend to have had some cloth and that she should have a cow, and when Mr. Stolion came to choose one of the best cows he had, and Mr. Stolion told him he might as well let his mother have two cows, for she had need of cows and the captain had need of cloth and commodities, whereupon the captain let him choose another cow and set him a price, namely 12 pounds. Mr. Stolion said he would give but 10 pounds but the captain told him he would abate 10 shillings. Mr. Stolion said he would give no more but 10 pounds. They parted and the captain promised he would come and speak with his mother, but because he could not well go to Mrs. Stolion, and having heard of the dearness of her commodities, the excessive gains she took, was discouraged from the proceeding, and accordingly, bid his man tell her he would have none of her cloth, and naming sundry particular instances of commodities sold by her at an excessive rate, left it to the consideration of the court whether she had not done him wrong in complaining of him, and if she might not be dealt with as an oppressor of the commonweal.

The court conceived the captain was to blame that he did not go to her according to his promise, especially that after he heard she was unsatisfied he did not attend her satisfaction. But withall that the captain might justly offer it to the consideration of the court whether such selling be not extortion and not to be suffered in the commonwealth.

1) The captain complained that she sold some cloth to William Bradley at 20 shillings a yard that cost her about 12 shillings for which she received wheat at 3 shillings, 6 pence a bushel, and sold it presently to the baker at 5 shilling a bushel who received it of William Bradley, only she forbearing her money six months.

2) That the cloth which Lieutenant Seely bought of her for 20 shillings a yard last year, she had sold this year for 7 bushels of wheat a yard, to be delivered in her chamber, which she confessed.

3) That she would not take wampum for commodities at 6 a penny though it were the same she had paid to others at 6, but she would have 7 a penny, as Thomas Robinson testified.

4) That she sold primers at 9 pence apiece which cost but 4 pence here in New England. Thomas Robinson testified that his wife gave her 8 pence in wampum at 7 a penny, though she had but newly received the same wampum of Mrs. Stolion at 6.

The court, seriously weighing all the particulars, charged against Mrs. Stolion, conceived that the nature and aggravations of the aforesaid charges was proper for a court of magistrates to consider of, and therefore respited and referred it to the court of magistrates to be held at New Haven the last Monday in March next.

A Woman Tavern-Keeper, 1673–1674[7]

Court records such as these illuminate the activities of extraordinary rather than ordinary men and women. Mrs. Stolion and Miss Greenland (described here) were such extraordinary women. Miss Greenland's business activities brought her frequently into the Maine provincial court as she ran afoul of the colonial laws regulating the sale of alcohol. Tavern-keeping was a relatively common occupation for women, who could turn their domestic skills and their own homes to profitable uses.

JULY 1, 1673.

Miss Greenland is ordered by the Court to take down her sign. Nor hath any license granted her by this Court.

JULY 7, 1674.

We present Miss Mary Greenland for selling wine, beer, and liquor by retail without a license.

The Court concludes her to have an admonition.

JULY 6, 1675.

We present Miss Mary Greenland for selling wine by retail without license.

This presentment is remitted in regard she hath some approbation for keeping of a public house of entertainment under the hands of the selectmen, and paying her fees, 5 shillings, is discharged.

We present Mr. John Bray keeping an ordinary licensed and not providing entertainment for strangers according to law, whereupon several persons were constrained to go to Miss Greenland's for entertainment.

Massachusetts Laws regarding Single Women, 1695–1696 and 1703–1704[8]

Single women who could not find work within their own households were expected to make their economic contributions in other ways. Although this permitted women a degree of flexibility, the 1695–1696 law indicates a recognition of women's unequal opportunities to earn money. The 1703–1704 statute reveals the possible fate of a women who did not work and suggests that more rigorous community standards were applied to women's than to men's work.

AN ACT FOR GRANTING A TAX UPON POLLS AND ESTATES

And be it accordingly enacted by the Lieutenant-Governor, Council, and Representatives in General Court assembled, and by the authority of the same, That there be raised, levied, collected, and paid into the public treasury of this province, a rate or tax upon polls and estates, real and personal, to be assessed upon the freeholders, inhabitants, and other of his majesty's subjects, resident within this his province, in manner, at time, and according to the several rules and proportions in this present act hereafter set down: that is to say, all male persons of the age of sixteen years and upward (except elders of churches, settled ministers, and others devoted to the ministry, the president, fellows, and students of Harvard College, grammar schoolmasters, and such who through age, infirmity, or extreme poverty in the discretion of the selectmen or trustees, are rendered incapable to contribute towards the public charge) at four shillings per poll; and all single women that live at their own hand, at two shillings each, except such as through age, or extreme poverty, in the discretion of the assessors as aforesaid, are unable to contribute towards the public charge.

AN ACT OF SUPPLEMENT TO THE ACTS REFERRING TO THE POOR, ETC.

Be it further declared and enacted by the authority aforesaid,
That the selectmen or overseers of the poor, or the greater part of them, be and are further empowered, by and with the assent of two justices of the peace, to set to work all such persons, married or unmarried, able of body, having no means to maintain them, that live idly and use or exercise no ordinary and daily lawful trade or business to get their living by. And no single person of either sex, under the age of twenty-one years, shall be suffered to live at their own hand, but under some orderly family government. Nor shall any woman of ill fame, married or unmarried, be suffered to receive or entertain lodgers in her house. And the selectmen or overseers of the poor, constables, and tithingmen, are hereby ordered to see to the due observance of this act, and to complain and inform against any transgressions thereof to one or more justices of the peace, or the court of general sessions of the peace, who are hereby respectively required and empowered, upon due conviction of the offender or offenders for living idly or disorderly, contrary to the true intent of this act, to commit or send such offenders to the house of correction or workhouse, there to remain and be kept to labour, until they be discharged by order of the court of general sessions of the peace, unless such person or persons so complained of shall give reasonable caution or assurance, to the satisfaction of the justice or court, that they will reform: provided, this act shall not be construed to extend to hinder any single woman of good repute from the exercise of any lawful trade or employment, for a livelihood, whereto she shall have the allowance and approbation of the selectmen or overseers of the poor, or the greater part of them, any law, usage or custom to the contrary notwithstanding.

Women in Poverty

The Wife of John Davess, 1681[9]

This fragment of a court record illustrates the economic dependence of a wife upon her husband. Without property rights or economic opportunity, a woman might be reduced to the abject poverty described here.

We present John Davess, living within the township of Cape Porpus, and his wife at Winter Harbor, the said Davess not taking care of her maintenance, notwithstanding several complaints have been made, and order taken for supply of her in her great necessity, and reforming that disorder, the woman being destitute of food and raiment, being constrained to fetch rockweed to boil and eat to maintain her life.

Abigail Day, 1691[10]

The town of Boston had early constructed an almshouse or poorhouse, although most paupers unable to care for themselves were sheltered in private homes until well into the eighteenth century. Cotton Mather here unwittingly comments on the lamentable conditions in this public institution and the pathetic vulnerability of the colonial poor woman.

Abigail Day received the censure of an admonition for

1) Untruths uttered in her speeches on many occasions;

2) Expressions full of scandalous discontent and impatience under her afflictions,
Especially saying of the laudable diet in the almshouse, where she is lodged, that she would thank neither God nor man for such victuals,

3) Defaming the man who keeps the almshouse, as if he had several times made attempts upon her chastity.

Her penitence for the two former heads of scandal appeared somewhat, but not enough.

She still insisted on the truth of what she hath said, in the third, though blaming her imprudent divulgation.

The man asserts his innocency, and she has no proof to support her charge of his guilt.

Indian Women, 1624[11]

The Europeans had first thought that the Indians, as they incorrectly called them, would do their work for them. Although a few Indians were enslaved, early hopes for an Indian labor force did not materialize among the dozens of tribes that dwelt in North America. Captain John Smith's account of Indian life is clearly distorted by his own European values, but it does furnish some reasons why Indians never became servants, as well as Smith's analysis of the different work done by male and female Indians of this particular eastern tribe. Notice how closely the work of both sexes was tied to the seasons and to available natural resources. What were the differences and similarities between work done by Indian and by colonial women?

The land is not populous, for the men be few; their far greater number is of women and children. Within sixty miles of Jamestown there are about some 5000 people, but of able men fit for their wars scarce 1500. To nourish so many together they have yet no means, because they make so small a benefit of their land, be it never so fertile.

Some being very great, as the Susquehannocks, others very little, as the Wighcocomocos; but generally tall and straight, of a comely proportion, and of a color brown when they are of any age, but they are born white. Their hair is generally black, but few have any beards. The men wear half their beard [heads] shaven, the other half long; for barbers they use their women, who with two shells will grate away the hair, of any fashion they please. The women's [heads] are cut in many fashions, agreeable to their years, but ever some part remains long.

They are very strong, of an able body and full of agility, able to endure to lie in the woods under a tree by the fire in the worst of winter, or in the weeds and grass.

They are inconstant in everything but what constrains them to keep. Crafty, timorous, quick of apprehension, and very ingenious. Some are of disposition fearful, some bold, all savage. They are covetous of copper, beads, and such like trash. They are soon moved to anger, and so malicious that they seldom forget an injury. They seldom steal from one another, lest their conjurers should reveal it and so they be pursued and punished. That they are thus feared is certain, but that any can reveal their offenses by conjuration, I am doubtful. Their women are careful not to be suspected of dishonesty without the leave of their husbands.

Each household knows their own lands and gardens, and most live off their own labors.

Their houses are in the midst of their fields or gardens, which are small plots of ground—some twenty acres, some forty, some one hundred, some two hundred, some more, some less. In some places from two to fifty of those houses [are] together or but a little separated by groves of trees. Near their habitations is little small wood or old trees on the ground by reason of their burning of them for fire. So that a man may gallop a horse among those woods any way but where the creeks or rivers shall hinder.

The men bestow their time in fishing, hunting, wars, and such man-like exercises, scorning to be seen in any women-like exercise, which is the cause that the women be very painful [toiling] and the men often idle. The women and children do the rest of the work. They make mats, baskets, pots, mortars, pound their corn, make their bread, prepare their victuals, plant their corn, gather their corn, bear all kind of burdens, and such like.

Their fire they kindle presently by chafing a dry pointed stick in a hole of a little square piece of wood, that firing itself will so fire moss, leaves, or any such like dry thing that will quickly burn.

In March and April they live much upon their fishing weirs, and feed on fish, turkeys, and squirrels. In May and June they plant their fields and live most off acorns, walnuts, and fish. But to amend their diet, some disperse themselves in small companies and live upon fish, beasts, crabs, oysters, land tortoises, strawberries, mulberries, and such like. In June, July, and August, they feed upon the roots of tuckahoe, berries, fish, and green wheat.

Betwixt their hands and thighs, their women use to spin the barks of trees, deer sinews, or a kind of grass they call pemmenaw; of these they make a thread very even and readily. This thread serves for many uses, as about their housing, apparel, also they make nets for fishing, for the quantity as formally braided as ours. They make also with it lines for angles.

Their hunting houses are like unto arbors covered with mats. These their women bear after them, with corn, acorns, mortars, and all bag and baggage they use. When they come to the place of exercise, every man does his best to show his dexterity, for by their excelling in those qualities they get their wives.

UNFREE WOMEN

Unfree women did the harshest and most disagreeable tasks within the colonial home and often outside of it as well. Indentured servants came from many groups of the European population. A few were of the middling sort who simply lacked the money for passage to the New World. Most, however, were from the dregs of European society—beggars, prostitutes, vagabonds, convicted criminals, enticed or kidnapped by "spirits" or by ship captains who made a profit on their transportation and sale. Servants were chattel, property which could be bought and sold during the time of their service. Although their legal rights were restricted—they could not marry, for example, without permission—they had some legal protection from their masters. Women servants had little protection, however, against the sexual advances of male employers or other men, and pregnancy could be punished by an extended period of servitude.

The trade in African slaves was also a profitable business which enriched Europeans and colonists. Slaves were also property but without the legal protections of the white servants. The agrarian economy of the southern colonies, resting upon the plantation system, meant that female slaves worked almost exclusively in the fields, doing the same backbreaking work as men. Slave labor in the North was often less arduous, but here there was also little differentiation on the basis of gender.

Servants

Advertisements for Servants, 1656[12]

This author's description of the pleasant and profitable life of servants in the southern colonies is reminiscent of the earlier promotional literature. He was directing his pleas to those servants who voluntarily contracted to come here, although many also came involuntarily, as noted. Although John Hammond's description was not entirely false and servants did have opportunities for upward mobility, note that he distinguished between the possibilities for male and female servants as well as between the work each did.

The labor servants are put to is not so hard nor of such continuance as husbandmen nor handcraftmen are kept at in England. I said little or nothing is done in winter time. None ever work before sun rising nor after sunset. In the summer they rest, sleep, or exercise themselves five hours in the heat of the day. Saturday afternoon is always their own. The old holidays are observed and the Sabbath spent in good exercises.

The women are not (as is reported) put into the ground to work, but occupy such domestic employments as housewifery as in England, that is, dressing victuals, righting up the house, milking, employed about dairies, washing, sewing, etc., and both men and women have times of recreation, as much or more than in any part of the world besides. Yet some wenches that are nasty, beastly, and not fit to be so employed are put into the ground, for reason tells us, they must not at charge be transported and then maintained for nothing, but those that prove so awkward are rather burdensome than servants desirable or useful.

Those servants that will be industrious may in their time of service gain a competent estate before their freedoms, which is usually done by many, and they gain esteem and assistance that appear so industrious. There is no master almost but will allow his servant a parcel of clear ground to plant some tobacco in for himself, which he may husband at those many idle times he had allowed him and not prejudice, but rejoice his master to see it, which in time of shipping he may lay out for commodities, and in summer sell them again with advantage.

I think it better for any that goes over free, and but in a mean condition, to hire himself for reasonable wages of tobacco and provision, the first year, provided he happen in an honest house, and where the mistress is noted for a good housewife, of which they are very many (notwithstanding the cry to the contrary) for by that means he will live free of disbursement, have something to help him the next year, and be carefully looked to in his sickness (if he chance to fall sick) and let him so covenant that exceptions may be made, that he work not much in the hot weather, a course we always take with our new hands (as they call them) the first year they come in.

If they are women that go after this manner, that is paying their own passage, I advise them to sojourn in a house of honest repute, but by their good carriage, they may advance themselves in marriage, by their ill, overthrow their fortunes. And although loose persons seldom live long unmarried if free, yet they match with as dissolute as themselves and never live handsomely or are ever respected.

Undutiful Servants, 1640 and 1641[13]

Because indentured servants did not often leave behind accounts of their own lives, we must rely on records left by others, such as Hammond's description, or these written by John Winthrop. From these, however, we can learn something about a servant's work and treatment and the particular difficulties of being a female servant. We can also learn a great deal about the attitudes of the master toward servants and the complicated dynamics of relationships within the colonial family and town.

MEMORANDUM ON THE CASE OF WELTHIAN RICHARD'S MAID

Mrs. Richards brought her maid Edie White to me for her misdemeanor. Her man John Gill, about 21 years of age, affirmed that she being set to keep the seven cows of her master, she left them in the woods and went away to the house of one Carpenter in Weymouth, and there lodged, and he wished her to go home, and brought her near home, but she went away again, and wandered in the woods till the seventh day at night, and then she went to one Dyer's house, but they would not entertain her but sent her home, but she came not home till the Lord's Day in the afternoon. This she confessed, and said she was afraid to go home, yet she saith her master and Mrs. never beat her since they were before me etc., but only her Mrs. give her a blow or two on the ear.

Her Mrs. charged her further with discovering the secrets of the family. One thing she confessed about a maid that drank too much there.

John Gill charged her also with ordinary lying and laziness.

She saith the reason why she lost the cows was that she sat down and slumbered, and the while they went away.

TESTIMONY OF ELIZABETH STURGIS

First, I, Elizabeth Sturgis, do affirm that when I lived with my master Cummings, I was sent to Captain Patrick's to help his wife, and having business in the cellar, he came down presently after me and took me about the middle and would kiss me and put his hand into my bosom, at which I was much amazed at his carriage to me, being but young, yet striving with him, he let me go then presently. After I went home to my master's and being troubled at it when we were in bed, I acquainted my dame's sister with his carriage to me. Afterwards my dame sending me thither again, I refused to go. My dame desirous to know the reason, her sister standing by told her, and she made her husband acquainted with his carriage to me, and her husband told a neighbor of it and that man told master Carter and Mr. Carter deals with him about it, whereupon he comes to my master and calls him to speak with him. Then my master calls me out and said to me, I wonder you should deal so with me, and I replied to him and said you cannot be ignorant of these things. And after many passages, he said if these things be true, I was in great temptation, and then he said to me, he could trouble me, but he would not and so he left.

Secondly, some time after I living at home with my father, I went into the lot to gather sucking stalks and he [Patrick] came suddenly upon me and asked me whether I spake those things that I had spake for any hurt to him or not. I said no, I aimed not to hurt him nor any other and the things being past, I intended to speak no more of them. Then he offered to kiss me. I refusing, he said unless I would kiss him, he would not believe but that I would speak of it again.

Thirdly, some time after, I being married, upon some occasion coming into the bay to my father's, I going to Watertown to the lecture, he [Patrick] overtook me on the way and spake to me to call in as I went back to see his wife, which I did. And suddenly he came in and desired me to go into the next room to speak with me about our plantation, and I was there, he came to kiss me. I desired him to forbear and told him such things were not fit, but he would and did and would have had me to set on his lap, but I did not. Then he replied to me that it was lawful so to do to express love one to another. Then I rose up to go away, but he said I should tarry, for he had sent for sack [wine] and I should drink with him. I told him I must be going. He told me if he had time and opportunities, he would make it appear to me the lawfulness of it. I still desiring to be gone, he wished me not to be offended, for if I did love him but as well as he did love me, I would not take it so ill but would rather pity him than be offended. Then he was at me to meet him in the evening and he would further labor to convince me of his love to me, but with much ado I got away and presently made my father and all the house acquainted with it and durst not go out that night for fear.

Servants in Court, 1697 and 1698[14]

Indentured servitude was a legal contract entailing rights and responsibilities for both servants and masters. The relationships between the two parties, then, often involved the judgments of local courts, in whose records servants' lives and fortunes—or misfortunes—were often revealed. The records of Chester County Court in Pennsylvania reveal that often, although not always, male and female servants were not provided with the same opportunities. The records also show the penalties for sexual misconduct which a female servant might receive even though she had few ways of protecting herself against sexual exploitation, as indicated also in Elizabeth Sturgis' testimony.

John Wood had a servant maid whose name is Elizabeth Allen, who was adjudged to serve five years from the Court to the said John Wood or his assigns.

Francis Chadsey brought a boy whose name is Alexander Steward, who was adjudged to serve eight years from the 14th day of September last past, if he be taught to read or write or else to serve but seven years. Also he had a servant maid whose name is Ann Bean, who was adjudged to serve five years from this Court to said Francis or his assigns.

William Cope brought a boy whose name is Thomas Harper, who was adjudged to serve five years and three quarters from the 14th day of September last past. If he be taught to read and to write or else to serve but five years from the said time to him or his assigns.

William Coeburn's servant lad whose name is James Canadee was brought to this Court to answer for the getting of his servant woman with child, whose name is Margaret Adamson, and being examined about it, he denied it, and she being called and strictly examined, declared that he was the father of the child and no other and that it was one day that her master and dame was here at meeting and left them both at home together, and after some debate, it was reserved till the next Court that the same James Canadee shall appear at the next County Court.

William Coeburn preferred a petition to the Court for to have satisfaction made him by the servant woman Margaret Adamson for what charges he had been had and expenses and for the loss of her time while she lay in and for her running away diverse times, and the said William Coeburn and Martha Reston were both attested and declared that they heard the said Margaret

Adamson swear several oaths since the last Court. And the Court orders that the said Margaret Adamson shall serve the said William Coeburn or his assigns the full term of four years from this Court for all the trouble and charges and loss of her time.

Slaves

The Middle Passage, 1699 and 1676[15]

This is a description by the captain of a Dutch slave ship which carried slaves from Africa to destinations in the New World. Many of these slaves were captured by other Africans in tribal wars; others, however, were kidnapped and stolen by European slave traders. None came voluntarily. The passage across the Atlantic was as traumatic as the uprooting from African communities and culture, as indicated by the following account and by the mortality table compiled for an English ship in 1676. What discrepancies exist between the captain's account and the table? What descriptions might the slaves themselves have given?

Not a few in our country fondly imagine that parents here sell their children, men their wives, and one brother the other. But those who think so deceive themselves, for this never happens on any other account but that of necessity, or some great crime. But most of the slaves that are offered to us are prisoners of war, which are sold by the victors as their booty.

When these slaves come to Fida [Africa], they are put in prison all together, and when we treat concerning buying them, they are all brought out together in a large plain, where, by our chirurgeons, whose province it is, they are thoroughly examined, even to the smallest member, and that naked too both men and women, without the least distinction or modesty. Those which are approved as good are set on one side, and the lame and faulty are set by as invalids. These are such as are above five and thirty years old, or are maimed in the arms, legs, hands, or foot, have lost a tooth, are grey-haired, or have films over their eyes; as well as all those which are affected with any venereal distemper, or with several other diseases.

The invalids and the maimed being thrown out, the remainder are numbered, and it is entered who delivered them. In the meanwhile, a burning iron, with the arms or name of the companies, lies in the fire, with which ours are marked on the breast.

I doubt not but this trade seems very barbarous to you, but since it is followed by mere necessity, it must go on, but we yet take all possible care that they are not burned too hard, especially the women, who are more tender than the men.

We are seldom long detained in the buying of these slaves, because their price is established, the women being one fourth or fifth part cheaper than the men.

When we have agreed with the owners of the slaves, they are returned to their prison, where from that time forwards, they are kept at our charge, cost us two pence a day a slave; which serves to subsist them, like our criminals, on bread and water. So that to save charges we send them on board our ships with the very first opportunity, before which their masters strip them of all they have on their backs so that they come aboard stark-naked as well women as men, in which condition they are obliged to continue, if the master of the ship is not so charitable (which he commonly is) as to bestow something on them to cover their nakedness.

You would really wonder to see how these slaves live on board, for though their number sometimes amounts to six or seven hundred, yet by the careful management of our masters of ships, they are so regulated that it seems incredible. And in this particular our nation exceeds all other Europeans. For as the French, Portuguese, and English slave-ships are always foul and stinking, on the contrary, ours are for the most part clean and neat.

The slaves are fed three times a day with indifferent good victuals, and much better than they eat in their own country. Their lodging-place is divided into two parts; one of which is appointed for the men, the other for the women; each sex being kept apart. Here they lie as close together as is possible for them to be crowded.

An account of the mortality of slaves aboard the ship James

1675	Day	Men	Women	Boys	Girls	
September	6	1				Departed this life suddenly
October	28			1		Departed this life of convulsion fits
December	20	1				Departed this life of a fever
January 1675/6	20	1				Rec'd from Wyemba very thin and consumed to nothing and so died
Ditto	26		1			Rec'd from Wyemba very thin and consumed to nothing and so died
February	8	1				Rec'd from Wyemba very thin and dropsical and so departed this life
Ditto	23		1			Bought to windward and departed this life of a consumption and worms

1675	Day	Men	Women	Boys	Girls	
Ditto	24			1		Rec'd from Wyemba with a dropsy and departed this life of the same disease
March	26		1			Rec'd from Wyemba thin and so continued until death
Ditto	5		1			Miscarried and the child dead within her and rotten and died two days after delivery
Ditto	13	1				Rec'd from Wyemba very thin and so continued until he departed this life
Ditto	15	1				Rec'd from Wyemba very thin and fell into a flux and so continued until his death
Ditto	18	1				Rec'd from Wyemba very thin and so fell into a consumption and departed this life
Ditto	30	1				Rec'd from Wyemba very thin and so continued wasting till death
Ditto	31			1		Very sick and fell over board in the night and was lost
April	6	1				Rec'd from Wyemba thin and consumed very low and died of a great swelling of his face and head
Ditto	14	1				Rec'd from Wyemba thin and died of a flux
Ditto	15		1			Rec'd from Wyemba, sickened and would not eat or take anything

1675	Day	Men	Women	Boys	Girls	
Ditto	16	1				Bought by me and died of a flux
Ditto	17	2				The one received from Wyemba and died of a flux
						The other received ditto who leaped overboard and drowned himself
Ditto	20		1			Received thin at Wyemba and died of consumption
Ditto	21			1		Received from Wyemba with a dropsy and so died
Ditto	26		1			Bought by myself and being very fond of her child, carrying her up and down wore her to nothing by which means fell into a fever and died

Slaves in New Amsterdam, 1664[16]

The Dutch were very active in the slave trade and logically established the institution of slavery in their colony at New Amsterdam. Director of the colony Peter Stuyvesant here describes the kinds of work expected of male and female slaves.

This day fortnight arrived here your Honors' vessel, the [Sparrow], with forty head of slaves sent to us by Vice Director Beck to procure provisions and all sorts of timber work, fix ox carts, and a new rosmill.

The negroes and negresses have all arrived safely and in health, but were, on an average, quite old, and as the skipper alleges, rejected by the Spaniards. The product of the greater part appears by the accompanying account of the public vendue. They would have brought more, had they not been so old. Five of the negro women, who were, in our opinion, unsaleable, have been kept back and remain unsold. In like manner, six negroes also, to help to cut the required timber and to perform some other necessary work for the honorable company.

The Execution of Maria Negro, 1681[17]

The sentence of death pronounced upon this black woman testifies to the brutality of the institution of slavery even in the North, as well as to the will of this woman to rebel. It should be noted also that Maria received at least a semblance of a legal trial for her crime of arson. What options might she have had to her confession?

AT A COURT OF ASSISTANTS HELD AT BOSTON, 6 SEPTEMBER, 1681

Maria Negro, servant to Joshua Lambe of Roxbury in the County of Suffolk in New England, being presented by the Grand Jury, was indicted by the name of Maria Negro for not having the fear of God before her eyes and being instigated by the Devil at or upon the eleventh day of July last in the night did wittingly, willingly and feloniously set on fire the dwelling house of Thomas Swann of said Roxbury by taking a coal from under a sill and carried it into another room and laid it on the floor near the door and presently went and crept into hole at a back door of thy master Lamb's house and set it on fire. Also taking a live coal between two chips and carried it into the chamber by which also it was consumed as by your confession will appear contrary to the peace of our Sovereign Lord the king, his Crown and dignity, the laws of this jurisdiction. The prisoner at the bar pleaded and acknowledged herself to be guilty of this fact. And accordingly, the next day being again brought to the bar, had sentence of death pronounced against her by the Honorable Governor, yet she should go from the bar to the prison whence she came and thence to the place of execution and there be burned.

NOTES

1. Rev. W. Simmonds, "The Fourth Book to Make Plain the True Proceedings of the Historie for 1609," in Edward Arber, ed., *Captain John Smith, Works, 1608–1631* (Birmingham, England, 1884), pp. 498–99.
2. Susan Myra Kingsbury, ed., *The Records of the Virginia Company of London*, vol. III (Washington, D.C., 1933), pp. 493–94.
3. Donald B. Stanford, ed., *The Poems of Edward Taylor* (New Haven, 1977) p. 467. Reprinted with permission of Donald B. Stanford.
4. *The Mayflower Descendant*, XI (Boston, 1909), pp. 42–43, 156–57.
5. Charles J. Hoadley, ed., *Records of the Colony and Plantation of New Haven* (Hartford, 1857), pp. 91–92.
6. Ibid., pp. 174–76.
7. Maine Historical Society, *Maine Province and Court Records*, vol. II (Portland, 1939), pp. 252, 284, 307.
8. *The Acts and Resolves, Public and Private, of the Province of the Massachusetts Bay*, vol. I (Boston, 1869), pp. 213, 538–39.
9. Maine Historical Society, *Maine Province and Court Records*, vol. III (Portland, 1947), p. 76.
10. Cotton Mather, *Diary*, vol. I, 1681–1709 (New York, 1957), p. 266 n.
11. "The Description of Virginia by Captain Smith," in Edward Arber, ed., *Captain John Smith, Works, 1608–1631* (Birmingham, England, 1884), pp. 65–70.
12. John Hammond, "Leah and Rachel or, The Two Fruitful Sisters, Virginia

and Maryland: Their Present Condition, Impartially Stated and Related, Originally Published in London, 1656," in Peter Force, ed., *Traces and Other Papers Relating Principally to the Origin, Settlement, and Progress of the Colonies in North America* (Washington, D.C., 1844), pp. 12, 14–15.

13. John Winthrop, *The Winthrop Papers*, vol. IV (Boston, 1943), pp. 232–33, 300–301. Reprinted with permission of the Massachusetts Historical Society.

14. *Chester County, Pennsylvania, Court Records*, vol. II (Danboro, Pa., 1972), pp. 12, 26.

15. Elizabeth Donnan, ed., *Documents Illustrative of the History of the Slave Trade to America* vol. I (Washington, D.C., 1930), pp. 206, 441–43.

16. Elizabeth Donnan, ed., *Documents Illustrative of the History of the Slave Trade to America*, vol. III (Washington, D.C., 1932), p. 429.

17. *Publications of the Colonial Society of Massachusetts* vol. VI (Boston, 1904), p. 321.

BIBLIOGRAPHY

Axtell, James, ed. *The Indian Peoples of Eastern America: A Documentary History of the Sexes.* New York, Oxford, 1981.

Clark, Alice. *The Working Life of Women in the Seventeenth Century.* London, 1968.

Dexter, Elisabeth A. *Colonial Women of Affairs: Women in Business and Professions in America before 1776.* Boston, 1931.

———. *Career Women of America, 1776–1840.* Francestown, N.H., 1950.

Lerner, Gerda. "The Lady and the Mill Girl: Changes in the Status of Women in the Age of Jackson." In Jean E. Friedman and William G. Shade, eds., *Our American Sisters: Women in American Life and Thought.* Lexington, Mass., Toronto, 1982, 183–95.

Norton, Mary Beth. "The Myth of the Golden Age." In Carol Ruth Berkin and Mary Beth Norton, eds., *Women of America: A History.* Boston, 1979, 37–47.

Ryan, Mary. *Womanhood in America from Colonial Times to the Present.* New York, 1979.

Spruill, Julia Cherry. *Women's Life and Work in the Southern Colonies.* New York, 1972.

Ulrich, Laurel Thatcher. *Good Wives: Image and Reality in the Lives of Women in Northern New England.* New York, 1982.

Wolloch, Nancy. *Women and the American Experience.* New York, 1984.

3 WOMEN AND RELIGION IN THE SEVENTEENTH CENTURY

Religion was a central experience in the lives of seventeenth-century Europeans, whose ideas and behavior were significantly shaped by church doctrine and practice. Rivalries between Protestant England and Catholic France and Spain spurred the exploration and settlement of the New World as each church sought to win the souls of "heathen" Indians. This religious conflict became readily translated into a struggle for political hegemony in this hemisphere and for the continents themselves. The English triumphed on the North American continent although they did not finally expel France until 1763 or buy out Spain until 1819. Protestantism, therefore, became the dominant religion.

Protestant churches provided order and stability in this new land from the early decades of the seventeenth century on since the familiar institutions of the Old World, particularly the state and the community, were often absent or only partially developed. In Puritan New England, for example, new communities were formed from church congregations, and church buildings served both religious and public functions. In the southern colonies the parishes of the Anglican churches sometimes also constituted the local political unit. In both North and South, church and political institutions cooperated to impose conformity on the disorderly. Although the Anglican churches and other Protestant sects such as Quakers were never as powerful as the Puritan, or Congregational, churches of New England, the influence of Protestantism was considerable in all of the European settlements throughout much of this century.

Within Protestant theology there was tension concerning woman's nature and position within the church and the society. At the heart of Protestant doctrine was the belief that salvation was achieved through the individual's direct and personal relationship with God, without the priests, rituals, and sacraments that Protestants associated with the Roman Catholic church. A corollary was the belief in the spiritual equality of all—men and women—before Christ. At the same time, however, Protestant thought had to accommodate the Biblical story of Eve's responsibility for humankind's fall from grace; in addition, the commentaries of St. Paul, another Biblical source, advised both silence and subjection for women. This tension is reflected in the sermons of Puritan ministers such as John Robinson and others, whose writings provided rules of conduct for both men and women.

A similar contradiction existed within the practice of most seventeenth-century Protestant churches, which allowed women to become members in full communion but did not allow them to vote on prospective ministers or other issues decided by the membership, or to become ministers or lay leaders themselves. Positions of power and prestige within the church, as within the state and family, were held by men.

These tensions and contradictions are reflected also in the work of later historians. For example, Laurel Thatcher Ulrich has found that religion offered the "good wives" of seventeenth-century New England independent and satisfying roles to play within their families, churches, and communities. Lyle Koehler, on the other hand, has contended that the Puritan church, like the community's other male-dominated institutions, repressed women, especially those who openly sought power and autonomy. He concedes, though, that often their religious faith provided these women with the strength to rebel.

Mary Maples Dunn distinguishes between the religious experiences of orthodox Protestant and Quaker women. The Quaker belief in conversion through an inner light did not make distinctions on the basis of gender, allowing Quaker women to become lay ministers and missionaries and to take part in women's meetings, which disciplined female members and regulated marriages. Congregationalist women, however, particularly as male hegemony became more firmly established in the place of early religious rebels like Anne Hutchinson, accepted their secondary position in the church as it became a "feminine" institution when men gravitated to politics and the marketplace where the locus of power had shifted.

The Puritan persecution of Quakers and witches illustrates the complex relationships women had with their churches. Although these incidents have long interested historians, only recently has it been recognized that women played the significant roles as both actors and victims in these religious dramas. Quaker women, acting as missionaries, were hounded and hanged by Puritan officials. In Salem village in 1692, both the accusers and the accused witches were female although here also the punishments were meted out by men.

Few historians contest the importance of religious experiences for women. For some, a faith in God provided spiritual sustenance and physical strength to survive in the wilderness of the New World. For others, religious doctrine promised not the hope of salvation but the terrors of damnation, emphasized by the harsh controls imposed by churches. Whether women were saints or sinners, powerful or powerless, the rewards or punishments of religion were great.

SAINTS

Seventeenth-century Protestants did not believe it was easy or even pleasant to be saved. The Puritans, for example, had come to the New World to establish churches in which only those saved, the "saints," could be members. Their criteria for sainthood became demanding: both an inner conversion experience in which the individual was "born again," cleansed of sin with God's grace, and outward behavior which was upright, sober, God-fearing, and obedient to community and church norms. The Puritan belief that humankind was born evil made it difficult to believe in one's own goodness, and the doctrine of predestination meant that salvation could not be achieved solely through one's own efforts but depended upon the will of an unknowable and omnipotent God. As the documents reveal, seventeenth-century women responded in many ways to these challenges posed by their religion.

Male Definitions

John Robinson, "On Marriage"[1]

Robinson (1567?–1625) was the pastor of the first Pilgrim settlers whose advice guided their lives both in Holland and the New World. Although sermons do not describe the ways in which people actually behaved, they did both reflect and reinforce the attitudes of Puritan congregations because of mandatory church attendance and the important role of the Puritan minister as community leader. Robinson's thoughts reflect the contradictions within Puritan theology about woman's nature, but they are less ambiguous on the relationship of husband and wife, which is based on the doctrine of woman's moral frailty. Robinson supported his position, as did all good Puritans, with frequent references to the Bible.

God hath ordained marriage, amongst other good means, for the benefit of man's natural and spiritual life, in an individual society between one man and one woman, and hath blessed it alone with this prerogative, that by it, in lawful order, our kind should be preserved and posterity propagated.

Not only heathen poets, but also wanton Christians, have nick-named women, necessary evils, but with as much shame to men as wrong to women, and to God's singular ordinance withal. When the Lord amongst all the good creatures which he had made, could find none fit and good enough for the man, he made the woman of a rib of him, and for a help unto him, Gen. ii 20, 21; neither is she, since the creation, more degenerated than he, from the primitive goodness. Besides, if the woman be a necessary evil, how evil is the man, for whom she is necessary!

Some have said, and that, in their own and others' judgment, both wittily and devoutly, that marriage fills the earth, and virginity, heaven, but others have better answered, How should heaven be full, if the earth were empty.

Many common graces and good things are requisite both for husband and wife, but more especially the Lord requires in the man love and wisdom, and in the woman, subjection, Eph. v. 22–25: The love of the husband to his wife must be like Christ's to his church; holy for quality and great for quantity, both intensively and extensively. Her person, and whatsoever is good in her he must love fervently, mending or bearing, if not intolerable, what is amiss; by the former of which two he makes her the better and himself by the latter. And if her failings and faults be great, he by being inured to bear them patiently, is the fitter to converse quietly and patiently with other perverse persons abroad. Neither sufficeth it, that the husband walk with his wife as a man of love, but before her also as a man of understanding, 1 Pet. iii. 7; which hath therefore afforded him, and means of obtaining it, above the woman, that he might guide and go before her, as a fellow heir of eternal life with him. It is monstrous if the head stand where the feet should be.

In the wife is specially required a reverend subjection in all lawful things to her husband, Eph. v. 22 & c. Lawful, I mean, for her to obey in, yea though not lawful for him to require of her. He ought to give honor to the wife, as the weaker vessel, i Pett. iii 7: but now, if he pass the bounds of wisdom and kindness, yet must not she shake off the bond of submission, but must bear patiently the burden, which God hath laid upon the daughters of Eve. The woman in innocency was to be subject to the man, but this should have been without all wrong on his part, or grief on hers. But she being first in transgression, i Tim. ii. 14, hath brought herself under another subjection, and the same to her, grievous, and in regard of her husband, often unjust, but in regard of God, always most just, who hath ordained that her desire should be subject to her husband, Gen. iii. 16, who by her subjection became subject to sin. And, albeit, many proud women think it a matter of scorn and disgrace, thus to humble themselves to God and their husband, and even glory in the contrary, yet therein they but glory in their shame, and in their husbands' shame also. And whilst they refuse a cross, choose a sin of rebellion, both against God and their husbands, which shall not escape unpunished from God.

Record of the First Church in Boston, 1691–1694[2]

This excerpt is only one page of hundreds in this record book, so it would be difficult to arrive at broad conclusions from it. Other sources too, however, suggest that by the end of the seventeenth century, a majority of church members were women. How does this list reflect the message of John Robinson's sermon?

MEN ADMITTED, AUGUST 30, 1691

Joseph Viccard, February 1691/2

Jeremiah Fitz, March 27, 1692

Jonathan Williams, May 29, 1692

James Allen Jr., August 14, 1692

Isaiah Toye, August 28, 1692

Joseph Prout, April 23, 1693

John Draper, July 16, 1693

JULY 17, 1693

Voted that our teacher do invite Mr. John Bayley to assist him in preaching constantly while among us 3 times in a month or oftener if he please.

VOTED THIS: NOVEMBER 28, 1693

at a meeting of the church at my house unanimously that our teacher invite Mr. Wadsworth to assist him constantly once a month or any other vacancy in preaching, and any other help he shall judge needful.

John Glover, Dec. 31, 1693

At a church meeting, at the meeting house, Jan. 12, 1693/4. Voted that Mr. Cooke and Mr. Adington be added to the former 3 for disposing of seats and that they have power to determine if fit places to be made so. Voted that our two deacons with our brother Bridge be assisting in judging of the convenience of making a middle door at the North side and shutting up the two corner doors and about a porch to the east door.

John Allen, March 11, 1693/4

John Eustic, March 25, 1694

WOMEN ADMITTED, AUGUST 30, 1691

Mary Patricke, December 6, 1691

Gutride Pease, April 10, 1692

Elizabeth Dyer, April 10, 1692

Elizabeth Atkinson, April 10, 1692

Mary Pecke, September 1692

Hannah Gouch, September 1692

Susanna Gardener, October 17, 1692

Mary Atkinson, October 17, 1692

Hannah Wiswall, October 30, 1692

Rebeckah Griffith, October 30, 1692

Elizabeth Quelch, November 27, 1692

Mary Dummer, February 26, 1692/3

Sarah Manning, February 26, 1692/3

Ruth Cooke, March 19, 1693

Mary Pemberton, March 26, 1692

Mary Green, March 26, 1692

Sarah Joice, April 9, 1693

Easter Green, April 9, 1693

Mary Frances, April 16, 1693

Martha Twinge, April 16, 1693

Mary Ashley, April 23, 1693

Naomi Harman, April 23, 1693

Jane Oakes, April 30, 1693

Patience Short, April 30, 1693

Joanna Croakam, May 28, 1693

Abigail Hatherly, May 28, 1693

Naomi Collins, August 20, 1693

Margaret Jackson, November 12, 1693

Anne Pierce, December 3, 1693

Sarah Tudman, December 3, 1693

Susan Farnham, January 26, 1693/4

Hannah Henley, February 18, 1694

Susanna Thaxter, April 8, 1694

Female Experiences

Anne Bradstreet (1612?–1672), "To My Dear Children"[3]

Few women have given such eloquent testimony to the intensity of their religious feelings as Bradstreet, America's "Tenth Muse." Indeed there were few other poets among the Puritans, who regarded poetry as an inconsequential form of literature. Bradstreet received her exceptional education in England and was influenced by the English religious poets. She was the wife of Simon Bradstreet, with whom she migrated to New England. Although her membership in the upper class and her education made her atypical of colonial women, her writings provide insight into the intimate relationship between the Puritan and her God, and the doubts it engendered. This autobiographical fragment was addressed to some of her eight children as she awaited the travail of another childbirth.

MY DEAR CHILDREN,

I, knowing by experience that the exhortations of parents take most effect when the speakers leave to speak, and those especially sink deepest which are spoke latest—and being ignorant whether on my death bed I shall have opportunity to speak to any of you, much less to all—thought it the best, whilst I was able to compose some short matters, (for what else to call them I know not) and bequeath to you, that when I am no more with you, yet I may be daily in your remembrance. I have not studied in this you read to show my skill, but to declare the Truth—not to set forth myself, but the Glory of God.

The method I will observe shall be this—I will begin with God's dealing with me from my childhood to this day. In my young years, about 6 or 7 as I take it, I began to make conscience of my ways, and what I know was sinful, as lying, disobedience to parents &c. I avoided it. If at any time, I was overtaken with the like evils, it was a great trouble. I could not be at rest till by prayer I had confessed it unto God. I was also troubled at the neglect of private duties, though too often tardy that way. I also found much comfort in reading the Scriptures, especially those places I thought most concerned my condition, and as I grew to have more understanding, so the more solace I took in them.

In a long fit of sickness which I had on my bed, I often communed with my heart, and made my supplication to the most High who set me free from that affliction.

But as I grew up to be about 14 or 15, I found my heart more carnal, and sitting loose from God, vanity and the follies of youth take hold of me.

About 16, the Lord laid his hand sore upon me and smote me with the smallpox. When I was in my affliction, I besought the Lord, and confessed my pride and vanity, and he was entreated of me, and again restored me. But I rendered not to him according to the benefit received.

After a short time I changed my condition and was married, and came into this country, where I found a new world and new manners, at which my heart rose. But after I was convinced it was the way of God, I submitted to it and joined to the church at Boston.

After some time I fell into a lingering sickness like a consumption, together with a lameness, which correction I saw that the Lord sent to humble and try me and do me good, and it was not altogether ineffectual.

It pleased God to keep me a long time without a child, which was a great grief to me, and cost me many prayers and tears before I obtained one, and after him gave me many more, of whom I now take the care, that as I have brought you into the world, and with great pains, weakness, cares, and fears brought you to this, I now travail in birth again of you till Christ be formed in you.

Among all my experiences of God's gracious dealings with me I have constantly observed this, that he hath never suffered me long to sit loose from him, and search what was amiss—so usually thus it hath been with me that I have no sooner felt my heart out of order, but I have expected correction for it, which most commonly hath been upon my own person, in sickness, weakness, pains, sometimes on my soul, in doubts and fears of God's displeasure, and my sincerity towards him, sometimes he hath smote a child with sickness, sometimes chastened by losses in estate, and these times (through his great mercy) have been the times of my greatest getting and advantage, yea I have found them the times when the Lord hath manifested the most love to me. Then have I gone searching, and have said with David, Lord search me and try me, see what ways of wickedness are in me, and lead me in the way everlasting. And seldom or never but I have found either some sin I lay under which God would have reformed, or some duty neglected which he would have performed. And by his help I have laid vows and bonds upon my soul to perform his righteous commands.

I have had great experience of God's hearing my prayers, and returning comfortable answers to me, either in granting the thing I prayed for, or else in satisfying my mind without it, and I have been confident it hath been from him, because I have found my heart through his goodness enlarged in thankfulness to him.

I have often been perplexed that I have not found that constant joy in my pilgrimage and refreshing which I supposed most of the servants of God have although he hath not left me altogether without the witness of his holy spirit, who hath often given me his word and set to his Seal that it shall be well with me. I have sometimes tasted of that hidden Manna that the world knows not, and have set up my Ebenezer, and have resolved with myself against such a promise, such tastes of sweetness, that Gates of Hell shall never prevail. Yet have I many times sinkings and droopings, and not enjoyed that felicity that sometimes I have. But when I have been in darkness and seen no light, yet have I desired to stay my self upon the Lord.

Return, O my Soul, to thy Rest, upon this Rock Christ Jesus will I build my faith, and, if I perish, I perish.

This was written in much sickness and weakness, and is very weakly and imperfectly done, but if you can pick any benefit out of it, it is the mark which I aimed at.

Elizabeth White, "God's Gracious Dealings," 1699[4]

Elizabeth White was clearly not the literary artist that Bradstreet was. Perhaps for this reason her account of her own spiritual progress is more representative of the Puritan attempt to reconcile the desire to achieve salvation with the belief in predestination. Note that for both women, spiritual crises coincided with crises in the female life cycle—marriage and childbirth, for example—and that for Elizabeth White, spiritual direction was often provided by male figures: father, husband, and Divinity.

From my childhood the LORD has inclined my heart to seek after the best things, and my father's chiefest care was to bring me up in the nature and admonition of the Lord. I was a great lover of histories, and other foolish books, and did often spare my sleeping time, in reading them, and sometimes I should think I did not do well in so doing, but I was so bewitched by them that I could not forbear, and hearing of a friend of mine, which was esteemed a very holy woman, that did delight in histories, I then concluded it was no sin, and gave myself wholly to this folly. I had sometimes thought I should put the Lord off from time to time with delays. I remember about a month before I was married, my father would have me receive the sacrament of the Lord's Supper, and I was very willing to it; until I considered what was requisite to be in those which did partake thereof, and then I began to doubt that I had not those things which were requisite wrought in me, as Knowledge, Faith, Love, Repentance, etc. When I had considered those things, I was filled with sorrow, and could not tell what to do. I was loath to disobey my father, and more loath to eat and drink my own Damnation. In this perplexity I set myself to seek the Lord for his Grace.

When I had thus done, I began to be comforted verily thinking that when I was married, I should have more leisure to serve God; and then going to the minister of the parish to be examined before I was admitted, and finding myself able to answer him, I thought all was well with me then, and so unworthy I went to the Lord's Table, not questioning but that I was in as good a condition as any of the rest which did receive. But blessed forever be the Lord, which broke my false confidence, and swept away my refuge of lies, which I then trusted in, and shewed me my sad condition. I thought I had a heart worse than the Devil and wondered that I was not consumed in some strange manner.

When I have seen a spider, which of all things is most loathsome to me, I have been ready to wish myself such a one, esteeming it to be in a far happier condition than I was in. I was afraid to be in the Dark, lest I should meet the Devil. I doubted whether I was elected, I had read that it was not him that willeth, nor of him that runneth, but of God that showereth mercy. Then I thought that if I were not elected, it was no purpose to strive; for what God hath decreed must be, yet I was unwilling to perish. I could not be so satisfied although I had but little hope to obtain mercy, yet I would not but ask it. And when I was with child, I was much dejected, having a sense of my approaching danger and wanting an assurance of everlasting happiness, but whilst I was considering of these things, I had this Scripture set home with abundance of sweetness, Psal. 53.15: "Call upon me in the Day of Trouble, and I will deliver thee and thou shall glorify me." And in the time of my extremity this word was set home upon my heart again, and my good God made me to experience it in a wonderful manner, for I had a speedy deliverance beyond my expectations. And when my child was weaned, I was in such a snare of deadness and darkness, that I thought if I was ever raised out of it, I should never question my condition again.

I had let out my affection in a wonderful measure to my child, and my Lord forsook me not, but dispelled my darkness, and filled me with rejoicing. I see nothing in myself that makes me more worthy of salvation than another. I know that I have deserved to lie in flames, as well as any that are now in the place of torments, and that nothing but mercy hath stept between my soul and everlasting burnings, and therefore I heartily wish that I might always be admiring of this free grace of God in choosing me before the foundation of the world was laid. O, the height and depth and breadth and length of this love of god in Christ Jesus.

Mary Rowlandson, "The Captivity," 1675[5]

This dramatic tale of Rowlandson (c. 1635–1678) and her children being captured by Indians on the Massachusetts frontier enjoyed great popularity both in the colonies and in England. Conflicts between the Indians and the Europeans were frequent, especially during the several French and Indian wars. A surprising number of Europeans decided to remain with their Indian captors rather than return to their colonial homes, preferring the Indian way of life. However, Rowlandson, the wife of a minister, believed that the providence of God had saved her from the dreadful perils she described here. Her plight was unusual, but her sustaining religious faith probably was not, nor were her attitudes about Indians. After three months in captivity, Rowlandson was reunited safely with her husband.

Oh, the doleful sight that now was to behold at this House: *Come, behold the works of the Lord, what desolations he has made in the Earth,* (Psalm xlvi. 8). Of thirty-seven persons who were in this one House, none escaped either present death, or a bitter captivity, save only one, who might say as he, Job

1.15, *And I only as escaped alone to tell the News*. There were twelve killed, some shot, some stabbed with their spears, some knocked down with their hatchets. When we are in prosperity, oh the little that we think of such dreadful sights, and to see our dear Friends and Relations lie bleeding out their heart-blood upon the ground. There was one who was chopped into the head with a hatchet, and stripped naked, and yet was crawling up and down. It is a solemn sight to see so many Christians lying in their blood, some here, and some there, like a company of Sheep torn by Wolves, all of them stripped naked by a company of hellhounds, roaring, singing, ranting and insulting, as if they would have torn our very hearts out; yet the Lord by his Almighty power preserved a number of us from death, for there were twenty-four of us taken alive and carried Captive.

I had often before this said, that if the Indians should come, I should choose rather to be killed by them than taken alive, but when it came to the trial, my mind changed; their glittering weapons so daunted my spirit, that I chose rather to go along with those (as I may say) ravenous Beasts, than that moment to end my days, and that I may the better declare what happened to me during that grievous captivity, I shall particularly speak of the several Removes we had up and down the wilderness.

Now away we must go with those Barbarous Creatures, with our bodies wounded and bleeding, and our hearts no less than our bodies. About a mile we went that night, up upon a hill within a sight of the Town where they intended to lodge. There was hard by a vacant house (deserted by the English before, for fear of the Indians). I asked them whether I might not lodge in the house that night to which they answered, what will you love English men still? This was the dolefulest sight that ever my eyes saw. Oh, the roaring and singing and dancing and yelling of those black creatures in the night, which made the place a lively resemblance of hell. To add to the dolefulness of the former day, and the dismalness of the present night, my thoughts ran upon my losses and sad bereaved condition. All was gone, my Husband gone (at least separated from me, he being in the Bay [at Boston], and to add to my grief, the Indians told me they would kill him as he came homeward), my children gone, my relations and friends gone, our house and home and all our comforts within door, and without, all was gone (except my life), and I knew not but the next moment that might go too. There remained nothing to me but one poor wounded Babe, and it seemed at present worse than death that it was in such a pitiful condition, bespeaking Compassion, and I had no re-freshing for it, nor suitable things to revive it.

But now, the next morning, I must turn my back upon the Town, and travel with them into the vast and desolate Wilderness, I knew not whither. It is not my tongue, or pen can express the sorrows of my heart, and bitterness of my spirit, that I had at this departure; but God was with me, in a wonderful manner, carrying me along, and bearing up my spirit, that it did not quite fail. One of the Indians carried my poor wounded Babe upon a horse, it went moaning all along, I shall die, I shall die. I went on foot after it, with sorrow that cannot be expressed. At length I took it off the horse, and carried it in my arms till my strength failed, and I fell down with it. Then they set me upon a horse with my wounded Child in my lap, and there being no furniture upon the horse's back, as we were going down a steep hill, we both fell over the horse's head, at which they like inhuman creatures laughed, and rejoiced to see it, though I thought we should there have ended our days, as overcome with so many difficulties. But the Lord renewed my strength still, and carried me along, that I might see more of his Power; yea, so much that I could never have thought of, had I not experienced it.

After this it quickly began to snow, and when night came on, they stopped. And now down I must sit in the snow, by a little fire, and a few boughs behind me, with my sick Child in my lap, and calling much for water, being now (through the wound) fallen into a violent fever. My own wound also growing so stiff, that I could scarce sit down or rise up, yet so it must be, that I must sit all this cold winter night upon the cold snowy ground, with my sick Child in my arms, looking that every hour would be the last of its life, and having no Christian friend near me, either to comfort or help me. Oh, I may see the wonderful power of God, that my Spirit did not utterly sink under my affliction. Still the Lord upheld me with his gracious and merciful Spirit, and we were both alive to see the light of the next morning.

Before I knew what affliction meant, I was ready sometimes to wish for it. When I lived in prosperity, having the comforts of the World about me, my relations by me, my Heart cheerful, and taking little care for anything, and yet seeing many, whom I preferred before myself, under many trials and afflictions, in sickness, weakness, poverty, losses, crosses, and cares of the World, I should be sometimes jealous lest I should have my portion in this life, and that Scripture would come to my mind, Heb. 12.6. *For whom the Lord loveth he chasteneth, and scourgeth every Son whom he receiveth.* But now I see the Lord had his time to scourge and chasten me.

SINNERS

It was always easier to tell a sinner than a saint, and the Protestant zeal for salvation, combined with the seventeenth-century intolerance of secular and religious dissent, made colonists zealous in the prosecution of those who transgressed the rules of church and state. For most of the seventeenth century, church and state worked together, especially in New England, to punish religious dissenters as well as violators of civil laws against such crimes as drunkenness, adultery, or disorderly conduct. These documents illustrate that many women refused to conform because of the strength of their religious convictions, their courage, or perhaps simply their perversity.

Heretics

Anne Hutchinson's Court and Church Trials, 1637–1638[6]

Hutchinson (1591–1643) was the most famous heretic of Massachusetts Bay colony. She was banished by the state and excommunicated by the church in 1637/38 for preaching antinomianism to groups of men and women in her home. Because antinomianism stressed salvation through inner regeneration rather than through conformity to external rules imposed by church and state, this heresy threatened the stability of the Puritan community. Hutchinson's open questioning of the moral and intellectual qualifications of the political and religious leadership threatened the male hegemony, especially since she herself had a wide and powerful following. The court record preserved by her great-great-grandson Thomas Hutchinson, governor of Massachusetts Bay on the eve of the American Revolution, illustrates the fear and distaste with which her bitter foe John Winthrop viewed her and the courage and wit with which she faced her prosecutors. The record of the church trial reveals the close connection in the Puritan mind between religious heresy—in this case, Hutchinson's alleged familism, a doctrine resembling antinomianism—and social and sexual disorder.

ANNE HUTCHINSON: THE COURT TRIAL, 1637

Governor John Winthrop: You have spoken diverse things so we have been informed very prejudicial to the honor of the churches and ministers thereof, and you have maintained a meeting and an assembly in your house that hath been condemned by the general assembly as a thing not tolerable nor comely in the sight of God nor fitting for your sex, and notwithstanding that was cried down, you have continued the same. Therefore, we have thought good to send for you to understand how things are, that if you be in an erroneous way we may reduce you that so you may become a profitable member here among us. Otherwise if you be obstinate in your course that then the court may take such course that you may trouble us no further. Why do you keep such a meeting at your house as you do every week upon a set day?

Mrs. Hutchinson: It is lawful for me so to do, as it is all your practices, and can you find a warrant for yourself and condemn me for the same thing? The ground of my taking it up was, when I first came to this land because I did not go to such meetings as those were, it was presently reported that I did not allow of such meetings but held them unlawful and therefore in that regard they said I was proud and did despise all ordinances, upon that a friend came unto me and told me of it, and I to prevent such aspersions took it up, but it was in practice before I came. Therefore I was not the first.

Gov.: For this, that you appeal to our practice you need no confutation. If your meeting had answered to the former, it had not been offensive, but I will say that there was no meeting of women alone, but your meeting is of another sort, for there are sometimes men among you.

Mrs. H.: There was never any man with us.

Gov.: Well, admit there was no man at your meeting and that you was sorry for it, there is no warrant for your doings, and by what warrant do you continue such a course?

Mrs. H.: I conceive there lies a clear rule in Titus [Titus ii. 3–51] that the elder women should instruct the younger and then I must have a time wherein I must do it.

Gov.: All this I grant you, I grant you a time for it, but what is this to the purpose that you, Mrs. Hutchinson, must call a company together from their callings to come to be taught of you?

Mrs. H.: Will it please you to answer me this and to give me a rule, for then I will willingly submit to any truth. If any come to my house to be instructed in the ways of God, what rule have I to put them away?

Gov.: But suppose that a hundred men come unto you to be instructed, will you forbear to instruct them?

Mrs. H.: As far as I conceive, I cross a rule in it.

Gov.: Very well and do you not so here?

Mrs. H.: No, sir, for my ground is they are men.

Gov.: Men and women all is one for that, but suppose that a man should come and say "Mrs. Hutchinson, I hear that you are a woman that God hath given his grace unto and you have knowledge in the word of God, I pray instruct me a little," ought you not to instruct this man?

Mrs. H.: I think I may. Do you think it not lawful for me to teach women, and why do you call me to teach the court?

Gov.: We do not call you to teach the court but to lay open yourself.

Mrs. H.: I desire you that you would then set me down a rule by which I may put them away that come unto me and so have peace in so doing.

Gov.: You must shew your rule to receive them.

Mrs. H.: I have done it.

Gov.: I deny it because I have brought more arguments than you have.

Mrs. H.: I say, to me it is a rule.

Mr. Endicot: You say there are some rules unto you. I think there is a contradiction in your own words. What rule for your practice do you bring, only a custom of Boston.

Mrs. H.: No, Sir, that was no rule to me, but if you look upon the rule in Titus, it is a rule to me. If you convince me that it is no rule, I shall yield.

Gov.: You know that there is no rule that crosses another, but this rule crosses that in the Corinthians. But you must take it in this sense that elder women must instruct the younger about their business, and to love their husbands and not to make them to clash.

Mrs. H.: I do not conceive but that it is meant for some public times.

Gov.: Well, have you no more to say but this?

Mrs. H.: I have said sufficient for my practice.

Gov.: Your course is not to be suffered for, besides that we find such a course as this to be greatly prejudicial to the state, besides the occasion that it is to seduce many honest persons that are called to those meetings and your opinions being known to be different from the word of God may seduce many simple souls that resort unto you, besides that the occasion which hath come of late hath come from none but such as have frequented your meetings, so that now they are flown off from magistrates and ministers, and this since they have come to you, and besides that it will not well stand with the commonwealth that families should be neglected for so many neighbors and dames and so much time spent, we see no rule of God for this. We see not that any should have authority to set up any other exercises besides what authority hath already set up and so what hurt some of this, you will be guilty of and we for suffering you.

Mrs. H.: Sir, I do not believe that to be so.

Gov.: Well, we see how it is. We must therefore put it away from you, or restrain you from maintaining this course.

Mrs. H.: If you have a rule for it from God's word, you may.

Gov.: We are your judges, and not you ours, and we must compel you.

THE CHURCH TRIAL, 1638

Mr. [John] Cotton [Hutchinson's former minister]: Consider in the fear of God, that by this one error of yours in denying the resurrection of these very bodies, you do the uttermost to raze the very foundation of religion to the ground, and to destroy our faith, yea all our preaching and your hearing and all our sufferings for the faith to be in vain, if there be no resurrection, then all is in vain, and we of all people are most miserable. Yea, consider if the resurrection be past, then you cannot evade the argument that was pressed upon you by our Brother Buckle and others, that filthy sin of the community of women, and all promiscuous and filthy coming together of men and women, without distinction or relation of marriage, will necessarily follow. And though I have not heard, neither do I think, you have been unfaithful to your husband in his marriage covenant, yet that will follow upon it, for it is the very argument that the Saduces bring to our Savior Christ against the Resurrection, and that which the Anabaptists and Familists bring, to prove the lawfulness of the common use of all women, and so more dangerous evils and filthy uncleanness and other signs will follow than you do now imagine or conceive.

Mrs. Hutchinson: I desire to speak one word, before you proceed. I would forbear but by reason of my weakness. I fear I shall not remember it when you have done.

Mr. Cotton: You have leave to speak.

Mrs. Hutchinson: All that I would say is this, that I did not hold any of these things before my imprisonment.

Mr. Cotton: I confess I did not know that you held any of these things, nor hear till of late. But it may be it was my sleepiness and want of watchful care over you, but you see the danger of it, and how God hath left you to yourself to fall into these dangerous evils, for I must needs say that I have often feared the height of your spirit and being puffed up with your own parts, and therefore, it is just with God thus to abase you and to leave you to these desperate falls, for the Lord looketh upon all the children of pride, and delights to abase them and bring them low.

Mrs. Oliver, 1638[7]

According to Winthrop, Hutchinson inspired other women to act in an unseemly fashion. Mrs. Oliver's protest against church rules, however, was not so threatening as Hutchinson's as Oliver had neither wealth nor an organized following. She remained in the colony to plague Winthrop with her disorderly conduct for a dozen years.

The devil would never cease to disturb our peace, and to raise up instruments one after another. Amongst the rest, there was a woman in Salem, one Oliver his wife, who had suffered somewhat in England for refusing to bow at the name of Jesus, though otherwise she was conformable to all their orders. She was (for ability of speech, and appearance of zeal and devotion) far before Mrs. Hutchinson, and so the fitter instrument to have done hurt, but that she was poor and had little acquaintance. She took offense at this, that she might not be admitted to the Lord's supper without giving public satisfaction to the church of her faith, etc., and covenanting or professing to walk with them according to the rule of the gospel. So as upon the sacrament day, she openly called for it, and stood to plead her right, though she were denied and would not forbear, before the magistrate, Mr. Endecott, did threaten to send the constable to put her forth. This woman was brought to the court for disturbing the peace in the church, etc., and there she gave such peremptory answers, as she was committed till she should find [guarantees] for her good behavior. After she had been in prison three or four days, she made means to the governor, and submitted herself, and acknowledged her fault in disturbing the church; whereupon he took her husband's bond for her good behavior, and discharged her out of prison. But he found, after, that she still held her former opinions, which were very dangerous.

About five years after, this woman was adjudged to be whipped for reproaching the magistrates. She stood without tying, and bore her punishment with a masculine spirit, glorying in her suffering. But after (when she came to consider the reproach, which would stick by her, etc.) she was much dejected about it. She had a cleft stick put on her tongue half an hour, for reproaching the elders.

Mrs. Anne Eaton, 1644[8]

Mrs. Anne Eaton was the wife of Theophilus Eaton, the governor of Connecticut. Her excommunication, despite her social status, indicates how serious were her offenses. Like Hutchinson, she was technically a heretic for disbelieving in infant baptism. In actuality, however, she was a difficult and obstreperous woman, unmindful of the strictures of both husband and clergy. Of particular interest and significance are the familial and household relationships described here. "Old Mrs. Eaton" was her mother-in-law and "Mrs. Mary Eaton" was the widow of Theophilus Eaton's son by his first marriage. Both of these women lived in Mrs. Anne Eaton's household along with the several servants mentioned. "Lady Moodey" had been excommunicated from a Salem church the previous year.

Our pastor, Mr. Davenport, stood up and spoke as followeth: Brethren, the public offense, which she knows is grievous to us, she still continueth in, departing from the Assembly whensoever baptism is administered or else absenting herself from the sermon and from all public worship in the congregation, though she knoweth that it is an offense to the whole Church. How she fell into the error, you partly know. Her will was gained to it before her judgement, and therefore she sought some arguments or other against the baptising of infants, and to that end spake with Lady Moodey and importuned her to lend her a book which having gotten into her hands, she read secretly, and as secretly engaged her spirit in that way. For she neither asked her husband at home according to the rule, Cor. xiv. 35 (whose faithfulness and sufficiency to have held forth light to her according to God, we all know), nor did she seek for any light or help from her pastor according to the rule, Mala. ii. 7.

Diverse rumors were spread up and down the town of her scandalous walking in her family, which were in the mouths of many before they came to my knowledge. At last with two or three of the brethren who had also heard of this common fame, considered what we were called to do, and concluded that it being a thing commonly and scandalously reported, the rule requireth that we should inquire, make search and diligently ask whether it were true, Deut. xvii, 13, 14, by proposition. Accordingly, Mr. Gregson, Mr. Hooke, and myself went to Mr. Eaton, told him what we heard commonly reported, and prayed him to certify us whether the things were so or not. We went together to speak to Mrs. Eaton and held forth the particulars and the rules broken by them, but without any fruit. Thus we are compelled to bring sundry particulars of which she was privately admonished into the public notice of the Church.

THE SEVERAL FACTS FOR WHICH THE CHURCH CENSURED MRS. EATON

That Mrs. Eaton sitting at dinner with Mr. Eaton and old Mrs. Eaton, Mrs. Eaton struck old Mrs. Eaton twice on the face with the back of her hand, which Mrs. Eaton saith she felt three days after; and Mr. Eaton sitting at table held his wife's hands, and whilst Mr. Eaton held his wife's hands, she cried with such vehemency of spirit, "I am afflicted, I am afflicted," as her mother [mother-in-law] saith she thought she might be heard over to Mr. Davenport's. Witness old Mrs. Eaton and herein is broken the Fifth Commandment, in breaking the rules of her relation to her mother; and also the Sixth Commandment is broken in her sinful rage and passion in striking her mother.

Mrs. Mary Eaton being knitting a pair of gloves and when she knit a piece of a glove, her mother said she had knit a glove and a piece, which Mrs. Mary denied, and said she had not knit so much. Her mother upon this grew outrageous, struck her, and knocked her head against the dresser, which made her nose bleed much. Besides others who were present, this was done before four Indians, who were then in the kitchen. Witnessed by old Mrs. Eaton, and Mrs. Mary and Elizabeth Browning, who saith though she was not in the kitchen when this was done, yet she was above in the chamber and heard Mrs. Mary cry and heard the blows up into the chamber, and when she came down, she saw Mrs. Mary's nose bleed very much, she asked what was the matter, and they told her Mrs. Eaton had beat Mrs. Mary. This is a breach of the Fifth Commandment in breaking the rule of the Apostle, Eph. vi, 4; Cor. iii, 21. And likewise she hath herein broke the Sixth Commandment, contrary to Matt. v, 21, contrary to the rule of the Apostle, Eph. iv, 31. Likewise, it is a breach of the Sixth Commandment, as it is a just offense to the Indians, and so a means of the murder of their souls, and so contrary to the rule of the Apostle, 1 Cor. x, 32.

That Mrs. Eaton hath unjustly charged Mrs. Mary, saying her belly was great and her breasts big almost to meet and she look blue under the eyes, and that she vomited, and that she looked very ill, and she feared her sickness would prove an ill sickness. Mrs. Mary saith she never vomited, and Mary Launch saith she knew she never vomited since she came into the house. Sister Maudlines saith that she living in the house about half a year, never saw any light carriage [behavior] in her that might give any suspicions to ground any just charge, and she took the more notice of her carriage because old Mrs. Eaton had often asked her about Mrs. Mary's carriage, because she had heard her mother had spoken many suspicious words concerning Mrs. Mary. Brother Lupton saith he never saw anything in Mrs. Mary but comely and well. Brother Bradley saith for light carriage in Mrs. Mary with any man he never saw any in the least, nor had cause for any such thought. And Brother Lupton said the same. Mrs. Eaton being demanded by Mr. Gregson, Mr. Davenport and Mr. Hooke why she charged Mrs. Mary with such things, she answered that she said it to set more upon her to prevent it, because she observed her temper and carriage (saying her carriage was wanton). Being earnest pressed to give an instance of any of these charges upon her, she then could give none. This charge is confessed in the answer Mrs. Eaton gives. This is a breach of the Ninth Commandment, as it is a slander and that of a high nature.

Mrs. Eaton says to her maids God would send their souls to hell; this is a sin against the Third Commandment, breaking that rule, Math. 7, 1. Witness Mary Breck and Ann Smart.

When Mr. Davenport was in preaching and speaking something against Anabaptism, Mrs. Eaton said as she sat in her seat, it is not so, and when Mr. Davenport said he would be brief, I would you would or I pray be so. Anna Eaton heard her mother speak thus, and told her brother, and he told his mother; old Mrs. Eaton saith that Theophilus telling his mother of it, she said it was not so. Anna Eaton saith that her mother did deny that she said so. But Mrs. Eaton since hath acknowledged that she did speak to that purpose; this is contrary to Isa. 30, 8, 9, 10.

Wayward Women

Virginia Law against Bigamy, 1624[9]

The Virginia company eagerly encouraged the migration of women to the young colony, but few came in its early years. This statute suggests that some of those who did come took advantage of their sex's scarcity. The law also illustrates the intimate connection between church and state which existed not only in Massachusetts Bay but in the southern colonies where the Church of England, or the Anglican church, was established. The King of England headed both his state and this church so that ecclesiastical and civil laws reinforced one another as they do here.

Whereas to the great contempt of the [Majesty] of God and ill example to others, certain women within this colony have of late contrary to the laws ecclesiastical of the realm of England contracted themselves to two several men at one time, whereby much trouble doth grow between parties, and the Governor and Counsel of State, thereby much disquieted, to prevent the like offence in others hereafter. It is by the Governor and Counsel ordered in Court, that every minister give notice in his church to his parishioners, that what man or woman soever shall hereafter use any words or speech tending to contract of marriage unto two several persons at one time (though not precise and legal, yet so as may entangle and breed scruple in their consciences) shall for such their offence under either corporal punishment (as whipping, etc.) or other punishment by fine or otherwise, according to the quality of the person so offending.

Christ Church Parish, Middlesex County, Virginia, 1649[10]

In the southern colonies the church parish had the responsibility of caring for those who needed public assistance, such as these women who were mothers of bastard children. These records also remind us of the powerlessness of servant women.

This vestry taking notice of Mary Hutton, servant to Mrs. Frances Sheppard, who hath brought three several bastard children which have been nursed at the charge of this parish, and hath never yet been presented for the same as the law directs, and there being further information now made that Joseph Smith, a tailor, and servant to the said Mrs. Sheppard, peremptorily owns himself father of the latter of the said three bastard children, to the end the same may be duly inquired into, do order that Joseph Harvey do deliver a copy hereof to the next Court held for this County that they may call before them ye said Mary and Joseph, and proceed against them as the law directs, etc.

The vestry doth also take notice of one Elizabeth Dowrey, servant to Mr. James Curtis, who hath also brought a bastard child, the which hath been nursed at ye charge of this parish, nor hath never yet been presented for ye same, as ye law directs. Therefore to the end ye same may be duly inquired into, do order that Joseph Harvey do deliver a copy hereof to ye next Court held for this County that they may call before them the said Elizabeth Dowrey and proceed against her as ye law directs, etc.

Dorothy Talbye, 1634[11]

As we have already seen, John Winthrop filled his journals with vivid descriptions of female misconduct, such as Talbye's, to serve as hideous examples for his readers. Although she was excommunicated by her church, we might question today whether the only torments which drove this pathetic woman to infanticide were spiritual.

Dorothy Talbye was hanged at Boston for murdering her own daughter, a child of three years old. She had been a member of the church of Salem, and of good esteem for godliness, etc., but falling at difference with her husband, through melancholy or spiritual delusions, she sometimes attempted to kill him, and her children, and herself, by refusing meat, saying it was so revealed to her, etc. After much patience, and diverse admonitions not prevailing, the church cast her out. Whereupon she grew worse; so as the magistrate caused her to be whipped. Whereupon she was reformed for a time, and carried herself more dutifully to her husband, etc.; but soon after she was so possessed with Satan, that he persuaded her (by his delusions, which she listened to as revelations from God) to break the neck of her own child, that she might free it from future misery. This she confessed upon her apprehension; yet, at her arraignment, she stood mute a good space, till the governor told her she should be pressed to death, and then she confessed the indictment. When she was to receive judgment, she would not uncover her face, nor stand up, but as she was forced, nor give any testimony of her repentance, either then or at her execution. The cloth, which should have covered her face, she plucked off and put between the rope and her neck. She desired to have been beheaded, giving this reason, that it was less painful and less shameful. After a swing or two, she catched at the ladder. Mr. Peter, her late pastor, and Mr. Wilson, went with her to the place of execution, but could do no good with her. Mr. Peter gave an exhortation to the people to take heed of revelations, etc., and of despising the ordinance of excommunication as she had done; for when it was to have been denounced against her, she turned her back and would have gone forth, if she had not been stayed by force.

First Church in Boston Records, 1638[12]

Women's names appeared alongside men's in a church's list of sinners. Women were often accused of different crimes, but they were subject to the same harsh discipline for misconduct as were men.

THE 15TH OF THE SECOND MONTH 1638

Judith Smith having been formerly in private admonished of sundry errors was then for her obstinate persisting therein in the Congregation and for sundry lies then expressed by her and persisted in, cast out of the Church with joint consent.

THE 29TH DAY OF THE 2ND MONTH 1638

Anne Walker, the wife of one Richard Walker and sometime the wife and widow of our brother Robert Houlton having before this day been often privately admonished of sundry scandals, as of drunkenish, intemperate, and unclean or wantonish behavior, and likewise of cruelty towards her children and also of manifold lies and still to this day persisting impenitently therein, was therefore now with joint consent of the Congregation cast out of the Church.

THE 11TH DAY OF THE 9TH MONTH 1638

Our brother Richard Turnor having been openly found drunken by the excessive drinking of strong water was this day cast out of the Church for the same offence.

THE 1ST OF THE 7TH MONTH 1639

The wife of our brother Robert Harding, admitted by the name of Philip Hammond widow, was excommunicated for speaking evil of authority both in Church and Commonweal. From having said in open Court that Mrs. Hutchinson neither deserved the censure which was put upon her in the Church, nor in the Commonweal. It was proved against her in the Church by the witness of our Brother Richard Truesdale and our brother Samuel Cole that she had also spoken.

ACTORS AND VICTIMS

Their vital roles as missionaries and lay preachers brought the wrath of Puritan religious and secular leaders down upon Quaker women, who alongside their male colleagues were harassed, physically assaulted, and martyred. These women shared the religious fervor of their culture but turned it into less acceptable channels than did Bradstreet, White, or Rowlandson. Like the Quaker women, accused witches were also guilty of nonconformity. They were the victims, however, not only of the male hierarchy but of female accusers as well.

Quakers

Mary Dyer, 1659[13]

Because of their belief in salvation through the inner light, which resembled antinomianism in its potential for social disruption, Quakers were forbidden by law to enter Massachusetts Bay under punishment of death. Dyer was first a follower of Hutchinson and then a Quaker. She became a preacher and missionary in the egalitarian Quaker tradition, and then a martyr in the wave of Quaker persecutions in Massachusetts Bay of 1655–1665. Although Dyer was at first reprieved, she returned to the colony and went to her death on the gallows. The author of this document, George Bishop, was a Quaker, who directed this indictment at a Puritan audience.

Not long after, viz., the 8th of the Eighth month following [1659], Mary Dyer, whom you had banished upon pain of death, and Hope Clifton, both of

Rhode Island, came to Boston, on the first day of the week, to visit Christopher Holder [another Quaker], who was then in prison. On the next morning after they came in, they were espied, and carried by the constable to the House of Correction; who, after your worship was ended, came again, and charged the keeper, "body for body, life for life," with Mary Dyer, till further order. So Mary was continued without being sent for, but Hope Clifton was had before your deputy-governor the next morning, who recommitted her, and one Mary Scott, a daughter of R. and C. Scott, of Providence, aforesaid.

And now the time of the sitting of your Court drawing near, wherein you acted this bloody tragedy, W. Robinson and M. Stevenson, came to Boston, viz., on the 13th day of the Eighth month, and with them Alice Cowland, who came to bring linen wherein to wrap the dead bodies of those who were to suffer, and Daniel Gould, from Salem, William King, Hannah Phelps, the wife of Nicholas Phelps aforesaid, and Mary Trask and Margaret Smith, of the same town—all these, as one, came together in the moving and power of the Lord, to look your bloody laws in the face, and to accompany those who should suffer by them.

So your prisons began to fill, and on the 19th of the same month, W. Robinson, M. Stevenson, and Mary Dyer were had before your Court, and demanded of by you, "Why they came again into your jurisdiction, being banished upon pain of death?" To which having severely answered, and declared that the ground or cause of their coming was of the Lord, and in obedience to Him, your governor said, "That he desireth not their death," and "that they had liberty to speak for themselves, why they should not be proceeded with, as to the giving of sentence against them"; yet he bid the jailer take them away.

The next day after your worship was ended, being heated by your priest and prepared to shed the blood of the innocent, you sent for them again, and your governor, speaking faintly, as a man whose life was departing from him, for the hand of the Lord was upon him, said to this effect, "We have made many laws, and endeavoured by several ways to keep you from us; and neither whipping, nor imprisonment, nor cutting off ears, nor banishment upon pain of death, will keep you from among us." And he said, "I desire not your death"; yet presently he said, "You shall be had back to the place from whence you came, and from thence to the place of execution, to be hanged on the gallows till you are dead."

And, on the 27th of the Eighth month aforesaid, ye caused the drums to beat, to gather your soldiers together for the execution; and after your worship was ended, your drums beat again, and your captain, James Oliver, came with his band of men, and the Marshal and some others, to the prison, and the doors were opened. And your Marshal and jailer called for W. Robinson and M. Stevenson, and had them out of the prison, and Mary Dyer out of the House of Correction, who parted from their friends in prison full of the joy of the Lord, who had counted them worthy to suffer for His name, and had kept them faithful unto death. And having embraced each other, with fervency of love and gladness of heart, and peace with God and praises to the Lord, they went out of your prisons, like innocent lambs out of the butcher's cart, to the slaughter.

So being come to the place of execution hand in hand, as to a wedding-day, all three of them with great cheerfulness of heart, and having taken leave of each other with the dear embraces of one another in the love of the Lord, your executioner put W. Robinson to death, and after him M. Stevenson, who died, both of them, full of the joy of the Lord.

But as for Mary Dyer, after she had parted joyfully from her friends at the foot of the ladder, expecting to die, and seeing her two friends hanging dead before her, her arms and legs tied, the halter about her neck, and her face covered with a handkerchief which your priest Wilson lent the hangman, and was with the Lord in joy and peace, an order came for her reprieve, upon the petition of her son, and unknown to her; which being read, and the halter loosened and taken off her neck, she was desired to come down. Some came presently and took her in their arms, and sat her on horseback, and conveyed her fifteen miles toward Rhode Island, and then left her with a horse and man, to be conveyed further.

Anne Coleman, Mary Tomkins, and Alice Ambrose, 1662[14]

Scenes such as these were immortalized in the nineteenth-century fiction of Nathaniel Hawthorne, whose ancestor played a leading role in Quaker persecutions. Like Dyer, these women were inspired and sustained in their faith, though inspired in very unconventional ways. The author again is George Bishop.

So on a very cold day, Walden, your deputy, caused these women to be stripped naked, from the middle upward, and tied to a cart, and after a while cruelly whipped them, whilst the priest stood and looked on, and laughed at it, which some of their friends seeing, they testified against it, for which Walden put two of them, Eliakim Wardel, of Hampton, and William Fourbish, of Dover, in the stocks. Having dispatched them in this town, you made way to carry them over the waters and through the woods to another town. The women refused to go unless they had a copy of the warrant, so your executioner sought to set them on horseback, but they slid off; then they endeavoured to tie each to a man on horseback, but that would not do either, nor any course they took, until the copy was given them, insomuch that the constable professed that he was almost wearied with them. But the copy being given them, they went with the executioner to Hampton, and through dirt and snow to Salisbury, halfway the leg deep, the constable forcing them after the cart's tail, at which he whipped them. Under which cruelty and sore usage, the tender women travelling their way through all, was a hard spectacle to those who had in them anything of tenderness; but the presence of the Lord was so with them, that they sung in the midst of the extremity of their sufferings, to the astonishment of their enemies.

At Hampton, the constable William Fifield, having received the women, there to whip them, said, "I profess you must not think to make fools of men," meaning thereby, upon the relation of the constable of Dover as to the work he had with them, as if he would not be outdone. The women answered, "They should be able to deal with him as well as the other." So the constable Fifield, who professed himself so stout, would have whipped them the next morning before daylight, but they refused, saying, "That they were not ashamed of their sufferings." Then he would have whipped them with their clothes on, when he had them at the cart, contrary to the warrant; but they said, "Set us free, or do according to the order," which was to whip them on their naked backs. Then he spake to a woman to take off their clothes; the woman said, "She would not do it for all the world," and other women also refused to do it. Then he said, "I profess I will do it myself." So he stripped them, and then stood, with the whip in his hand, trembling as a condemned man, and did the execution as a man in that condition.

Witches

Salem Witchcraft, 1692[15]

These are probably the most famous trials in the American past, resulting in the execution of twenty persons, mostly women, and the imprisonment of 150 more. The variety of roles which women played in this incident are illustrated in this account by a former Salem minister, Deodat Lawson. Traditionally, historians have attributed the witchcraft trials to Puritan fanaticism, political upheaval, or social tensions within the community. Other explanations may occur to us, however, if we look at the witchcraft hysteria from the perspective of women involved, especially the young accusers.

On the nineteenth day of March last [1692], I went to Salem Village and lodged at Nathaniel Ingersol's near to the Minister Mr. P's [Parris's] house, and presently after I came into my lodging, Capt. Walcut's daughter Mary came to Lieut. Ingersol's and spake to me, but, suddenly after as she stood by the door, was bitten, so that she cried out of her Wrist, and looking on it with a Candle, we saw apparently the marks of Teeth both upper and lower set, on each side of her wrist.

In the beginning of the Evening, I went to give Mr. P. a visit. When I was there, his Kinswoman Abigail Williams (about 12 years of age) had a grievous fit; she was at first hurried with Violence to and fro in the room (though Mrs. Ingersol endeavoured to hold her) sometimes making as if she would fly, stretching up her arms as high as she could, and crying "Whish, Whish, Whish!" several times. Presently after she said there was Goodwife N. [Nurse] and said, "Do you not see her? Why there she stands!" And the said Goodw. N. offered her The Book but she was resolved she would not take it, saying often, "I won't, I won't take it, I do not know what Book it is. I am sure it is none of God's Book, it is the Devil's Book, for ought I know." After that she run to the Fire, and begun to throw Fire Brands about the house.

On Lord's Day, the twentieth of March, there were sundry of the afflicted Persons at Meeting, as Mrs. Pope, and Goodwife Bibber, Abigail Williams, Mary Walcut, Mary Lewes, and Doctor Grigg's Maid. There was also at Meeting Goodwife C. [Corey] (who was afterward Examined on suspicion of being a Witch). They had several Sore Fits, in the time of Public Worship, which did something interrupt me in my First Prayer, being so unusual.

In Sermon time when Goodw. C. was present in the Meetinghouse, Ab. W. called out, "Look where Goodw. C. sits on the Beam suckling her Yellow Bird betwixt her fingers!" Anne Putnam, another girl afflicted, said there was a Yellow-bird sat on my hat as it hung on the Pin in the Pulpit. But those that were by, restrained her from speaking loud about it.

On Monday, the 21st of March, the Magistrates of Salem appointed to come to Examination of Goodw. C. The worshipful Mr. Hathorne asked her, Why she afflicted those Children? She said, she did not Afflict them. He asked her, who did then? She said, "I do not know. How should I know?" The number of the afflicted persons were about that time Ten, viz. four married women, Mrs. Pope, Mrs. Putnam, Goodw. Bibber, and an ancient woman, named Goodall, three Maids, Mary Walcut, Mary Lewes at Thomas Putnam's, and a maid at Dr. Grigg's. There were three girls from 9 to 12 years of age, each of them, or thereabouts, viz. Elizabeth Parris, Abigail Williams and Ann Putnam. There were most of them at G. C.'s [Corey's] Examination, and did vehemently accuse her in the Assembly of afflicting them, by biting, pinching, strangling, etc. And that they did in their Fit see her Likeness coming to them, and bringing a Book to them, she said, she had no Book. They affirmed, she had a Yellow-Bird, that used to suck betwixt her Fingers, and being asked about it, if she had any Familiar Spirit, that attended her, she said, she had no Familiarity with any such thing. She was a Gospel Woman, which Title she called herself by; and the Afflicted Persons told her, ah! She was a Gospel Witch. Ann Putnam did there affirm, that one day when Lieutenant Fuller was at Prayer at her Father's House, she saw the shape of Goodw. C. and she thought Goodw. N. praying at the same time to the Devil. She was not sure it was Goodw. N., she thought it was, but very sure she saw the Shape of G. C. The said C. said they were poor, distracted children, and no heed to be given to what they said. Mr. Hathorne and Mr. Noyes replied, it was the judgement of all that were present, they were Bewitched, and only she, the Accused Person said, they were Distracted. It was observed several times, that if she did but bite her underlip in time of Examination, the persons afflicted were bitten on their arms and wrists and produced the marks before the Magistrates, Ministers, and others. And being watched for that, if she did but Pinch her fingers, or grasp one hand hard in another, they were pinched and produced the marks before the Magistrates, and Spectators. They accused her of her Familiarity with the Devil, in the time of Examination, in the shape of a Black man whispering in her ear; they affirmed, that her Yellow-bird sucked betwixt her Fingers in the Assembly; and order being given to see if there were any sign, the Girl that saw it said, it was too late now; she had removed a Pin and put it on her head, which was found there sticking upright.

[Goodwife Corey] was that Afternoon committed to Salem-Prison; and after she was in Custody, she did not so appear to them, and afflict them as before.

On Thursday the twenty-fourth of March (being in course the Lecture Day, at the Village) Goodwife N. [Nurse] was brought before the Magistrates, Mr. Hathorne and Mr. Corwin, about Ten of [the] Clock, in the forenoon, to be Examined in the Meeting House. The Reverend Mr. Hale begun with prayer, and the Warrant being read, she was required to give answer, Why she afflicted those persons? She pleaded her own innocency with earnestness. Thomas Putnam's wife, Abigail Williams, and Thomas Putnam's daughter accused her that she appeared to them, and afflicted them in their fits. And her motions did produce like effects as to biting, pinching, bruising, tormenting, at their breasts, by her leaning, and when, bended back, were as if their backs was broken. The afflicted persons said, the Black Man whispered to her in the Assembly, and therefore she could not hear what the Magistrates said unto her. They said also that she did then ride by the Meeting-house, behind the Black Man. Others also were there grievously afflicted, so that there was once such a hideous screech and noise as did amaze me, and some that were within told me the whole assembly was struck with consternation, and they were afraid, that those that sat next to them, were under the influence of Witchcraft. This woman also was that day committed to Salem Prison.

John Hale's "Modest Enquiry into the Nature of Witchcraft," 1647–1692[16]

Hale was also a minister who visited Salem during the hysteria. He did not question the existence of witches and was at first a supporter of the trials, but he became a doubter after his own wife was accused. His "Enquiry" reflects these doubts and also provides examples of the kinds of female behavior that often triggered accusations.

Several persons have been charged with and suffered for the Crime of Witchcraft in the Governments of Massachusetts, New Haven, or Stratford and Connecticut, from the year 1646 to the year 1692.

The first was a Woman of Charleston, Anno 1647 or 1648 [Margaret Jones]. She was suspected partly because that after some angry words passing between her and her Neighbors, some mischief befell such Neighbors in their Creatures, or the like; partly because some things supposed to be bewitched, or have a Charm upon them, being burned, she came to the fire and seemed concerned.

The day of her Execution, I went in company of some neighbors, who took great pains to bring her to confession and repentance. But she constantly professed herself innocent of that crime. Then one prayed her to consider if God did not bring this punishment upon her for some other crime, and asked, if she had not been guilty of Stealing many years ago; she answered, she had stolen something, but it was long since, and she had repented of it, and there was Grace enough in Christ to pardon that long ago, but as for Witchcraft, she was wholly free from it, and so she said unto her Death.

Another that suffered on that account some time after, was a Dorchester Woman. And upon the day of her Execution Mr. Thompson, Minister at Brantry, and J. P., her former Master, took pains with her to bring her to repentance. And she utterly denied her guilt of witchcraft, yet justified God for bringing her to that punishment. For she had when a single woman played the harlot, and being with Child, used means to destroy the fruit of her body to conceal her sin and shame, and although she did not effect it, yet she was a Murderer in the sight of God for her endeavours, and shewed great penitency for that sin; but owned nothing of the crime laid to her change.

There was another Executed of Boston Anno 1655 for that crime [Mrs. Ann Hibbins]. And two or three of Springfield, one of which confessed; and said the occasion of her familiarity with Satan was this: She had lost a Child and was exceedingly discontented at it and longed, Oh that she might see her Child again. At last the Devil in likeness of her Child came to her bedside and talked with her, and asked to come into the bed to her, and she received it into the bed to her that night and several nights after, and so entered into covenant with Satan and became a Witch. This was the only confessor in these times and that Government.

Another at Hartford, viz. Mary Johnson, confessed herself a Witch. Who upon discontent and slothfulness agreed with the Devil to do her work for her, and fetch up the Swine. And upon her immoderate laughter at the running of the Swine, as the Devil drove them, as she herself said, was suspected and upon examination confessed. I have also heard of a Girl at New Haven or Stratford, that confessed her guilt. But all others denied it unto the death unless one Greensmith at Hartford.

NOTES

1. Robert Ashton, ed., *The Works of John Robinson*, vol. 1 (Boston, 1851), pp. 236–42.

2. Richard B. Pierce, ed., *Records of the First Church in Boston, 1630–1868* (Boston, 1961), p. 93.

3. John Harvard Ellis, ed., *The Works of Anne Bradstreet* (Charlestown, Mass., 1867), pp. 3–7, 10.

4. "The Experience of God's Gracious Dealings with Elizabeth White as They Were Written Under Her Own Hand, and Found in Her Closet After Her Decease, December 5, 1669," (Boston, 1741), pp. 1–16.

5. Mary Rowlandson, *Narrative of the Captivity and Removes of Mrs. Mary Rowlandson* (Lancaster, Pa., 1828), pp. 16–22, 87.

6. C. F. Adams, ed., *Antinomianism in the Colony of Massachusetts Bay, 1636–1638* (Boston, 1894), pp. 235–41, 314–15.

7. John Kendall Hosmer, ed., *Winthrop's Journal*, vol. II (New York, 1908), pp. 285–86.

8. *Papers of the New Haven Colony Historical Society*, vol. 5 (New Haven, 1894), pp. 133–34.

9. Susan Myra Kingsbury, ed., *Records of the Virginia Company of London*, vol. IV (Washington, D.C., 1935), p. 487.

10. C. C. Chamberlayne, ed., *The Vestry Book of Christ Church Parish, Middlesex County, Va., 1663–1767* (Richmond, Va., 1927), p. 49.

11. John Kendall Hosmer, ed., *Winthrop's Journal*, vol. I (New York, 1908), p. 283.

12. Richard B. Pierce, ed., *Records of the First Church in Boston, 1630–1868* (Boston, 1961), pp. 22, 25.

13. George Bishop, *New England Judged by the Spirit of the Lord* (Philadelphia, 1885), pp. 98–103, 110–11.

14. Ibid., pp. 230–32.

15. George Lincoln Burr, ed., *Narratives of the Witchcraft Cases, 1647–1706* (New York, 1914), pp. 152–61.

16. Ibid., pp. 408–10.

BIBLIOGRAPHY

Battis, Emory. *Saints and Sectaries: Anne Hutchinson and the Antinomian Controversy in the Massachusetts Bay Colony*. Williamsburg, Va., 1962.

Dunn, Mary Maples. "Saints and Sisters: Congregational and Quaker Women in the Early Colonial Period." *American Quarterly* 30 (Winter 1978): 582–601.

———. "Women of Light." In Carol Ruth Berkin and Mary Beth Norton, eds., *Women of America: A History*. Boston, 1979, 114–36.

Erikson, Kai. *Wayward Puritans: A Study in the Sociology of Deviance*. New York, 1966.

Koehler, Lyle. *A Search for Power: The "Weaker Sex" in Seventeenth-Century New England*. Urbana, Chicago, London, 1980.

———."The Case of the American Jezebels: Anne Hutchinson and Female Agitation during the Years of the Antinomian Turmoil, 1636–1640." In Linda K. Kerber and Jane deHart Mathews, eds., *Women's America: Refocusing the Past*. New York, Oxford, 1982, 36–50.

Ulrich, Laurel Thatcher. *Good Wives: Images and Reality in the Lives of Women in Northern New England, 1650–1750*. New York, 1982.

4 WOMEN AND THE LAW IN THE SEVENTEENTH CENTURY

As is the case with all social institutions, the law and legal institutions in each of the American colonies evolved with, shaped, and were shaped by the total environment. A product of society, the colonial legal system reflected the needs and interests of the community, or of particular groups within the community. An agency of social control, it organized and regulated human relations and behavior, intervening in areas that are considered private by present-day jurisprudence. Despite a resurgence of interest in American legal history within the last twenty years, most scholarship ignores the colonial period or treats it incidentally, assuming that the era from the American Revolution to the Civil War was formative in the history of American law. As a result of such benign neglect and because documentary records are, in many cases, lost or inaccessible, historians know relatively little about early American legal developments.

The common-law tradition, still the basis for the legal systems of most of the states of the United States, was transplanted by the first English settlers. A body of rules, the roots of which are traceable to Anglo-Saxon times, the common law was originally and principally the work of the royal courts of justice, usually called the Courts of Westminster after the place where they sat from the thirteenth century. Decision by decision, the Court of Exchequer, the Court of Common Pleas, and the Court of King's Bench gradually constructed a new law, many of the elements of which were derived from different local English customs, others from Roman law. Because the royal courts dealt principally with the legal problems of the upper ranks of British society, beginning in the fourteenth century a system of rival courts sprang up, as private individuals, unable to obtain justice from the royal courts or else dissatisfied with a court's remedy, appealed for relief to the royal official known as the chancellor. The chancellor, a special agent of the king, was not bound by the same strict common-law rules which prevailed in the royal courts and was therefore able to dispense justice based upon equity. By the sixteenth century, equity had become institutionalized in the Court of Chancery. Within this structural framework, the English legal system evolved principally through decisions rendered by the Courts of Westminster and the Court of Chancery and, to a far lesser extent, through statute and custom, developed the legal concepts and categories that distinguish it from the Romano-Germanic system.

Although the Indians had their own tradition of laws and legal concepts and each cultural group that settled in America introduced its own law, the English colonies by and large accepted the structure and concepts of the common-law system. A different geographical milieu, different economic and social conditions, and a different ethnic and racial composition necessitated adjustments in the English legal system, however. Obsolete doctrines and procedures, made by and for a feudal society, were incompatible with conditions in America and were consequently abandoned by colonial courts and assemblies. For example, the feudal English land law, characterized by primogeniture and entail, was established in scattered jurisdictions. Because the colonies needed as many settlers as possible to develop the vast land and abundant natural resources, though, colonial law generally followed the local English practice of gavelkind tenure, which provided for descent of land to all children rather than to the eldest son. Although the colonies followed the English practice of criminalizing sin, they did not re-create the system of church courts that prevailed in England to enforce regulations of personal conduct and behavior. Whereas in England professional lawyers and judges administered the law according to strict common-law rules, in America colonial court proceedings, frequently presided over by laymen unversed in judicial precedent and rules of action, were apparently much more informal. Moreover, each of the thirteen colonies was founded during a different phase of the historical evolution of the common-law system. Because the common-law regime was constantly changing, different parts of it were imported into the several colonies, depending upon the date of their founding. Furthermore, different conditions in each of the colonies produced legal mutations ultimately creating thirteen separate legal systems.

To what extent these factors, combined with the wide availability of equity jurisprudence in the colonies, affected the legal status of colonial American women is the subject of debate among historians of the law. The earliest attempt to examine the legal status of women in the colonial period of American history was Richard B. Morris's *Studies in the History of Early American Law* (1930). Concerned exclusively with the role of married women, Morris's pioneering work presumed that because of the imbalanced gender ratio before 1700, and because of conditions peculiar to a frontier society, women in the English colonies enjoyed a relatively elevated legal status in comparison to their English counterparts or their descendants of the succeeding Victorian era.

Recent scholarship points to a different conclusion. It has been suggested, if not fully proved, that from the beginning women in colonial Anglo-America occupied a position of social and legal inferiority. The work of Marylynn Salmon, for example, indicates that the colonists in fact tried to re-create the traditional paternalistic legal codes of their home countries. In some cases, Salmon argues, women actually lost ground. When, instead of adhering to English standards, colonial jurists made changes, those changes were often reductive. The position taken by Joan R. Gundersen and Gwen Victor Gampel represents the middle ground in the scholarly debate. Based on their analysis of court, town, and probate records for New York and Virginia, they conclude that until the mid-eighteenth century, white married women in both colonies enjoyed significantly more control over property and greater protection for their dower, paraphernalia, and guardianship rights than did their English contemporaries. Gundersen and Gampel suggest, however, that by 1750, as a result of a variety of economic and demographic factors, women's legal status had diminished considerably, although in certain particulars American adaptations of the English legal system survived to the end of the colonial period. At the other extreme is Lyle Koehler's contextual examination of women in seventeenth-century New England. On the basis of a comparative analysis of town records, court dockets, and tax lists, Koehler concludes that the legal status of New England females was inferior to that of English females.

What these great disparities in scholarly findings mean is not entirely clear. They seem, however, to suggest the mutability of the common law, not only as it made the Atlantic crossing but as it was transplanted in the several colonies. Changes in the character of social and economic conditions apparently mitigated the constraints of the common law in some colonies, while in others the law became even more restrictive. Whether American law diverged from or duplicated English law, the familiar mold that formed the legal rights of colonial women was the common-law tradition of coverture.

Based on the assumption that marriage required total unity of interest between husband and wife and that the interests of the partners were always coincidental, the laws of coverture designated the husband as head of the family and gave to him dominion over his wife. In practice this meant that at marriage a woman's legal identity was subsumed under that of her husband, who thereafter performed all legal functions for the two of them. By contrast, unmarried women and widows were not subject to any substantial disabilities. As femes sole women could contract; sue and be sued; act as administrators of estates and as guardians of children; hold, bequeath, inherit, and buy property; work, keep their earnings, or spend them as they pleased. They were, in short, legally independent of male control.

DOMESTIC RELATIONS

The theoretical basis for the married woman's loss of legal rights was the feudal doctrine of coverture. Based in part on Biblical notions of the unity of flesh of husband and wife, the doctrine rested on Genesis 2:22–23: "And Adam said, this is now bone of my bones, and flesh of my flesh; she shall be called Woman, because she was taken out of man. Therefore shall a man leave his father and his mother, and shall cleave unto his wife and they shall be one flesh." The fictional unity of husband and wife was reinforced by the feudal system of hierarchical relations. Within the feudal hierarchy each individual had a defined status, with particular rights and duties attached to it. The common law incorporated these status relationships. In common law the husband had the status of master of the household; his wife held a subordinate position analogous to the relation of a vassal to his lord. By law he was required to provide for her support according to his rank and status; she was required to render obedience to her baron or lord. Because she remained under his protection and cover, she was called in law a feme covert and her condition during marriage was known as her coverture.

Man and Woman Are One

The Laws' Resolution of Women's Rights, 1632[1]

Colonial law played a major role in supporting and sustaining social institutions such as the family. Directly or indirectly, the law helped define gender roles and thereby invigorated traditional notions of male dominance and authority. As in all other aspects of seventeenth-century life, however, the private law of domestic relations was also profoundly influenced by moral and religious ideas. In explaining the moral basis for the common-law doctrine of coverture, for example, seventeenth-century legal tracts, such as *The Laws' Resolution of Women's Rights*, first published in 1632, invariably turned to Christian theology to show that the scriptures decreed the subordination of women in families and their total exclusion from political and economic power.

SECT. II: THE CREATION OF MAN AND WOMAN

God the first day, when he created the world made the matter of it, separating light from darkness: the second day he placed the firmament which he called heaven, between the waters above the firmament and the waters under the firmament: the third day he segregated the waters under the firmament into one place, calling the waters seas, and the dry land earth, which he commanded to bring forth fructifying herbs, plants and trees: the fourth day he made the sun, the moon and the stars in the firmament, to be for signs, seasons, days and years, and to give light upon the earth: the fifth day he made by his word the fishes of the sea, whales and every feathered fowl of the air, commanding them to increase: the sixth day he made cattle, creeping things, the beasts of the earth: and now having made all things that should be needful for them, he created man, male and female made he them, bidding them multiply and replenish the earth, and take the joint sovereignty over the fishes of the sea, the fowls of the air, and over all beasts moving upon the earth, Genesis, 1.

In the second chapter Moses declares and expresses the creation of women, which work in good sense, signifies not the woe of man as some affirm, but with Man: for so in our hasty pronouncing we turn the preposition with to woe, or we oftentimes: and so she was ordained to be with man as a help, and a companion, because God saw it was not good that man should be alone. Then when God brought woman to Man to be named by him, he found straight way that she was bone of his bones, flesh of his flesh, giving her a name, testifying she was taken out of man, and he pronounced that for her sake man should leave father and mother and adhere to his wife which should be with him one.

NOW MAN AND WOMAN ARE ONE

Now because Adam hath so pronounced that man and wife shall be but one flesh, and our Law is that if a feofment be made jointly to John at Stile and to Thom. Noke and his wife, of three acres of land, that Tho. and his wife get no more than one acre and a half, quia una persona, and a writ of conspiracy does not lie against one only, and that is the reason, Nat. br. fo, 116 a writ of conspiracy doth not lie against baron and feme, for they are but one person, and by this a married woman perhaps may either doubt whether she be either none or no more than half a person. But let her be of good cheer, though for the near conjunction which is between man and wife, and to tie them to a perfect love, agreement and adherence, they be by intent and wise fiction of law, one person, yet in nature and some other cases by the law of God and man, they remain divers, for as Adam's punishment was several from Eve's, so in criminal and other special causes our law argues them several persons, you shall find that persons is an individuum spoken of any thing which hath reason, and therefore of nothing but Vel de Angelo, vel de homme, fol. 154 in Dyer, who cites no worse authority for it than Callepinus own self, seeing therefore I list not to doubt with Plato, whether Women be reasonable or unreasonable creatures, I may not doubt but every woman is a temporal person, though no woman can be a spiritual Vicar....

SECT. III: THE PUNISHMENT OF ADAM'S SIN

Return a little to Genesis, in the 3rd Chapter whereof is declared our first parents transgression in eating the forbidden fruit: for which Adam, Eve, the serpent first, and lastly, the earth itself is cursed: and besides, the participation of Adams punishment, which was subjection to mortality, exiled from the garden of Eden, injoined to labor, Eve because she had helped to seduce her husband has inflicted on her an especial bane. In sorrow shall thou bring forth thy children, thy desires shall be subject to thy husband, and he shall rule over thee.

See here the reason of that which I touched before, that women have no voice in Parliament, they make no laws, they consent to none, they abrogate none. All of them are understood either married or to be married and their desires are subject to their husband, I know no remedy though some women can shift it well enough. The common law here shaketh hand with Divinity.

Separation from Bed and Board

William Fitzhugh to Kenelm Chiseldine, June 8, 1681[2]

Throughout the colonial period of American history, marriage was seen as an institution designed to promote both individual happiness and the best interest of the community. Because the purpose of marriage could not be fulfilled if the prospect for dissolution existed, most colonies conformed to the English practice and prohibited absolute divorce. There were, however, significant differences. In England ecclesiastical courts regulated matrimonial litigation; no such courts existed in America. Under the English system a valid marriage could not be dissolved for any reason; in America practice varied widely. As in England, the Anglican colonies, including Virginia, Carolina, and New York after the reception of common law, adhered to the view that marriage was a sacrament; once consummated it could not be dissolved except by a private bill passed by the legislature. Apparently the first such case in Virginia involved Giles Brent, Jr., the half-Indian son of Giles and Mary Kittamaqund Brent, and his wife Mary Brent, an English cousin. Rather than grant a full divorce the court approved separation with maintenance by the husband. The Brent decision established a precedent for the courts' handling of problems of a similar nature, as the letter of William Fitzhugh, a lawyer, planter, and merchant from Westmoreland County in Virginia, to Kenelm Chiseldine, Attorney General of Maryland, suggests. Fitzhugh's sister-in-law, the victim of wife-abuse, was probably Elizabeth James, the second wife of Ebenezer Blackston or Blakiston of Cecil County, Maryland. John

Newton was the third husband of Fitzhugh's mother-in-law, Rose Tucker
Gerard Newton.

Mr. Kenelm Chiseldine   June 8th. 16[81]

Sr. The Cruelty of Mr. Blackston towards my sis[ter] in law is grown so no-
torious and cruel, that there [is] no possibility of keeping it any longer private
w[ith?] the preservation of her life, his cruelty alread[y] having occasioned her
to make two or three attemp[ts] to destroy her self, which if not timely prevent[ed] will inevitably follow, therefore Sr. in relatio[n] of my affinity to her,
as also at the instance a[nd] request of Mr. Newton, to propose some remedy
I think there's some means to be used for a s[e]paration, because of his continued cruelty, whic[h] is England is practical, here in Virginia it i[s] [a] rare
Case, of which nature I have known but o[ne] which was between Mrs. Brent
and her husband Mr. Giles Brent; the case thus managed: She petitio[ns] the
governor and council, setting forth his inhumane usage, upon which petition,
the court orders her to live separate from him, and he to allow her a maintenance, according to his quali[ty] and estate, and to make his appearance at
the nex[t] general court before which court he died, and so [no farther] [pro-
ceedings] therein Mr. [Newton can give you a full account of his cruelty and
barbarity] [towards h]er, & has evidences ready to prove, therefore [I] advised
him to consult you for the manner of pro[ceeding] therein, and earnestly request
you will assist him in [it] [It] cannot properly be called a Divorce but a sep-
ara[tion] rather, for I find in Cooke on Littleton folio 235 [sever]al sorts of
divorces a Vinculo Matromonii [a divorce *a vinculo matrimonii* meant divorce
with permission to remarry], but [div]orces propter Saevitiam and causa Ad-
ulterii are more properly separation, because no dissolutions a Vinculo Matromonii but only a Mensa et thoro [a divorce *a mensa et thoro* granted permission
to be separated but did not allow remarriage], and the Cov[erture] continues,
and consequently a Maintenance allowed [her] and dower after his decease,
as is plentifully set [fourth?] by those that treat thereof. You may find one
precedent in Cooke Car. fo. 461.462 between Porter and his [wife?], where upon
prosecution it was decreed, Quod propter Sevitiam of her said Husband &c. I
question not but you [are] furnished with precedents of like nature, therefore
[your] assistance and advice in this affair is desired by

To. Mr. Kenelm Chiseldine   Sir Your W. ff.
Attorney General of Maryland

New Haven Code, 1655[3]

Under the influence of the Protestant Reformation, which denied the
sacramental basis of marriage, the Puritan colonies of New England
treated marriage as a civil contract, subject to dissolution on limited
grounds, including desertion, cruelty, adultery, and bigamy. Like Massachusetts, which passed the first divorce law, most New England statutes actually granted separation rather than full divorce and restricted
the couples' legal right to remarry. By contrast, Connecticut's more

liberal law, shown below, made divorce more accessible and consequently more frequent than in most of the other American colonies.

It is ordered, &c. That if any married person proved an adulterer, or an
adulteress, shall by flight, or otherwise, so withdraw or keep out of the jurisdiction, that the course of justice (according to the mind and law of God here
established) cannot proceed to due execution, upon complaint, proof, and prosecution, made by the party concerned, and interested, a separation or divorce,
shall by sentence of the court of magistrates be granted and published, and
the innocent party shall in such case have liberty to marry again. Mat. 19. 9.

And if any man marrying a woman fit to bear children, or needing and
requiring conjugal duty, and due benevolence from her husband, it be found
(after convenient forbearance and due trial) and satisfyingly proved, that the
husband, neither at the time of marriage, nor since, has been, is, nor by the
use of any lawful means, is like to be able to perform or afford the same, upon
the wife's due prosecution, every such marriage shall by the court of magistrates, be declared void, and a nullity, the woman freed from all conjugal
relation to that man, and shall have liberty in due season, if she see cause, to
marry another, but if in any such case, deceipt be charged and proved, that
the man before marriage knew himself unfit for that relation, and duty, and
yet proceeded, sinfully to abuse an ordinance of God, and in so high a measure
to wrong the woman, such satisfaction shall be made to the injured woman,
out of the estate of the offender, and such fine paid to the jurisdiction, as the
court of magistrates shall judge meet. But if any husband after marriage, and
marriage duty performed, shall by any providence of God be disabled, he falls
not under this law, not any penalty therein. And it is further declared, that
if any husband shall without consent, or just cause shown, willfully desert his
wife, or the wife her husband, actually and peremptorily refusing all matrimonial society, and shall obstinately persist therein, after due means have
been used to convince and reclaim, the husband or wife so deserted, may justly
seek and expect help and relief, according to 1. Cor. 7. 15. And the court upon
satisfying evidence thereof, may not hold the innocent party under bondage.

Anne Walker v. George Walker, 1708[4]

Although examples of absolute divorce are rare, some colonial courts
did agree to legal separations for couples with serious marital differences. In such cases the custody of children was almost always given
to the father. The historical origins of paternal custody rights are
derived from feudal times when, in order to preserve landed estates
intact, rules were adopted entitling the father to custody of the child
heir's person and property. Until the adoption in the nineteenth century of modern custody practices, fathers continued to have almost
unlimited rights to the custody of their children, as the response of the
Virginia council to a case brought before it by Anne Walker suggests.
Anne, a member of the Church of England, objected to having her
children raised as Quakers by their father, George Walker, an Eliza-

beth County Quaker. Despite the general suspicion of Quakers in the seventeenth century, the council decided in favor of the father's rights.

Williamsburgh April 25th, 1708

Anne Walker. This day was exhibited to us in council a petition which said petition we take to be from you and accordingly we have had your husband this day before us in council to answer the said petition upon hearing of which he only desires to have that authority over his children that properly belongs to every Christian man: that is to bring up his children in whatever Christian religion he may be of that is privileged by our Christian laws: and it seems to be hard that any person whatever shall endeavor or undertake to prevart or persuade any mans children against the instructions and admonitions of the father: your husband seems to be very willing to give you all manner of liberty to enjoy your religion provided you leave the instruction of all his children to him and that you will not cause them to read any books except the Scripture but such as he allows of and that you forbear to incense and persuade any of his children against his religion as long as he professes to be a Christian and continues in the exercise of it and also forbear to interpret or expound any part or portion of Scripture to any of his children without his leave or advice if he be willing to expound such portions as may happen to come in dispute or that any of his children may desire to be informed in: we therefore as your friends not being willing to give further trouble: if your husband will give you liberty to enjoy your religion without interruption: he ought to have all the liberty above desired: but if you can prove that he is not a Christian and so consequently not within the verge of our Christian laws then we are willing to hear you on Wednesday morning next but we should be glad you could be reconcilled without such proceedings.

Answer by Governor and Council to Mrs. Walker's Petition.

PROPERTY RELATIONS

Whatever the common-law status of men and women before they married, the act of marriage produced important changes in that status. As a result of the marriage, a woman incurred various common-law disabilities while her husband enjoyed a correspondingly increased legal capacity. The harshest aspects of the common-law disabilities operated in the law of real property, which had its origins in feudal society. According to the feudal system introduced into England by William the Conqueror, ultimate ownership of the land was in the king. Lands were granted by him to his followers on condition that the possessor render military service to his king when called upon to do so. Because they were presumed incapable of bearing arms, women were incapacitated from holding lands. The principle of seisin, as it came to be called, entitled the husband to possession, use, and income of all real property, whether acquired before or after marriage. Despite the demise of feudalism, the proprietary rights of the husband over family property were maintained in England. Different social and economic conditions in America, however, made certain feudal rights obsolete. The abundance of land, for example, and the desire of landholders for freedom to dispose of their property freely led to the abandonment or modification of some of the more cumbersome English land-law practices. As a result, married women, at least those from upper-class families, won limited legal capacity to deal with their property.

The common-law restrictions on the wife's right to own and control real property, which grew out of the feudal system of landholding in exchange for military service, did not apply where personal property was concerned. Nonetheless, out of concern for family stability, the common law gave to the husband the right to the wife's personal property, including money, household goods, and personal chattels which she brought to the marriage as dower. Once reduced into his possession the wife's personal property was his, absolutely and exclusively, to sell or bequeath at his pleasure. Denied the limited protections that the common law provided in real estate transactions, the wife thus lost all economic control over her personal property, except for her paraphernalia, which consisted of her wearing apparel, bed, and ornaments suitable to her social station.

The common-law notion of the union of husband and wife had other far-reaching legal ramifications. As a result of it a husband could not contract with his wife because to do so would constitute recognition of her separate existence. Theoretically, at marriage the wife disappeared as a legal entity. The law denied to her the ability to enter into legal relationships with others, including the ability to borrow money or to buy tangible goods, and it limited her liability for contracts entered into. The reasoning behind the practice was based first on the right of the husband to the person of his wife. If she could bind herself by her contracts she could be held liable for them; her inability to pay damages if awarded could lead to her confinement in prison, thus depriving the husband of the company of his wife. It was based second on the law's assumption that the wife was in the power of her husband and any contract made by her during coverture might be the product of coercion.

In practice these disabilities were also modified somewhat in America. In some colonies, for example, married women were able, under certain conditions, to incur contractual obligations. The criterion by which the validity of such contracts was judged tells us something about how early Americans conceived of power relationships within the household. It might also suggest different familial conditions in America, at least in some colonies. Inheritance practices are another important guide to understanding the structure of the family and interfamilial relations, because through the transmission of family property an individual expresses personal feelings and attitudes toward the surviving spouse and children. The general features of the English laws governing inheritance were in force throughout the American colonies. The rules strongly favored husbands over wives and sons over daughters. In order to protect family continuity and to preserve paternal authority, real property usually descended through male heirs according to an essentially equitable inheritance system. Although daughters seldom inherited real property since at marriage it would be carried out of the family, they usually shared in the division of personal property.

Real Property

Mary Dowe, Hartford, 1674[5]

Widespread landholding in the colonies created pressures to change some of the elaborate rules governing property rights, particularly as they pertained to the landowners' rights to divide up and sell off land. Under the spur of necessity, colonial assemblies sometimes allowed married women to manage landed estates in behalf of an absent or disabled spouse. Because they appreciated the advantages of speedy alienation of land, most of the colonies also modified conveyancing practices, although no uniform system of conveyance developed until the late eighteenth century. Connecticut, for example, gave to the husband an absolute title to the real property of the wife and allowed him alone to execute the conveyance. Even in Connecticut, however, married women living apart from their husbands were, like Mary Dowe, sometimes allowed conveyancing privileges by the General Court. It should be noted, however, that the point of such practices was not to give married women full legal equality but to enhance the efficiency of the land market, or, as in this case, to protect the rights of the creditor.

Mary Dowe, of Hartford, informing this Court that her husband being gone to sea and not being heard of for near two years, and leaving her destitute of supplies necessary for the maintenance of herself and children, she is fallen into debt and knows not how to pay the same without it be by sale of her house and lot, and therefore desires this Court to impower her so to do,—The Court considering the premises do see good reason to grant her desire, and do accordingly give her full power to grant, bargain and sell the said house and lot, and her deed therein shall be esteemed good and valid in the law.

An Act Empowering Femes Covert to Make Good
Acknowledgment of Sales of Land, 1674[6]

At marriage real property that belonged to the wife was, by the principle of seisin, vested in the husband. Although he was entitled to the possession, use, and income from such property during the coverture, he could not permanently dispose of it without his wife's consent. In England, transfer of the title to such land was accomplished by the complicated practice of fine and recovery: by a suit, either actual or fictitious, the wife formally surrendered her ownership rights and relinquished legal title to the marital property of her husband. In the interest of the market, the colonies abandoned fine and recovery in favor of the more simple form of the joint deed, which named the husband and wife together as sellers and carried both signatures. This Virginia statute of 1674 influenced a similar North Carolina statute of 1715 and the Georgia act of 1760. Although the American practice does not signal any major change in attitude, it does anticipate the modern view of marriage as an economic partnership of equals.

WHEREAS the legal way in England of passing estates where the inheritance is in a feme covert, is by way of fine and recovery, and it being the usual way in this country for many years, we having no fines and recoveries, that sales have been made by the husband and wife of the inheritance of the wife by conveyance from them, and the said conveyances acknowledged in the general or county courts of the husband and the wife, the wife being first privately examined by the court whether she acknowledge the same freely, but there being no act of assembly to authorize the same; *Be it therefore enacted by the governor, council and burgesses of this grand assembly, and by the authority thereof*, that all such sales and acknowledgments that by husband and wife have at any time heretofore been made in manner and form as aforesaid, or shall hereafter be made, shall be good and effectual against the said husband and wife, their and every of their heirs and assignees, and against all other persons claiming by, from, or under them, or any of them, and that to all intents and purposes as if the same had been done by fine and recovery or any other way whatsoever.

Elizabeth Eyre, New Haven, 1696, and Elizabeth Baldwin, Milford, 1699[7]

Throughout the colonies the most radical conveyancing privileges were enjoyed by widows. Women predeceased by their husbands had the same legal status as femes sole, and were consequently able to transfer their own real property by an ordinary conveyance, or dispose of it by will, gift, or bequest. As the following cases indicate, however, the approval of such transactions did not necessarily reflect any fundamental social change in attitudes toward women, but were meant instead to serve a useful purpose in protecting the economic interests of the widow and her family.

ELIZABETH EYRE, NEWHAVEN, 1696

Mrs. Elizabeth Eyre of Newhaven, widow, petitioned this Court to grant to her liberty and power to make sale of a parcel of land about eight miles distant from the said town of Newhaven in a tract of land called the third division, which parcel of land descended to her by gift from her grandmother, Mrs. Allerton deceased. This Court having considered the petition of the said Mrs. Eyre and her pleas therein recited, do grant her request, and do hereby grant her free liberty and full power to make sale of the aforesaid land, and do order that a conveyance thereof under her hand shall be effectual to all intents and purposes to confirm the said land and every part thereof to any person or persons whatsoever, to his or their heirs that shall purchase the said land of her.

ELIZABETH BALDWIN, MILFORD, 1699

Liberty and full power is by this Assembly granted to Elizabeth Baldwin of Milford, widow, to make confirmation according to law of a certain parcel of land unto the purchaser, which was sold by her husband in his life time to a neighbor of his and for which he received a good part of the pay.

Liberty and full power is by this Assembly granted to Elizabeth Wells widow and relict of Joseph Wells late of Hartford deceased, and administratrix to the estate of her deceased husband, with the advice of Mr. Thomas Hooker and Captain Cyprian Nickols, to sell some of the land belonging to the said estate for the payment of debts that are due therefrom, they amounting to about forty pounds.

Liberty and full power is by this Assembly granted to Mrs. Elizabeth Eyre of Newhaven, widow, to sell three acres and a half of upland, and two acres and a half of meadow, to satisfy a debt due for monies borrowed to procure the enlargement of her husband who was taken by the French in the late war; the sale thereof being made with the advice of Major Mansfield and Mr. John Allin.

Petition of Ann Stewart, 1692[8]

Although the husband was legally prohibited from selling his wife's property without her consent, the law left him otherwise free to use her property as he saw fit, even to squander it if he so desired. Both in England and in America, the wealthy landed classes tried to protect female family members from profligate husbands by resorting to extra-legal devices, such as a bequest, a jointure, or a marriage settlement, by which a married woman was allowed to own property separately from her husband. Practically speaking, however, such procedures were not available to the average family and as a result, until the passage in the nineteenth century of married women's property acts, every married woman was vulnerable to severe financial hardships in the event her husband mismanaged their estate. Ann Stewart of Albemarle County, North Carolina, was one of the victims of the laws of coverture.

THE PETITION OF ANN STEWART, 1692

Albemarle County Court

To the honorable the Lords proprietors, deputies and the rest of the wor-

shipful commissioners now setting for the County of Albemarle, the petition of Ann Stewart humbly shows that your petitioner being possessed of a considerable estate and marrying one John Stewart who has squandered and made away all the estate so that she is altogether without a maintenance but what she is assisted with by her children: and what little she is capable to get of her self: she being likewise a cripple and without one of her legs now such is the case that many persons do allege that the abovesaid Stewart is much indebted to them: so that your petitioner is discouraged so from endeavouring for a livelihood for herself and children, lest the creditors of the said Stewart should lay claim to it for payment of their debts lest I be secured against them by your honors and worships will please to provide to the contrary which I humbly hope you will and your petitioner shall as in duty ever pray.
May 3th, 1692 Ann Stewart

Personal Property

Hall v. Peyton, 1658[9]

Because by marriage the wife was stripped of the legal right to own and dispose of her property, common law made the husband liable for her debts contracted before marriage. The law was intended both to guarantee the claims of creditors and to protect the wife from unfair imprisonment for debt. On the other hand, under the law the husband could, without her consent, bring suit for the chattels belonging to his wife, or for her choses in action (choses in action refers to personal property to which the owner has a right of immediate possession or possession in the future). What he got possession of through such action became simply his to dispose of. The case of Hall v. Peyton below is typical of such action. It suggests the nature of the power relationships within the household.

HALL V. PEYTON (1658)

Upon the petition of Walter Hall, against Henry Payton, concerning a boat which Henry Fox lent to the said Payton, and which the said Walter Hall has right unto, by marrying the relict of the said Henry Fox, etc: it being proved that there has been an attachment granted and served upon a debt of the said Paytons in Lieutenant James Lindseys hand thereby to bring the said Henry Payton to answer and he never appearing. And upon the oath of Walter Pakes who affirms in open court that he was buying the said boat of Henry Fox about a month or thereabouts before the boat was lent to the said Payton, and profered 500 [pounds of] tobacco, for the said boat and sail, and the said Fox profered the said boat for 600 [pounds] tobacco to the deponent. It is ordered that the petitioner have a new attachment for twelve hundred pounds tobacco and in case the said Payton appear not either by himself or attorney at the next Provincial Court, then the petitioner to have judgment for six hundred pounds tobacco, with costs and damages.

Hall v. Knapp, 1644; David and Jane Sherwood, 1693;
White v. Parrat, n.d.[10]

Typically under English common law the right to file suit was denied to femes covert. The case of Hall v. Knapp, in which John Hall sued alone to recover a debt owing to his wife, shows how the rule operated. Not all American colonies adhered to the rule, however. Court records from northern and southern colonies reveal that women frequently joined with their husbands in filing suits to settle legal obligations incurred before marriage. In, for example, the case of David and Jane Sherwood, the Sherwoods filed a joint suit for her legacy; similarly in the case of White v. Parrat, the husband and wife joined in action for the recovery of the antenuptial debt owed her. The effect of such modifications in the law was to give to American married women more control over property than was generally enjoyed by contemporary English women.

HALL V. KNAPP, 1644

John Hall demands 3 pounds due to him from Roger Knapp in the right of his wife which he did acknowledge, whereupon it was ordered that he should pay the said 3 pounds, only abating 14s. which he has done in work for John Woolen, brother to the said John Halls wife.

DAVID AND JANE SHERWOOD, 1693

Know all men by these presents that I David Sherwood of North Carolina having lawfully intermarried with Jane Long late of Virginia for divers good causes me thereunto moving have constituted appointed and made Mr. Stephen Manwaring my true and lawful attorney to sue for or to receive such sum or sums of tobacco or other goods as shall be found due or anyways owing to me the said David Sherwood in the right of my wife Jane left to her by Mary Long deceased in the hands of Mr. Robert Ceester or in whosoevers hands the same shall be found and upon receipt thereof to give full and absolute discharges for the same against me and my wife Jane Sherwood and what my said attorney shall lawfully do for the recovering of the same we do hereby ratify and confirm as witness our hands and seals the eighteenth of October Anno Domini 1693.

Sealed signed and delivered   David Sherwood
  in the presence of   The mark of Jane Sherwood
Thomas Gough

The mark of Jon. Williams

WHITE V. PARRAT [DATE UNDETERMINED]

North Carolina SS.   To the General Court

Thomas White and Diana his wife plantiffs versus Francis Parrat defendant in a plea of the case complains that the said Francis Parrat contracted [with] the said Diana while she was sole for [torn] drink to the value of forty eight shillings and nine pence as by his account does appear and which the said

Francis Parrat has not paid and to render does refuse though often demanded to the plantiffs damage threescore shillings for which he has brought his suit [and] craves judgment for the same with cost of suit and he shall pray.
[*Illegible*] day   Vera Copia   W. Glover   Clerk
   [*Endorsed:*]
   [*Torn*] versus P[arrat]
   To be renewed

Contracts

Samuel Chase, Baron and Feme, 1700[11]

Because of her incapacity to own property on her own account, at common law a married woman could not make contracts, unless she acted as the agent of her husband, in which case her contracts, previously authorized or subsequently ratified by him, were valid because they were his contracts. In the excerpt below from *Baron and Feme. A Treatise of the Common Law Concerning Husbands and Wives*, Samuel Chase explains the theory behind the practice.

Coverture is *tegere* in Latin, and is so called for that the wife is *sub potestate viri* [under or subject to the power of another]. The law of nature has put her under the obedience of her husband, and has submitted her will to his, which the law follows, *cue ipsa in vita sua contradicer e tradicere non potuit*, [whom in his lifetime she could not gainsay] and therefore will not bind her by acts joining with her husband, because they are judged his acts and not hers; she wants free will as *minors* want judgment, and yet the law of the land for necessity sake makes bold with this law of nature in a special kind, and therefore allows a fine levied by the husband and his wife, because she is examined of her free will judicially by an authentical person trusted by the law, and by the King's Writ, and so taken in a sort as a sole woman, as also when she comes in by receipt, Hob. 225.

A feme covert in our books is often compared to an infant, both being persons disabled in the law, but they differ much; an infant is capable of doing an act for his own advantage, so is not a feme covert. A lease made by an infant without rent is not void, but voidable; but its void in the case of a feme covert. If a feme covert enter into bond, non est factum [a plea denying execution of instrument sued on] may be pleaded to it; but if an infant enter into bond he must plead the special matter that he was under age. An infant may bind himself for conveniences, as necessaries for himself and family, and the law gives him authority so to bind himself; but a feme covert cannot do so without the consent actual or implied of the husband, because thereby she is to bind another that has all the property in her estate, as with the opinion of the Lord Chief Just Hales in *Scot and Manby's* case. And yet a feme covert is a favorite of the law, and therefore the law gives her *rationabile Estoveriun* [alimony], til dower assigned: and its said in some of our books an action lies not by the executors against her for her *paraphernalia*. [Paraphernalia is the separate property of a married woman, other than that which is included in her dowry, i.e., apparel and ornaments suitable to her rank and station.]

March et. ux. v. March, 1682; Hall v. Estate of Wilkes, 1648; Nevill v. Beach, 1644; Vos v. Hendricx, 1653[12]

Procedurally, as a result of coverture wives could neither sue nor be sued at law unless they were joined with their husbands. By contrast, upon marriage the husband acquired the right to sue on antenuptial contracts of his wife (March *et. ux.* v. March, 1682). He could sue for the value of his wife's services (Hall v. Estate of Wilkes, 1648). At the same time, however, he became liable for all of his wife's premarital contracts (Nevill v. Beach, 1644; Vox v. Hendricx, 1653).

MARCH ET. UX. *V. MARCH, 1682*

Joseph Fletcher in behalf of John March and Jemima his wife plaint aga[inst] Hugh March serve defendant in an action of appeal from the judgment of the county court at Ipswich after the attachment courts judgment reasons of appeal and evidences in the case produced were read committed to the jury and are on file with the records of this court the jury brought in their verdict they found confirmation of the former juries special verdict viz. If the acquittance in the deed does acquit Hugh March from his promise upon marriage to Joseph Fletcher on the behalf of John March and Jemima his wife then we find for the defendant costs of courts otherwise we find for the plaintiff one hundred thirty and two pounds in or as money and costs of courts the magistrates on perusal of this verdict finds for the plaintiff and his costs granted was six pounds eleven shillings.

HALL V. ESTATE OF WILKES, 1648

John Hall having formerly pleaded for a portion for his wife of 10 pounds out of the estate of Mr. Wilkes, due to her by promise, as did appear by the testimony of William Paine and Bridget Wilkes upon oath, and at the last court renewed his plea, and produced another witness, viz., Johnathan Marsh, who was also heard and examined upon oath, but the cause for some reasons then shown, was not issued, therefore he did not renew his desire that the court would be pleased to put an issue to it, and Goodey Hall being present was asked why her master Wilkes promised her 10 pounds if she served out her time. She said because he knew she deserved it. The indenture wherein Goodwife Hall was bound to Mr. Wilkes was called for and also read in court, wherein it appeared that she was to serve him for 5 years and to have 3 pounds a year, which the court judged competent wages, her passage being also paid for by Mr. Wilkes, so that the act was altogether free on Mr. Wilkes his part. But he having promised and engaged himself to do it, as appears fully by testimony of the witnesses upon oath, therefore it becomes a due debt to her. Therefore the sentence of the court is that Mr. Robert Newman, executor of the estate of Mr. Wilkes, pay to John Hall as a debt due from Mr. Wilkes to his wife, 10 pounds.

NEVILL V. BEACH, 1644

John Nevill made oath, that Anne now wife of Ellis Beach, at some time in or near November anno 1642, at Snow-hill, did contract with the deponent to carry her the said Anne to Elizabeth River in Virginia in a boat of Colonel Trafford, and to have therefore at his arrival in Virginia stockings and shoes and other clothes to give him content: and that this deponent did carry down the said Anne and Ellis Beach and did land them at Mr. Mottrams in York, with the consent of the said Anne, at the motion of the said Ellis; and was there ready to have carried them on to Elizabeth River, if there had been provisions of victuals and that there was no provisions of victuals to carry the boat about, and that he was upon that voyage from the time of setting forth til he left it off for want of provision near about a month and that he used all moral diligence to get a passage back to Maryland, and it was near about 3 weeks more ere he returned to Snow-hill and that he made no profit all that time of his labor.

Ellis Beach appeared to the suit of John Nevill; and said that he made no bargain with the plaintiff nor did use his labor; the 86 pounds he acknowledges.

And the judge beside the 86 pounds found for the plaintiff 20 pounds tobacco for damage of evidence, and 1 pair good new shoes 1 pair good new Irish stockings; 1 good new locram shirt, and 1 pair of new drawers of frise worth 7 shillings 6 pence in English: by the judgment of 2 neighbors, or else 2 pair of good canvas drawers for it: to be delivered to the plaintiff at the next arrival of any vessel in this river with such goods; or in case none arrive sooner, then sometime before the first of December next; or in default thereof 700 pounds tobacco to be levied upon him by execution.

VOS V. HENDRICX, 1653

Matewis Vos, curator as before, v/s Anneke Hendricx, wife of Jan van der Bil, who appears for the wife. Plaintiff demands payment of 24fl. 18st. book-debts. Deft. being in doubt, whether he has not already paid, he is condemned to pay within a month from date or prove, that he has paid.

Contract between Folckje Jurriaens and Seger Cornelissen, 1660[13]

Under both the common law and Roman–Dutch law, a married woman could not bind herself, her husband, or the community without the consent or subsequent ratification of her husband. The Roman–Dutch rule was, however, subject to several important exceptions. If, for example, a married woman contracted for necessaries for the joint household, as appears to be the case below, by such contract she bound herself and her husband.

CONTRACT BETWEEN FOLCKJE JURRIAENS, WIFE OF JAN VAN HOESEN, AND SEGER CORNELISSEN IN REGARD TO THE PURCHASE OF WHEAT

On this day, the 28th of October 1660, appeared before me Dirck van Schelluyne, notary public, and before the hereinafter named witnesses, Folckie Jurriaensz, wife of Jan van Hoesen, dwelling in Beverwyck, of the first part, and Seger Cornelisz, farmer, dwelling in the colony of Renselaerswyck, of the second part, and declared that they, the appeares, had contracted and agreed with each other in the manner following: Seger Cornelisz promises to deliver next winter, at the latest before the month of May 1661, to Folckie Jurriaensz aforenamed the quantity of three hundred skipples of winter wheat the skipple reckoned at three guilders, for which she, Folckie Jurriaensz, promises to pay to said Seger Cornelissz, on his order, on or before the 1st of June 1661, punctually and without further delay, the quantity of one hundred and twelve and a half good, merchantable winter beaver skins, reckoned at eight guilders a piece (whole); thereto binding their persons and estates, nothing excepted, subject to all courts and judges. Appeared likewise Adriaen Symonsz, trader, at present here, dwelling at Amsterdam in New Netherland, who declared that in connection with the foregoing agreement he becomes surety and co-principal for the full satisfaction and payment of the aforesaid one hundred and twelve and a half beaver skins, on the day of payment aforesaid, renouncing therefore the *beneficium ordinis et excussionis*, the effect whereof he understands, binding and subjecting himself as above. Thus done and executed in Beerwyck in New Netherland, in presence of Mr. Phillip Pietersz Schuyler and Jurriaen Teunisz, innkeeper, as witnesses hereto called.

<table>
<tr><td></td><td>This mark X was made by FOLCKIE
JURRIAENSZ, aforesaid</td></tr>
<tr><td>Philip Pieterse Schuyler</td><td>This mark X was made by SEGER</td></tr>
<tr><td>Jureyaen Tunsen</td><td>CORNELISZ, aforesaid
ARYAN SYMENSE
D. V. SCHELLUYNE, *Not. Pub.* 1660</td></tr>
</table>

Lease of a House from Catryna Jochems, 1661[14]

The far-reaching exceptions of the general rule on contracts in New Netherland resulted in the broad extension of the contractual power to married women on a scale unprecedented in other colonies. Although most New Netherland women merchants were widows, a few, like Catryna Jochems, apparently the owner of a freehold, and Maria Becker, probably a female trader engaged in the lucrative fur trade, were wives.

LEASE OF A HOUSE FROM CATRYNA JOCHEMS, WIFE OF ABRAHAM STAETS, TO MARIA BECKER, WIFE OF JOHANNES BECKER

On this day, the 10 of September 1661, Catryna Jochemsz, wife of Mr. Abraham Staats, lets, and Maria Becker, wife of Johannes Becker, hires the lessor's house and lot, standing and lying in the village of Beverwyck near the house of Folckert Jansz and known to the lessee; for the time of one year beginning on the first of November next, for the sum of one hundred and fifty guilders, to be paid in good, merchantable beavers, reckoned at eight guilders apiece. It is further stipulated that in case the lessor wishes to build a little house on the lot for her own convenience, she may do so at her pleasure and during the trading season next summer she may also retain the use of the little house at present standing there. Also, in case of a longer lease, this lessee is to have the preference, provided she pay as much as others. Furthermore, a window is to be made on the north side of the house at the expense of the lessor; and as said house and lot is to be delivered to the lessee in proper repair, window, roof, and floor tight, she, the lessee, promises to deliver up the same at the end of this lease in the same condition, unavoidable accidents excepted; thereto binding their respective persons and estates, nothing excepted, to the authority of all courts and judges. Done in Beverwyck, dated as above.

TRINTEN IOCHIGIMS
MARYKEN D'BECKER
In my presence,
D. V. SCHELLUYNE, *Not. Pub.* 1661

Estates and Wills

Will of Marten Cornelissen and his Wife, 1676–1677[15]

Under common law, testamentary rights were restricted to persons not under special prohibition by law or custom. Infants, idiots, madmen, and women fell into that special category. In each case the law presumed them incapacitated from bequeathing their property by reason of a deficiency of liberty or free will. Roman-Dutch law of New Netherland, however, allowed an exception by permitting husbands and wives to execute joint wills, an example of which follows below. The practice automatically gave to the wife one-half of the joint estate if her husband predeceased her and allowed her to dispose of the other half unless the will stipulated otherwise.

In the name of God, Amen. Know all men by the contents of this present public instrument that in the year after the birth of our Lord and Savior Jesus Christ 1676/7, on the 12th day of the month of January, before me, Adriaen van Ilpendam, notary public residing in New Albany (appointed by the Right Honorable Edmond Andros, [governor] general of the parts of America) pursuant to nomination for this place of Albany, colony of Renselaerswyck and the district thereof, and before the subscribing witnesses, came and appeared the worthy Maerten Cornelisz, born in the city of Ysselsteyn, and his wife Maeycke Cornelis, born at Barrevelt, both dwelling at the Claverrack, to me, the notary, well known, both being sound of body, standing and walking, having perfect use and command of their faculties, reason, memory and understanding; which appearers, considering the shortness and frailty of human life, the certainty of death and the uncertainty of the time and hour thereof, and wishing therefore to dispose of their worldly goods to be left behind while through God's grace they still are able, as they do of their own free will and inclination, without persuasion or misleading of any persons, have now ordained and concluded this their last will and testament in form and manner following: First and foremost commending their immortal souls, whenever they may be separated from their bodies, to the gracious and merciful hands of God, their Creator and Redeemer, and their bodies to a Christian burial, at the same time revoking, annulling and canceling hereby all and every such testamentary disposition and bequest as they before the date hereof either jointly or severally may have made and executed, holding the same null and of no effect, and now making a new disposition, they, the testators, out of mutual and particular love, which during their marriage estate they have steadily borne and do now bear toward each other, declare that they have reciprocally nominated and instituted, as by these presents they do, the survivor of the two their sole and universal heir to all the property, whether personal or real, claims, credits, money, gold and silver, coined and uncoined, jewels, clothing, linen and woolens, household furniture etc., nothing excepted, which the one dying first shall leave behind as well here in this country as elsewhere, to do therewith as with his or her own property, without contradiction or opposition of any persons; which they do for the reason that they (through God's blessing) have obtained most of the estate by great labor and diligence during their marriage with each other. Likewise [they will] that no persons whatever, whether magistrates, orphan masters, friends, or others shall have the right to demand of the survivor any accounting or inventory of the estate, much less security or sureties, so long as he or she remains in his or her widowed estate; and if so be that the survivor again enter into wedlock, he or she shall be holden to settle a just half of the estate (as the same may be found) on the children left behind, that all of them, share and share alike, may receive their legitimate portion of the father or mother's estate, provided that the survivor shall receive the income and profits thereof until the children shall arrive at their majority or marriage estate, til which time the survivor shall be holden to bring them up in the fear of the Lord and (so far as he or she can) to have them taught reading and writing, together with some handicraft whereby under God they may earn their living with honor. And if so be that the testators after this date make further dispositions, declarations, or bequests, whether in writing under their hands or signatures or before two or more trustworthy witnesses by word of mouth, or in the aforesaid conditions make any change, increase or diminution, they will and desire all that to have the same power, value and effect and by every person to be considered and holden as though written and set forth in this will. All which aforesaid conditions they, the testators, declare to be their last will and testament, willing and desiring that after the death of the first of the two the same may have full force and effect, whether as will, codicil, donation, gift in anticipation of death, or otherwise, as may be most compatible, although certain formalities demanded by law or usage may not be observed herein, desiring that the utmost benefit may be received herefrom, and one or more copies hereof to be made in proper form to serve as occasion may require. Thus done and executed in New Albany at the house of Pieter Loockermans and in the presence of Mr. Jan Verbeeck and Pieter Loockermans, called and bidden as trustworthy witnesses hereto, who with the testators in presence of me the notary, have subscribed this with their own hands the year, month and day aforesaid.

This is the mark X of MAERTEN COENELISZ, made with his own hand
This is the mark X of MAEYCKE CORNELIS, made with her own hand

As witnesses:
Jan Verbeeck
Pieter Loockermans
Quod attestor
ADRIAEN VAN ILPENDAM, *Not. Pub.*

Will of Jonathan Amory, 1697[16]

Although the economic concessions granted to femes covert were limited, seventeenth-century probate records suggest that in the southern colonies wives also enjoyed greater economic influence within the family, a condition which is reflected in the disposition of family property. Many testators either left to their wives a major part of the estate or, like Jonathan Amory, made their wives executrix. Amory (1654–1699), a member of a merchant trading and shipping family of Ireland, South Carolina, and Boston, gave to his widow control over the estate, thus making her responsible for preserving family property.

In the Name of God Amen. The twenty third day of November and year of our Lord one thousand six hundred and ninety seven, I Jonathan Amory of the province of Carolina merchant being weak in body, yet of sound and perfect memory praised be God do make this my last will and testament in manner and form following viz. First I bequeath my soul and spirit unto the hands of the Almighty God, my heavenly Father, and my body to the earth to be buried at the discretion of my executrix; and my worldly goods to be disposed of as follows. I give and bequeath unto my son Mr. Joseph Croskeys all that piece of land that lies next the Rattrap which was bought of Andrew Lawson and lies on the left hand of the broad path as you go into the country, to him and his assigns forever, I likewise request my executrix to make a title to him of that piece of land which lies next to my dwelling house, which I gave to him with my daughter. I also give him my best silver head cane, I give to Sarah Rhett daughter to Capt. Wm. Rhett ten pounds paid into the hands of her mother to buy her a gold chain. I give to Dr. Atkin Williamson ten pounds I give unto Dr. Thomas Todd ten pounds, I give to the poor of Charles Town fifteen pounds, I give and bequeath unto James Noble twenty pounds, I give unto my loving wife Martha my dwelling house, in Charles Town and all the land paled in about the same during her natural [life] and after her death I give grant and devise the said house and land to my sons Thomas and Robert

Amory and the survivors of them, their heirs and assigns for ever. I give and bequeath unto my said loving wife all her wearing apparel and all the plate and household goods belonging to my said dwelling house...I also nominate and appoint my said wife Martha sole executrix during her life and after her decease I nominate my two sons Thomas and Robert my executors I do also hereby impower and authorize my said executrix to sell and dispose for ever all or any part of my real estate provided that the shares of the money raised thereby be secured to my sons behalf in witness whereof I have here unto set my hand and seal, day year and place above expressed
published and declared in the presence of

Geo. Logan
Ara Hidling
Joane Hearne
Jonathan Amory

Petition of Elizabeth Bateman, 1695[17]

Women received an economic identity of their own primarily through widowhood. The ancient right of dower, meant as compensation to the wife for the loss of her property, finds its roots in the medieval practice of a gift made by the bridegroom to the bride at the church door. In the thirteenth century the law developed that unless she had accepted less at the church door, the widow was entitled to a third of the lands of which the husband was seized during the marriage. Still later in the century, it was decided that she might be entitled to more but could not be entitled to less than one-third. The right of dower made the Atlantic crossing and was incorporated into the laws of the colonies. According to colonial laws if the husband did not fulfill his obligation or if he died intestate, his widow was free to seek relief from the courts. In the case of the Widow Bateman, the husband apparently left her less than she was by law entitled to. She therefore renounced her bequest and sued for a third life interest, which the court granted. The willingness of the courts to protect the widow's thirds was perhaps due to concern that indigent women might become a public charge.

Albemarle
To the honorable court now sitting the petition of Elizabeth Bateman widow most humbly shows that Jonathan Bateman late husband to your petitioner some small time before his death did make a will by which he bequeathed certain legacies to your petitioner and his children, but your petitioner upon due consideration finds it for many reasons not convenient for her to stand by or unto that will wherefore she craves that your honors will be pleased according to [law] to grant her the third of the said Jonathan her late husband's estate and she shall as in duty bound for ever pray.

A WILL OF JONATHAN BATEMAN PROVED BY THE EVIDENCE AND ORDERED TO BE RECORDED

And Elizabeth Bateman widow and relict of the said Jonathan Bateman declining her legacy given in the said will and craving to have her thirds of her deceased husband's estate. Ordered that the said Elizabeth Bateman have her thirds of her said husband's estate and the remain to be divided among the rest of the legatees. And that administration with the will anexed to be granted to the executor appointed in the said will and that Jno. Whitby Tho. Durant Francis Foster and Mr. Joseph Sutton or any three of them apprise the said estate and the Mr. Jno. Durant or Mr. Ralph Flecher administer to the said apprisors their oathes and account of the said estate to be given to the next general court. And Jno. Lilly and Thomas Hassold have undertaken for the executor for the true performance hereof.

PUBLIC RELATIONS

The advances made by women in the areas of the wife's right to property and in her limited contractual capacity did not reflect any fundamental social change in attitudes toward women. The old concept of natural male dominance persisted in many areas of the law in which women received different treatment from their husbands. Deemed to be citizens in the most common sense of the word, women were not, however, extended the right to take part in the government, either as voters or as officeholders. Generally ignored by political philosophers in their discussions of civic powers and responsibilities, women were expected to experience the political world through their fathers, their husbands, or their sons. The public sphere consequently remained an exclusively male domain, although some women were engaged informally in political activities.

Citizens without Rights

Petition of Abbigarll Dexter, 1681[18]

Extant public records suggest that some women were active participants in political struggles of the seventeenth century, such as Bacon's Rebellion in Virginia. Many women were clearly interested in political issues of the times. A few deliberately championed the cause of political rights for women. Perhaps the first to do so was Margaret Brent, a member of a distinguished Maryland family. Named executrix by the dying Governor Leonard Calvert, Mistress Brent in 1647 demanded a seat in the provincial assembly, probably so that she could look after the Calvert interest. Her request denied, Brent continued to play a prominent role in public affairs. Although her case is the best known, there are other examples of ordinary women protesting their exclusion from the political world. The fact that she was required to pay taxes but denied the right to vote led the Widow Dexter to object to the town meeting of Providence, Rhode Island.

To the town met June the 6th 1681: Honored Gentlemen if the poor and low condition, of a poor widow has no influence upon the hearts of your rate makers, but to rate me where there is no justice for it before God nor man, that they should rate me to sergeant's wages, and house rent, I cannot see just cause, for these reasons, first the sergeant has neither power, nor occasion to warn me to your meetings, knowing I am not allowed any vote there, secondly all my lands meadows and orchard lie common to your benefit, and not mine nor the orphans of my deceased husbands. Thirdly if I should have came to have voted today in your election, perhaps it would have been said what had I to do there: and if I have not to do to vote and make use of the house you rate me for the use thereof, I leave to your wisdoms to judge of: praying your consideration of it and your determination of the same,

Your poor widow and friend
Abbigarll Dexter

This bill is granted that no widows shall be rated to house rent nor sergeants wages.

An Act for the Prevention of Undue Election of Burgesses, 1699[19]

The rationale for sexually discriminatory laws in the public sphere was found in the laws of coverture, which regarded women as wards of their husbands and therefore presumed them incapable of making free political choices through the exercise of the franchise. The result, as the Virginia law of 1699 suggests, was that the colonial franchise was everywhere denied to women, whether sole or covert. By contrast, although there was de facto exclusion of women from the franchise in England, there were no legal prohibitions on woman suffrage there.

AN ACT FOR THE PREVENTION OF UNDUE ELECTION OF BURGESSES

For the prevention of undue election of Burgesses to serve in the general assembly in this his majesty's colony and dominion.

Be it enacted by the governor, council and Burgesses of this present general assembly, and the authority thereof, and it is hereby enacted, that no person or persons shall be enabled to give a vote for the election of a burgess or burgesses to serve in the general assembly hereafter to be called but those who are freeholders in the respective county or town for which the said burgess or burgesses shall be elected and chosen, and if any person shall presume to give his vote for the election of a burgess or burgesses in any county or town who is not a freeholder in such county or town he shall forfeit and pay the sum of five hundred pounds of tobacco for every such offence. *Provided always*, and it is the true intent and meaning of this act that no woman sole or covert, infants under the age of twenty-one years, or recusant convict being freeholders shall be enabled to give a vote or have a voice in the election of burgeses any thing in this act to the contrary notwithstanding.

Kent County Court Proceedings, 1668[20]

Like the political structure, the court system was exclusively a male arena. Although women regularly appeared before colonial courts as criminal and civil litigants, they never sat as judges and they were denied the right to serve on juries on the same basis as men. For certain crimes such as abortion, infanticide, or witchcraft, it was common to impanel a jury of women to search the body of the accused woman for witch marks or to ascertain if she was pregnant or had recently delivered a child. The jury of matrons summoned to examine Hannah Jenkins served simply in an information-gathering capacity. Their findings were then reported to an all-male jury which rendered the actual verdict.

At a court held the 13 October 1668 for the Lord proprietor in the 37 year of his Dominion and at Mr. Richard Blunts for Kent County present

> Capt. John Vicaris
> Mr. Morgan Williams
> Mr. Matthew Read   *Commissioners*
> Mr. Richard Blunt
> Mr. Thomas Osborne
> Mr. John Dabb

Whereas information has been given to some of the commissioners of this county that Hannah Jenkins, daughter in law to Mr. George Harris of this county, has been delivered of a man child.

The court finding a suspicion of murder ordered a jury of women to be called to search the body of the said Hannah whether she was delivered of a child or not which accordingly was done.

The names of the jury women

Mary Vicaris	Elizabeth Winchester
Rebecka Denny	Hannah Dabb
Christian Ringgold	Kathorine Osborne
Elizabeth Coppage	Ann Blunt
Dorothy Williams	Mary Southerne
Margrett Jones	Kathorine Scale

The jury's verdict is that the said Hannah Jenkins is clear from child bearing and never had a child to the best of their knowledge.

Mary Vicaris Forewoman

Hannah Jenkins desires her father in law, Mr. George Harris, to be her attorney which the court does allow of:

According to the jury's verdict the court does order that the said Hannah Jenkins shall be cleared by proclamation and ordered the sheriff to do it.

Citizens before the Law

Brabling Women, 1662[21]

In compensation for the various disabilities women suffered under the laws of coverture, they were, at least theoretically, privileged from liability for certain of their actions. For example, because the law presumed that the wife's actions were done by the husband's coercion, he was liable for the torts she committed in his company. In fact, few married women escaped punishment for legal wrongs. Even for defamation, a common complaint against women in the seventeenth century, the colonies attempted to extend liability to the wife for the defamatory statements attributed to her alone. This Virginia statute of 1662 offers such an example.

WHEREAS oftentimes many brabling women often slander and scandalize their neighbors for which their poor husbands are often brought into chargeable and vexatious suits, and cast in great damages; *Be it therefore enacted by the authority aforesaid* that in actions of slander occasioned by the wife as aforesaid after judgment passed for the damages the women shall be punished by ducking; and if the slander be so enormous as to be adjudged at a greater damage than five hundred pounds of tobacco, then the woman to suffer a ducking for each five hundred pounds of tobacco adjudged against the husband if he refuse to pay the tobacco.

Mary Lathan and James Britton Executed for Adultery, 1643[22]

Because men defied the law more often, they appeared in court more frequently than did women. Women were, however, regularly brought to trial, usually for religious dissent or for sexual misconduct. In all of the American colonies adultery, which represented the most serious threat to conjugal relations, was a capital crime. Defined as sexual congress with a married or betrothed woman, the offense was commonly punished by fines, lashes, or the pillory. Mary Lathan and her lover James Britton were among a small minority of couples executed for their crime.

At this court of assistants one James Britton, a man ill affected both to our church discipline and civil government, and one Mary Lathan a [proper] young woman about 18 years of age, whose father was a godly man and had brought her up well, were condemned to die for adultery, upon a law formerly made and published in print. It was thus occasioned and discovered. This woman, being rejected by a young man whom she had an affection unto, vowed she would marry the next that came to her, and accordingly, against her friends' minds, she matched with an ancient man who had neither honesty nor ability, and one whom she had no affection unto. Whereupon, soon after she was married, divers young men solicited her chastity, and drawing her into bad company, and giving her wine and other gifts, easily prevailed with her, and among others this Britton. But God smiting him with a deadly palsy and fearful horror of conscience withal, he could not keep secret, but discovered this, and other the like with other women, and was forced to acknowledge the justice of God in that having often called others fools, &c. for confessing against themselves, he was now forced to do the like. The woman dwelled now in Plymouth patent, and one of the magistrates there, hearing she was detected, &c. sent her to us. Upon her examination, she confessed he did attempt the fact, but did not commit it, and witness was produced that testified (which they both confessed) that in the evening of a day of humiliation through the country for England, &c. a company met at Britton's and there continued drinking sack, &c. til late in the night, and then Britton and the woman were seen upon the ground together, a little from the house. It was reported also that she did frequently abuse her husband, setting a knife to his breast and theatening to kill him, calling him old rogue and cockold, and said she would make him wear horns as big as a bull. And yet some of the magistrates thought the evidence not sufficient against her, because there were not two direct witnesses; but the jury cast her, and then she confessed the fact, and accused twelve others, whereof two were married men. Five of these were apprehended and committed, (the rest were gone,) but denying it, and there being no other witness against them than the testimony of a condemned person, there could be no proceeding against them. The woman proved very penitent, and had deep apprehension of the foulness of her sin, and at length attained to hope of pardon by the blood of Christ, and was willing to die in satisfaction to justice. The man also was very much cast down for his sins, but was loth to die, and petitioned the general court for his life, but they would not grant it, though some of the magistrates spoke much for it, and questioned the letter, whether adultery was death by God's law now. This Britton had been a professor in England, but coming hither he opposed our church and government, &c. and grew dissolute, losing both power and profession of godliness.

1.21.] They were both executed, they both died very penitently, especially the woman, who had some comfortable hope of pardon of her sin, and gave good exhortation to all young maids to be obedient to their parents, and to take heed of evil company, &c.

Petition of Christopher Merchant, 1684[23]

Like adultery, fornication was equally offensive in both male and female. Judged together, when convicted the offending couple ordinarily received the standard punishment of a ten-pound fine or a public whipping. If however, the woman became pregnant, she was then subject to the harsh laws regulating bastardy, while the father of the child often escaped the court's notice. Prohibited by law from marrying during their term of service, female indentured servants like Anne Basten of North Carolina were among the most frequent offenders against the law.

Upon the petition of Christopher Merchant that a servant maid named Anne Basten who is a servant to the estate of Capt. Jno. Willoughby being delivered of a bastard child during her service ordered therefore that at the end of term which she has now served she shall continue and abide in her now [service] one whole year more to the estate of the said Capt. Willoughby from thence to be fully complete and ended.

Women Servants Got with Child, 1662[24]

In some colonies the law punished bastardy by binding female servants to additional years service. The rape of women servants by unscrupulous masters seeking to take advantage of the law, however, led to its revision in Virginia. Despite the change in the provisions of the law, women remained the most conspicuous victims of the laws against bastardy.

ACT VI. WOMEN SERVANTS GOT WITH CHILD BY THEIR MASTERS AFTER THEIR TIME EXPIRED TO BE SOLD BY THE CHURCHWARDENS FOR TWO YEARS FOR THE GOOD OF THE PARISH.

WHEREAS by act of assembly every woman servant having a bastard is to serve two years, and late experience shows that some dissolute masters have gotten their maid with child, and yet claim the benefit of their service, and on the contrary if a woman got with child by her master should be freed from that service it might probably induce such loose persons to lay all their bastards to their masters; It is therefore thought fit and accordingly enacted, and be it enacted henceforeward that each woman servant got with child by her master shall after her time by indenture or custom is expired be by the churchwardens of the parish where she lived when she was brought to bed of such bastard, sold for two years, and the tobacco to be imployed by the vestry for the use of the parish.

Elizabeth Greene, 1664[25]

Ignorance of reliable methods of birth control led many women, particularly young, single women like Elizabeth Greene of Calvert County, Maryland, to murder their bastard children rather than face the rigorous penalties for fornication and bastardy. Executions, often public, were intended to provide a warning and to serve as a deterrent.

The jury for the Right Honorable the Lord Proprietary do present Elizabeth Greene of Garriden in Calvert County spinster the sixth day of May in the

year of our Lord God 1664 being big with child by Gods providence was delivered of a certain living man child which said living man child she the said
Elizabeth Greene did throw into the fire, and so that the said Elizabeth Greene
the living man child by throwing into the fire in manner and form aforesaid,
then and there feloniously and of malice forethought did kill and murder
contrary to the peace of his said Lordship his rule and dignity—

The Grand Jury discharged the Petite Jury called (vizt)

Foreman Mr. Richard Smyth	Thomas Bennit
Joseph Horsley	William Hatten
Wm. Dorrington	William Watts
Francis Armstrong	Robert Jones
Robert Blinckhorne	William Black
William Groome	William Harper

The presentments was again read to the said jurors, and the evidence
called examined and sworn as afore—the jurors withdrew to consider on the
said bills and their charge—

The jurors being called and answering all of them to their call by their
several names—the foreman delivers in their verdicts endorsed on the back-
side of each bill with this word (vizt) guilty—

Pope Aluey Arthur Nottooll and Elizabeth Greene all called by their
names to the bar—

Pope Aluey first demanded of him what he had to say for himself. To
which he craves benefit of clergy, which was granted him, and the book
being given and demanded whether he read or not, answer was made that
he read—

Arthur Nottooll being demanded what he had to say for himself to which
he craves benefit of clergy, which was granted him, and the book being
given, and demanded whether he read or not, answer was made, that he
read—

Ordered thereupon that the said Pope Aluey and Arthur Nottooll be forthwith burned in the brawn of their right hands with a red hot iron. Which
was by the under sheriff immediately executed—

Then it was demanded of Elizabeth Greene, what she had to say for herself, answered that she threw herself on the mercy of the board, being again
demanded if that was all she had to say, she answered yes—Then sentence
of death past upon her by the governor and judge in these words following
(vizt) Elizabeth Greene you shall be carried to the place from when you
came, from there to the place of execution, and there be hanged by the neck
til you are dead, and so God have mercy upon your soul.

On the morrow being the 8th July 1664 warrant issued to the sheriff of
St. Marys County for the performance of execution (vizt)

Whereas Elizabeth Greene was at our court of sessions arraigned for murder and there found guilty by the verdict of the jury, upon which sentence of
death was passed as by the judgment given on the 6th day of July 1664 does
upon our record appear,—

NOTES

1. *The Laws Resolutions of Women's Rights: Or the Laws Provision for Women* (London, 1632), pp. 3–6.

2. Richard Beale Davis, ed., *William Fitzhugh and His Chesapeake World, 1676–1701. The Fitzhugh Letters and Other Documents, 1676–1701.* (Chapel Hill, N.C., 1963), pp. 97–99. Reprinted with permission of the Virginia Historical Society.

3. J. Hammond Trumbull, ed., *The True-Blue Laws of Connecticut and New Haven* (Hartford, 1876), pp. 216–17.

4. "Miscellaneous Colonial Documents," *Virginia Magazine of History and Biography* XVI (No. 1, 1908), pp. 79–81.

5. J. H. Trumbull and C. J. Hoadley, eds., *Public Records of the Colony of Connecticut (1636–1776)*, 15 vols. (Hartford, 1850–1890), II, p. 239.

6. William W. Hening, *The Statutes-at-Large, Being a Collection of All the Laws of Virginia* (1619–1792), 13 vols. (Philadelphia, New York, 1823), I, p. 317.

7. Trumbull and Hoadley, eds., *Public Records of the Colony of Connecticut*, IV, pp. 182 and 293.

8. Mattie Erma Edwards Parker, ed., *North Carolina Higher-Court Records, 1670–1696* (Raleigh, 1968), pp. 383–84. Reprinted with permission of the Historical Publications Section of the North Carolina State Department of Archives.

9. William Browne et al., eds., *Archives of Maryland* (Baltimore, 1883–1912), XLI, p. 79.

10. C. J. Hoadley, ed., *Records of the Colony and Plantation of New Haven from 1638 to 1649* (Hartford, 1857), I. p. 142; Parker, ed., *North Carolina Higher-Court Records, 1670–1696*, pp. 250 and 327. Reprinted with the permission of the Historical Publications Section of the North Carolina State Department of Archives.

11. Samuel Chase, *Baron and Feme. A Treatise of the Common Law Concerning Husbands and Wives* (London, 1700), pp. 3–4.

12. Hoadley, ed., *Records of the Colony and Plantation of New Haven from 1638 to 1649*, I, p. 397; Browne et al., eds., *Archives of Maryland*, IV, pp. 269 and 274; Berthold Fernow, ed., *The Records of New Amsterdam from 1653 to 1674*, 7 vols. (New York, 1897), I, p. 63.

13. *Early Records of the City and County of Albany and Colony of Rensselaerswyck*, 3 vols. (Albany, 1916–1919), III, pp. 41–42.

14. Ibid., p. 109

15. Ibid., pp. 359–61.

16. Amory Family Papers, 1697–1823, Library of Congress, Washington, D.C.

17. Parker, ed., *North Carolina Higher-Court Records, 1670–1696*, pp. 128 and 170. Reprinted with permission of the Historical Publications Section of the North Carolina State Department of Archives.

18. Horatio Rogers and Elway Field, eds., *Early Records of the Town of Providence* (Providence, 1899), XV, pp. 230–31.

19. Hening, *The Statutes-at-Large, Being a Collection of All the Laws of Virginia*, III, p. 172.

20. Browne et al., eds., *Archives of Maryland*, XIV, p. 250.

21. Hening, *The Statutes-at-Large, Being a Collection of All the Laws of Virginia*, II, pp. 166–67.

22. John Winthrop, *The History of New England From 1630 to 1649*, James Savage, ed., 2 vols. (Boston, 1826), II, pp. 157–58.

23. Parker, ed., *North Carolina Higher-Court Records, 1670–1696*, p. 345. Reprinted with permission of the Historical Publications Section of the North Carolina State Department of Archives.

24. Hening, *The Statutes-at-Large, Being a Collection of All the Laws of Virginia*, II, p. 167.

25. J. Hall Pleasants, ed., *Archives of Maryland*, XLIX, p. 235.

BIBLIOGRAPHY

Billias, George A., ed. *Law and Authority in Colonial Massachusetts*. Barre, Mass., 1965.

Botein, Stephen. *Early American Law and Society*. New York, 1983.

Flaherty, David H., ed. *Essays in the History of Early American Law*. Chapel Hill, N.C., 1969.

———. "Law and the Enforcement of Morals in Early America." *Perspectives in American History* 5 (1971): 201–53.

Friedman, Lawrence M. *A History of American Law*. New York, 1973.

Greenberg, Douglas. *Crime and Law Enforcement in the Colony of New York, 1691–1776*. Ithaca, N.Y., 1976.

Haskins, George L. *Law and Authority in Early Massachusetts: A Study in Transition and Design*. New York, 1960.

Hemphill, C. Dallett. "Women in Court: Sex-Role Differentiation in Salem, Massachusetts, 1636 to 1683." *William and Mary Quarterly*, 3d ser., 39 (1982): 164–75.

Koehler, Lyle. *A Search for Power: The "Weaker Sex" in Seventeenth-Century New England*, Urbana, Chicago, London, 1980.

Morris, Richard B. *Studies in the History of American Law with Special Reference to the Seventeenth and Eighteenth Centuries*. New York, 1930.

Salmon, Marylynn. "Equality or Submersion: Feme Covert Status in Early Pennsylvania." In Carol R. Berkin and Mary Beth Norton, eds., *Women of America: A History*. Boston, (1979): 92–113.

Sirmans, M. Eugene. "The Legal Status of the Slave in South Carolina, 1670–1740." *Journal of Southern History* 28 (1962): 462–73.

5 WOMEN AND THE FAMILY, 1700–1815

The family remained an absolutely central institution of American life through most of the eighteenth century. Broadly speaking, it retained intact many of the features of the traditional family. Parents and children continued to form the core of the family. Marital norms and the basic arrangements of family life were, on the whole, little altered. The husband continued to act as head of the household, and the wife to occupy a subordinate position. The second half of the eighteenth century, however, was a period of important transition in family life. Under the pressures of mobility, expansion, and war, some of the inherited traditions and values around which the traditional family was structured slowly began to erode.

One of the most important factors in producing change was the separation of work from the individual household, a consequence of urban industrial development. As the colonial economy shifted from its agricultural base to a commercial base by the late eighteenth century, alterations in work patterns became increasingly apparent, especially in the northeast, after the turn of the century. More and more, men's work was carried on outside the home, in small factories and incipient industries, while women continued to perform their primary work in households, giving rise to what one scholar has called the canon of domesticity. Without repudiating the patriarchy, books of advice to the wife and mother emphasized the domestic sphere as her peculiar domain and maintained that her chief concern there was the rearing of children.

The American Revolution accelerated and extended these changes. A war for independence and nation building, the Revolution caused social and economic disruptions of lasting consequence. The struggle to achieve autonomy from Britain inevitably involved alterations in traditional patterns of authority. Part of the psychological preparation for the rejection of kingly authority involved modifications in the familial metaphor that had long served to explain imperial relations: England the mother country, the king the sovereign father, the colonies the children. Persuaded by Thomas Paine's audacious characterization of George III as a "brute," Americans of the revolutionary generation rejected the notion of the king as the legitimate father of his subjects and their own status as children within the empire, declaring themselves ready "to assume the equal and independent station to which the laws of nature and nature's god entitle them."

Not surprisingly, the explicit generational argument used to explain independence had social parallels in the decline of parental authority over children. Sons, and to a lesser extent daughters, struggled to realize a measure of personal autonomy, at least in the selection of a mate. That tendency toward independence in the marital choice was reinforced by the rise of romantic love. In place of the traditional criteria of rational love based on spiritual unity, equality of station, and love learned after marriage, love and companionship came to enjoy high priority in the selection of a spouse. The transformation was articulated as romantic love, evidence of which is found in the tender, sometimes passionate language of love letters of the eighteenth century.

Value shifts such as these inevitably led to a different concept of the family, one which emphasized the primacy of affection in familial relations and stressed the importance of the child within the home. The development of the affectionate child-centered home in turn affected the roles of individual family members. The definition of the role of women within the family was in part determined by the Revolutionary War experience and by the needs of the new republic. Historians who have studied the female experience in the Revolutionary War are not in agreement as to whether it helped or harmed their status within the family. Recent studies by Mary Beth Norton and Linda Kerber, among others, have argued that by producing a temporary breakdown in the system of sexual spheres, the American Revolution made many women more acutely conscious of the proscriptions that circumscribed their lives, particularly their inferior status before the law and the social limitations that prevented them from speaking out on a variety of issues that vitally affected their lives. War-time experiences forced the revolutionary generation to reassess many of the old ideas about the place of women in society. As society's expectations of women began to change, a new ideology that celebrated the social value of motherhood began to emerge. Although it did not challenge the notion that women belonged in the home, it recognized the significance of what they did there. In their capacity as moral mothers, women were given primary responsibility for shaping the minds, morals, and manners of their children, thereby contributing to republican stability by rearing virtuous citizens.

By contrast, Joan Hoff Wilson sees in the Revolution no advances for women. Instead she insists that the didactic role assigned to them increasingly confined women to the home and contributed significantly to the formation of the cult of domesticity that emerged in the nineteenth century. These scholarly differences are perhaps more apparent than real. Even if the new attitudes did not produce significant change in the lives of most women, for many affluent white women they opened up new educational opportunities and in that way served as a step in the process of women's political socialization.

The postwar period exacerbated many of these tensions, producing further strains on familial relationships. Following the Peace of Paris, which ended the American Revolution, a surging tide of settlement rolled across the trans-Allegheny frontier. For the settlers, the frontier had different meanings. Despite the hazards and hardships, for the men who dominated the westward movement the frontier promised adventure and the opportunity for economic advancement. For the children, particularly the sons who made the decision to leave the security of established communities, it meant earlier economic independence and the loosening of family ties. For the women, who often joined the enterprise reluctantly, it meant separation from family and friends, acute loneliness, and unparalleled drudgery.

As the restless line of settlement advanced, American civilization collided and later fused with the non-English cultures of Louisiana and West Florida. Successively under the sovereignty of France, Spain, and the United States, Louisiana encompassed a vast domain extending from the Mississippi River to the Rockies and from the Gulf of Mexico to the Canadian border, although population was concentrated in New Orleans and about twenty settlements in Lower Louisiana. Successive French and Spanish regimes had created a society there that was different both from the mother countries and from the English seaboard colonies. Although Gallic and Hispanic familial arrangements were based upon the same fundamental concept of male superiority that regulated the English family, frontier conditions and marital laws modified somewhat the status of women in the family, particularly where property rights were concerned. Despite the tremendous powers of assimilation exerted by the Anglo-Americans, some of the basic differences persisted and survive today in the civil law of the state of Louisiana.

Although the same historical forces operated among black and Indian women, the effects on life and culture were not always the same. Indeed demographic studies done in recent years reveal both striking similarities and differences between those cultures and contemporary white culture. On the one hand, the same rough balance between the sexes that characterized the white population by the eighteenth century also prevailed among the black population. Contrary to conventional wisdom, the black family in antebellum America carried out many of the traditional family functions observed in white families. On the other hand, the oppressive nature of slavery produced special patterns of courtship and marriage, such as distinctive sexual attitudes and practices and a higher rate of involuntary marital breakup. Studies of various Indian societies reveal that although Indian familial patterns continued to be significantly different from either black or white culture, both black and Indian practices were changed as a result of prolonged contact with white culture.

PATTERNS OF MARRIAGE

In the history of the American family, the eighteenth century represented an extended period of transition. In a number of fundamental ways, patterns from the past persisted: in the economic determinants of marriage among some upper-class families, in the economic subjection of women, in the sovereignty of the rights of the husband within the family. Changes in attitudes and in practices were, however, occurring, almost imperceptibly in some places, more rapidly in others: in the affectionate nature of marital relationships, in the changing patterns of parental control over marriage, in the marital age structure. These changes in turn produced significant shifts in child-bearing and child-rearing practices, which became increasingly apparent after 1750.

The economic and demographic changes that were transforming family life among the upper and middle classes apparently operated differently among racial groups and along class and regional lines. As a result of the centrality of slavery to the social and economic life of the South, the patriarchy persisted there when it was apparently declining elsewhere. Its continuance produced substantive differences in the white family structure, and divergent family values and patterns of behavior among both black and white families. Because of their semiautonomous existence, Indian tribes were able, by and large, to maintain their own tribal marriage customs, although contact with whites did result in certain changes in family attitudes and practices.

Independence: Personal and Political

Abigail Franks to Naphtali Franks, 1743[1]

With the infusion of romance in courtship, American men and women in the eighteenth century came increasingly to regard marriage as an affectionate relationship from which they expected to derive emotional satisfaction. The primacy of affection led to a significant decline in parental authority, which manifested itself in the growing tendency of sons and daughters to reject parental advice in mate selection. It also produced a decline in religious love, which was reflected in the growth of interfaith marriages. Forced to choose between spiritual unity and romantic love, Phila Franks, the twenty-year-old daughter of Jacob Franks, a wealthy Jewish merchant, and twenty-four-year-old Oliver DeLancey, the son of a prominent Episcopalian family from New York, married outside the faith, as did many couples of all religious denominations. The angry letter of Phila's mother Abigail to her oldest son Naphtali, or "HeartSey," reveals that the couple was secretly married against the wishes of her parents, and probably his parents as well.

Flatt bush [Tuesday] June 7th, 1743

Dear HeartSey

My wishes for your felicity are as great as the joy I have to hear you are happily married. May the smiles of Providence wait always on y[ou]r inclinations and your dear Phila's whom I salute with tender affections pray[ing] kind Heaven to be propitious to your wishes in making her a happy mother. I shall think the time tedious until I shall have that happy information for I don't expect to hear it by the return of these ships and therefore must injoin your care in writing by the first opportunity (after the birth of whatever it shall please God to bless you with) either by via Carolina Barbados or any other. I am now retired from town and would from my self (if it were possible to have some peace of mind) from the severe affliction I am under on the conduct of that unhappy girl. Good God what a shock it was when they acquainted me, she had left the house and had been married six months. I can hardly hold my pen while I am writing it; it is what I never could have imagined, especially after what I heard her so often say that no consideration in life should ever induce her to disoblige such good parents. I had heard the report of her going to be married to Oliver Delancey but as such reports had often been of either of your sisters, I gave no heed to it further than a general caution of her conduct which has always been unblemished and is so still in the eye of the Christians who allow she has disobliged us but has in no way been dishonorable being married to a man of worth and character. My spirit was for sometime so depressed that it was a pain to me to speak or see anyone. I have overcome it so far as not to make my concern so conspicuous, but I shall never have that serenity nor peace within I have so happily had hitherto. My house has been my prison ever since I had not heart enough to go near the street door. It's a pain to me to think of going again to town and if your father's business would permit him to live out of it I never would go near it again. I wish it was in my power to leave this part of the world, I would come away in the first man of war that went to London. Oliver has sent many times to beg leave to see me but I never would though now he sent word that he will come here. I dread seeing him and how to avoid I know no way. Neither if he comes can I use him rudely. I may make him some reproaches but I know myself so well that I shall at last be civil though I never will give him leave to come to my house in town. And as for his wife I am determined I never will see nor let none of your family go near her. He intends to write to you and my brother Isaac to endeavour a reconciliation. I would have you answer his letter if you don't hers for I must be so ingenious [as] to confess nature is very strong and it would give me a great concern if she should live unhappy though it's a concern she does not merit.... My compliments to Mrs. Compton and Captain Riggs. I beg they will be so good to forgive me that I don't answer their agreeable favor by this: my spirit is too depressed to write. It is with reluctancy I do write to anyone at present, therefore, whoever I omit you must excuse me to them. I think I've spun this to a considerable length and shall conclude with the repetition of my prayers for your health and happiness I am,

My Dear Son,
Your Affectionate Mother,
Abigail Franks

Sally Hanschurst to Sally Forbes, 1762[2]

Although marriage bound both partners, it legally and physically subjected the wife to her husband. Because the choice of a mate determined her life experience, marriage had therefore a different meaning for a woman. The following letter from Sally Hanschurst to her friend Sally Forbes in Sterling, New York reflects young women's awareness of the special importance of the marriage choice and also the greater emphasis placed by women on the role of affection in marriage.

Dear Sally

Don't thing [sic] my Sollitude intirly unprofitable as it affords me Some time for reflection—and I often run over in my mind, the many Disadvantages that Accrues to our Sex from an alliance with the other—not but that I look upon the marriage State Capable of Affording a Great Deal of Happiness were [sic] there is a Strict Union of Souls, but this Seldom happens, and when the reverse it must of Consequence bring on a Train of Disappointments—I am not ignorant of the number of your acquaintance among there are many I believe well calculated to please both in person and Conversation, and some others perhaps though possessed of affluent fortunes that are such Dull Stupid earth Born Souls, that one had better Spend the Residue of these Days in Exile than be there [sic] Companion, the first has doubtless been Rejected by you for some prudential Reasons, the last your good Sense has taught you to Despise—my Dear as you are very Sensible Happiness does not Consist in Worldly Wealth, but the Riches of the Mind, I hope the one that falls to your lot will be imbued with every virtue one that will know to esteem you as he ought, Detesting all the Fashionable Vices that our Modern Gentlemen Seem so ambitious to acquire—if you should fail in this my most ardent wish, and I am Disappointed

in Some little expectations I believe we most [sic] have Recourse to a Retired Life as the English Constitution won't admit of a Recluse—I imagine the Town must seem Duller than Common at present the Spirit of the Inhabitants have been so imbued with Theatrical Entertainments which are now over—however we have this Satisfaction in past pleasure the hopes of there returning. I am with Respect
Dear Sally your S.H.

Anne Randolph to St. George Tucker, 1788[3]

The same common set of attitudes respecting love and marriage apparently prevailed everywhere, although certain regional variations persisted, owing to differences in demographic and cultural conditions. In the eighteenth century, northern society was relatively egalitarian, whereas the South had developed a highly structured society composed of planters, yeoman farmers, tenants, and slaves. In order to justify their own social and political dominance, planters relied heavily on patriarchal ideology and the patriarchal family structure. Women did not share directly in the power of the patriarchy but they did play a significant role in perpetuating it by linking patriarchal clans through marriage and by giving birth to heirs to pass on the family name. Marriages became, as a consequence, more kin-oriented as successful planters looked for marriage partners among blood relatives as a means of cementing kinship bonds. The marriage of sixteen-year-old Judith to Richard Randolph, her nineteen-year-old cousin, was, in several respects, typical of marriages among middle- and upper-class planter families. Endogamous, it united a couple of nearly equal age, from the same social rank, even from the same kinship network. Although Judith's mother, Anne Randolph, strongly objected to the premature union, her concerns were ultimately subordinate to the couple's happiness. The marriage, which took place the following year, was marred by family tragedy.

Richmond, September 23, 1788

Dear Sir,

I was not surprised at the information your very friendly and polite letter contained, having, like you, suspected it some time ago. It has ever been my wish to keep my daughters single 'til they were old enough to form a proper judgment of mankind; well knowing that a woman's happiness depends entirely on the husband she is united to; it is a step that requires more deliberation than girls generally take, or even mothers seem to think necessary; the risk though always great, is doubled when they marry very young; it is impossible for them to know each others disposition; for at sixteen and nineteen we think everybody perfect that we take a fancy to; the lady expects nothing but condescension, and the gentleman thinks his mistress an angel. As young people cannot have a sufficient knowledge of the world to teach them the necessity of making a proper allowance for the foibles to say no worse, of humanity, they are apt to be sour when the delirium of love is over and reason is allowed to reascend her throne; and if they are not so happy as to find in each other a similarity of temper and good qualities enough to excite esteem and Friendship, they must be wretched, without a remedy. If the young people who have been the cause of my giving you my sentiments thus freely should ever be united I hope they will never repent of the choice they have made.

I have given Judy Richard's letters; but have desired her not to answer them before she has her Father's leave.

With good wishes for your self and family I am dear sir your Affectionate Humble Servant

Ann Randolph

Cultural Interaction: Continuity and Change

Thomas Anburey, Travels, 1789[4]

The existence of slavery in the South profoundly affected the nature of the southern patriarchy and presumably familial relations among both blacks and whites. Despite laws prohibiting it, miscegenation was apparently extensive, as Thomas Anburey, a British officer serving in America during the Revolution, discovered. Although they had succeeded in establishing independent family units, the sexual exploitation of black wives and mothers made it difficult for many slave families to maintain a regular family life. Such exploitation typically involved fornication between white men and black women, making it necessary for whites to insist that the family unit be defined by race rather than by paternity. This, according to one scholar, was the principal reason for the universal insistence on the absolute purity of southern women, which was at the heart of the chivalric tradition.

JONES PLANTATION, NEAR CHARLOTTESVILLE, VIRGINIA, 1779.

Having mentioned that there are mulattoes of various tinges, it may not be amiss to inform you from whence it arises, and no doubt but you will be surprised, when I tell you it is by planters having intercourse with their negroes, the issue of which being a mulatto, and having a connection with that shade becomes lighter; as an instance, I remarked at Colonel Cole's, of which I have made mention, there were mulattoes of all tinges, from the first remove, to one almost white; there were some of them young women, who were really beautiful, being extremely well made, and with pretty delicate features; all of which I was informed were the Colonel's own. I could not help reflecting that if a man had an intercourse with his slaves, it was shameful in the extreme, to make his own offspring so; for these mulattoes work equally the same as those who come from Africa: To be sure, you may say, it is a pleasant method to procure slaves at a cheap rate, I imagine there could not be less than 20 or 30 mulattoes of this description at Colonel Cole's notwithstanding he has a very agreeable and beautiful wife, by whom he has eight children.

David Zeisberger's Account of Indian Marital Practices,
1779, 1780[5]

White observers of Indian marriage customs in the eighteenth century reported the persistence of certain features, such as the rituals of courtship, the isolation of menstruating women, and sexual abstinence during nursing. Their accounts also note important changes, however, such as the increase of drinking and moral vice and the disuse of the cradleboard, which are attributable to prolonged contact with European colonists. David Zeisberger, a Moravian missionary who spent fifty years among the Delaware and Mohican Indians of New York, Pennsylvania, and Ohio, left this reliable description of change and persistence in native culture.

When, in a young female, the first menstrual discharge occurs, generally between the twelfth and sixteenth year, the Delawares generally separate such daughters from all companionship the Monsied [Monseys] being more strict and having more ceremonies in the observance of the custom than the Miamis. They build for such a girl, separate hut, apart from the rest, where her mother or some old female acquaintance cares for her and guards her so that none may see her. Wherefore, she is also kept within the hut the whole of the menstrual period, with the blanket over her head. She is given little to eat, but regularly dosed with emetics. She is not allowed to do any work during the whole time, which generally lasts twelve days. At the end of the time, they bring her into her home, looking black, grimy and dishevelled, because she has been lying about in dust and ashes the whole time. Washed and dressed in new garments, she is allowed to be in the home, but required to wear a cap with a long shield, so that she can neither see any one readily, nor be seen. Such a covering she must wear for two months, at the end of which time she is informed that she may marry.

The Shavanose [Shawanese] and Mingoes, however, also observe much the same customs, follow a different course in this matter. The young woman in question is allowed to remain in the house. She prepares food for those in the house, of the corn and fruits she has raised. Of such food she does not, however, herself partake, but goes to her hut, apart from the others, and there prepares and eats her food.

Every month, during her menstrual period, a Delaware woman lives by herself in a separate hut, which is usually very poorly built, and remains there two or three days, food being taken to her. When the time is over they bathe and wash their clothes and are allowed to return to their husbands. During the menstrual period, they are not permitted to do any cooking or domestic work. None will eat what a woman in this condition prepares, for food prepared under such circumstances is said to be unwholesome and to cause pain in the abdomen. The women do not go into company, but keep to their huts until their time is over. Hence, it occasionally happens that a woman engaged in baking will leave everything and go to her hut. This custom does not obtain among the Mingoes; their women continue their usual work and remain in the house.

In the wooing of a bride, custom demands that if an Indian would proceed honorably and at the same time have assurance that his wife when married will remain with him, he first sends a present of blankets, strouds, linen and whatever else the Indians commonly use for clothing and perhaps a few belts or fathoms of wampum. If he has no cloth, wampum alone will do. These things he gives to an Indian to whom he has declared his purpose and who hands them to a friend of the person fixed upon, speaks for him and presses his suit. Thereupon, the friends assemble, examine the present, propose the matter to the girl, who generally decides agreeably to the wish of her parents and relations. The suitor is then informed that his proposal has been accepted. If it is decided to decline the proposal, the present is simply returned and understood to be a friendly negative. In case the match is agreeable, the girl is led to the dwelling of the groom, without further ceremony. After the bride has joined her husband, the things constituting the present are divided among the friends and the belts of wampum cut and a piece given to each. The friends return the civility by a present of Indian corn, beans, kettles, dishes, spoons, sieves, baskets, hatchets, brought in solemn procession into the hut of the newly married couple. Commonly, the latter lodge in a friend's house until they can erect a dwelling of their own.

This custom still obtains among the Indians. Within the last years, however, disorderly living and evil have become so common that faith is not kept and many of the usages, that were good and preserved a certain decency, have fallen into disuse. At the present time, even if the Indian would take a wife in honorable fashion and proceed in accordance with the above described custom, the parties concerned will not deny his suit in view of the presents, even though the friends and the girl are not willing to accept him. The friends will urge the girl to live with the man a short time, and tell her that if she is not pleased, to leave him again. Thus it happens that women will go from one to another for the sake of the gifts. Yet there are many cases where husband and wife are faithful to one another throughout life.

Occasionally, parents who have a son will agree with parents who have a daughter that in due time their children shall marry. As, however, they can neither persuade nor compel their children against their wishes, it in the end depends upon the children whether the match shall be consummated.

Among the Mingoes it is not unusual to fix upon children of four or five years of age, with a view to future marriage. In this case the mother of the girl is obliged to bring a basket of bread every week into the house of the boy and to furnish him with firewood. The parents of the boy must supply the girl with meat and clothes, till they are both of a proper age. Their marriage, however, solely depends upon their own free will, for there is never any compulsion. If either man or woman is unwilling to follow up the engagement entered into by parents, no marriage results.

Although there are many Indians who live peaceably with their wives, especially if they have children for whom they care (for if a man has several children he will try to get along with his wife) the younger Indians at the present time generally live together only a very short time after a marriage. Hence, fornication is very common among them. Satan's influence in this respect being very strong.

If it is asked why the Indians at the present time are more given to vice and disorderly living than formerly, when they were as ignorant heathen as they are now, two reasons may be given. First, much evil unquestionably has been taught them by white people, especially the traders, who were content to live among the Indians as long as there were no Indian wars. Through the examples of the traders, also the Indians acquired the habit of drinking to excess. Secondly, the Indians had formerly great respect for the aged and the chiefs, from whom they learned that unfaithfulness in the marriage relationship was a great crime and that whoever was guilty of such evil would live neither long nor happily. At the present time they show little reverence to the aged and each one thinks himself to be wise in his own conceits....

CONJUGAL RELATIONS

Under the impact of the American Revolution women's domestic roles gained added significance. The exigencies of the situation forced a temporary suspension of prescribed roles. Urged by colonial leaders to actively participate in the war effort, patriot women supported the colonial boycott of British goods. Beginning with the first boycotts in the 1760s, they made and wore homespun, which they produced either in the home or in the manufacturing houses established in several major cities for the employment of poor women. As men left the home to participate in political or military activities, patriot and loyalist women alike took over many of the essential tasks normally performed by men. As a result, normal patterns of domestic life were disrupted. The changes that ensued were not sweeping, nor were they everywhere the same for all women. For the most part, familial organization and the rights of the husband within the family remained constant. Women's perception of themselves and society's expectations of them were, however, significantly altered.

The impact of the Revolutionary War on black women is equally ambiguous. The war itself created unprecedented opportunities for liberty both as a result of the promise of freedom in exchange for military service offered by successive British commanders as a means of breaking southern resistance, and the colonial tradition of accepting slaves and free blacks for military service in exchange for their freedom. Thousands of slaves took advantage of the situation to escape to British lines or to seek freedom on their own in northern urban areas.

Building upon a vigorous tradition of religious opposition to slavery, during the Revolutionary War years most of the northern states took steps to end slavery. With no rooted religious antislavery tradition to draw upon, the southern states took steps to secure the slave system. Convinced that the recovery of their wartorn economies was inextricably linked to the restoration of slave labor, Georgia and South Carolina resorted to the massive importation of slaves from Africa and, for a period of time, from the Chesapeake. Left with a large surplus of slaves by the transition from tobacco to wheat, planters from the Chesapeake entered upon the domestic slave trade, and thereby helped to extend slavery into the back country of Georgia and South Carolina and into the rapidly developing regions of Kentucky and Tennessee. Although the forced separation of family members and demographic conditions on the new frontier made family formation difficult, black migrants were able eventually to reconstruct family and community life.

Persistence of the Patriarchy

Robert Barclay, A Catechism and Confession of Faith, 1788[6]

In post-Revolutionary America the normative version of married life continued to stress male domination. Even Quakers, who gave women greater freedom within the meeting structure than did most of their contemporaries, continued, like other religious denominations, to insist upon the subordination of wives to their husbands. The most popular Quaker catechism in the eighteenth century, Robert Barclay's *A Catechism and Confession of Faith*, used scriptural citations to support the subjection of women. The metaphor in Ephesians 5:22–25, which compares wifely submission to the subjection of the church to Christ, was commonplace in most Quaker writings on the subject of marriage.

Q. What between husbands and wives?

Eph. 5.22 to 25, and 28. 31, 33

A. Wives, submit yourselves unto your own husbands as unto the Lord. For the husband is the head of the wife, even as Christ is the head of the church; and he is the Saviour of the body. Therefore, as the church is subject unto Christ, so let the wives be subject to their own hubands in everything. Husbands, love your wives, even as Christ also loved the church, and gave himself for it; so ought men to love their wives as their own bodies; he that loveth his wife, loveth himself. For this cause shall a man leave his father and mother, and shall be joined unto his wife, and they two shall be one flesh. Nevertheless, let every one of you in particular so love his wife, even as himself; and the wife see that she reverence her husband.

Col. 3. 19 3   Husbands, love your wives, and be not bitter
Pet. 3. 1, 7   against them. Likewise, ye wives, be in
subjection unto your own husbands; that if any
obey not the word, they also may be without the
word be won by the conversation of the wives,
while they behold your chaste conversation
coupled with fear. Likewise you husbands, dwell
with them according to knowledge, giving honor
unto the wife, as unto the weaker vessel, and as
being heirs together of the grace of life, that
your prayers be not hindered.

Betsy Foote Washington Journal, 1779, 1789[7]

In many families, particularly among the southern gentry, conjugal relationships apparently conformed to the ideal of the obedient wife who submitted to her husband's control with pleasing good nature. As she contemplated marriage to her cousin Lunde Washington (who managed Mount Vernon for George Washington until 1785), Betsy Foote revealed to her journal her intention to conform to the contemporary model of domesticity by bending to her husband's will and in all things striving to please him. Ten years later she attributed the success of her marriage to self-abnegation.

November, 1779

I have lately promised to enter into the holy state of matrimony and may a blessing of the Almighty attend this momentous step I have taken—may my gracious God direct and influence my heart and its affections that I may make it my study to please my husband in every way that is not against the divine Laws and as there is a probability of my living in houses not my own for some time—may the divine goodness assist me, so that I may study to live in peace and friendship with the family where I live—may it be one of my daily petitions to the throne of grace to conduct myself as a dutiful obedient wife.

I will make a memorandum of these petitions and put them in a little book in case I should desire any time hence to add more of them—in that I may remember what was my thought at the time of my changing my state—I hope I have prepared myself for the worst that may happen—that is—if my marriage should prove an unhappy one—I trust I have so sincere a desire to please my Saviour that I hope I shall be enabled to bear with whatever is the divine will—and as I believe nothing happens by chance, so it is my duty to bear with what the Almighty permits with the same resignation as if I knew he had willed it, but as my gracious God has been infinitely merciful to me, so I humbly hope my marriage may be a happy one—and that my husband may never be against my being as religious as my inclinations may lead me—I pray God.

The summer of 1784

I have now been married better than four years—and I think have had the satisfaction of conducting myself to the approbation of my husband—and God grant I may continue to do it—hope I shall with the Divine assistance. I can truly say I have never had cause to repent of my marriage—so far from it, that I do think there is not one other man scarce to be found that would have suited me so well as my dear Mr. Washington and I have reason to think that he is perfectly satisfied with the choice he has made.

Summer 1789

One of my first resolutions I made after marriage was never to hold disputes with my husband—never to contend with him in my opinion of things—but if ever we differed in opinions not to insist on mine being right, and his wrong—which is too much the custom of my sex—they cannot bear to be thought in the wrong—which is the cause why there is so much contention in the married state—and the Lordly Sex—they can never be in the wrong in their own opinion—and cannot give up to a woman but I blame my sex most. It is their business to give up to their husbands—our mother even when she transgressed was told her husband should rule over her—then how dare any of her daughters to dispute the point—I never thought it degraded my understanding to give up my opinion to my husbands—that is not to contend with him—there is no necessity for a woman appearing to be afraid of her husband—indeed I think they err very much when they are so—I think a woman may keep up the dignity of a wife and mistress of a family without ever disputing with her husband—I never could take any pleasure in having my own way—it ever was more pleasing to have my husband's opinion to coincide with mine. I was once told by a very near male relation that I only affected to conform to my husband's will, to be thought an obedient wife—but this is not the case—a much more laudable motive has influenced my conduct—and I hope will always influence it—a desire to do my duty—to conform to the Scripture direction given to wives has been the ruling principle that has conducted my actions in the married state.

Challenges to the Patriarchy

Susanna Haswell Rowson, "Women as They Are," 1804[8]

Inspired, perhaps, by Revolutionary War experiences and republican ideology, some women began to challenge the conventional notions of femininity and domestic virtue. Susanna Haswell Rowson, the daughter of a British military officer, spent her early years in America and eventually made her home there. During her years as a writer from 1786 to 1822, she produced eight novels, seven theatrical works, two collections of poetry, six pedagogical works, and many fictional and occasional pieces. Addressed to women, her work had the theme of limited feminism. In "Women as They Are" in *Miscellaneous Poems*, she attacked the stereotypes of the woman of fashion and the household drudge because neither role permitted the expression of the total woman, and she chastised parents who encouraged their daughters to grow up idle-brained or seductresses.

WOMEN AS THEY ARE

"CHILDREN, like tender osiers, take the bow,
And as they first are fashioned, always grow"

Thus spoke the bard; and t'is a moral truth,
That precept and example, taught in youth,
Dwell on the mind till life's dull scene is past;
Clinging about us even to the last.
And women, pray for folly don't upbraid them,
Are just such things, as education made them.

The girl, who from her birth is thought a beauty,
Scarce ever hears of virtue, sense or duty;
Mamma, delighted with each limb and feature,
Declares, she is a fascinating creature;
Forbids all study, work, or wise reflection;
T'will spoil her eyes, or injure her complexion.
"Hold up your head, my dear; turn out your toes;
Bless me, what's that? a pimple on your nose;
It smarts, dear, don't it? how can you endure it?
Here's some Pomade Divine, to heal and cure it."
Then, every little master, that comes near her,
is taught to court, to flatter, or to fear her.
Nurse or Mamma cries, "See, my dearest life,
There's Charley, you shall be his little wife;
Smile my sweet creature; Charley, come and kiss her,
And tell me, is she not a pretty miss, sir?
Give her that orange, fruit, fine clothes, and toys,
Were made for little ladies, not for boys."

Thus, ere one proper wish her heart can move,
She's taught to think of lovers, and of love;
She's told she is a beauty, does not doubt it;
What need of sense? beauties can wed without it.
And then her eyes, her teeth, her lips, her hair,
And shape, are all that can be worth her care;
She thinks a kneeling world should bow before her,
And men were but created to adore her.
But call her to the active scenes of life,
As friend, as daughter, mother, mistress, wife;
You scarce can find, in the whole course of nature,
A more unfortunate or helpless creature.
Untaught the smallest duty of her station,
She stands, a cypher in the vast creation.
Her husband might perhaps expect to find
The angel's form contained an angel's mind.
Alas, poor man! time will the veil remove;
She had no fault. No! you were blind with love;
You flattered, idolized, made her your wife;

She thought these halcyon days would last for life.
At every small neglect, from her bright eyes
The lightning flashes; then she pouts and cries;
When the angel sinks, I fear, alas, in common,
Into a downright captious, teasing woman;
And if a reasonable friend was sought,
To counsel, sooth, or share each anxious thought,
Poor man! your disappointment I lament;
You've a long life before you—to repent.

. . . .

Methinks I hear some man exulting swear,
"Why, this is really 'Women as they are'."
Pardon me, sir, I'll speak, I'm not afraid;
I'll tell you what they are, what might be made.
When the Creator formed this world in common,
His last, best work, his master-piece, was woman.
Taken from the side of man, and next his heart,
Of all his virtues she partakes a part;
And from that source, poor woman got a share
Of vice and folly, mingled here and there.
But would you treat us, scorning custom's rules,
As reasonable beings, not as fools,
And from our earliest youth, would condescend
To form our minds, strengthen, correct, amend;
Teach us to scorn those fools, whose only joys,
Are placed in trifling idleness and noise.
Teach us to prize the power of intellect;
And whilst inspiring love, to keep respect;
You'd meet the sweet reward of all your care;
Find in us friends, your purest joys to share;
You then would own the choicest boon of Heaven,
The happiest lot that can to man be given,
To smooth the rugged path, and sweeten life
Is an affectionate and faithful wife.

Slave Petitions for Freedom, 1774[9]

The irony of Revolutionary War rhetoric, which protested British attempts to enslave white Americans, was not lost on black Americans. In a series of petitions addressed to the General Court of Massachusetts, groups of slaves called for the abolition of slavery. Invoking the ideology of natural rights, they based their attack on the barbarous effects of slavery on black family life. As a result of both religious antislavery attacks and revolutionary ideology, during the war most northern states, like Massachusetts, eradicated slavery by judicial, legislative, or constitutional action.

To his Excellency Thomas Gage Esq. Captain General and Governor in Chief in and over this Province.
To the Honorable his Majesty's Council and the Honorable
House of Representatives in General Court assembled
May 15, 177—
The Petition of a great number of blacks of this Province who by divine permission are held in a state of slavery within the bowels of a free and christian Country
Humbly Showing
That your Petitioners apprehend we have in common with all other men a natural right to our freedoms without being deprived of them by our fellow men as we are a freeborn people and have never forfeited this blessing by any compact or agreement whatever. But we were unjustly dragged by the cruel hand of power from our dearest friends and some of us stolen from the bosoms of our tender parents and from a populous pleasant and plentiful country and brought hither to be made slaves for life in a Christian land. Thus are we deprived of every thing that has a tendency to make life even tolerable, the endearing ties of husband and wife we are strangers to for we are no longer man and wife then our masters or mistresses think proper married or unmarried. Our children are also taken from us by force and sent many miles from us where we seldom or ever see them again there to be made slaves of for life which sometimes is very short by reason of being dragged from their mother's breast. Thus our lives are imbittered to us on these accounts. By our deplorable situation we are rendered incapable of showing our obedience to Almighty God. How can a slave perform the duties of a husband to a wife or parent to his child. How can a husband leave master and work and cleave to his wife. How can wives submit themselves to their husbands in all things. How can the child obey their parents in all things. There is a great number of us sincere ... members of the Church of Christ. How can the master and the slave be said to fulfill that command, live in love let brotherly love continue and abound, bear you one another's burdens. How can the master be said to bear my burden when he bears me down with the heavy chains of slavery and operates against my will and how can we fulfill our part of duty to him while in this condition. And as we cannot serve our God as we ought while in this situation, neither can we reap an equal benefit from the laws of the land which do not justify but condemns slavery or if there had been any law to hold us in bondage, we are humbly of the opinion there never was any to enslave our children for life when born in a free country. We therefore, beg your Excellency and Honors will give this its due weight and consideration and that you will accordingly cause an act of the legislative to be passed that we may obtain our Natural right, our freedoms and our children.

Petition of Margareta Powell to Governor Thomas Johnson, 1779[10]

In the South the legal status of slavery was left untouched by the Revolution, although the anarchic conditions produced by the war made it possible for thousands of slaves to escape. For many, perhaps even for most slave families in the South, the Revolutionary War was a period of great suffering. Taking advantage of wartime disruptions, British and American armies, partisan bands, and gangs of banditti plundered river banks and backcountry plantations of slaves, many of whom were subsequently transported and sold. The petition of a former Maryland slave, Margareta Powell, poignantly describes the fate of thousands of slaves who were forcibly separated from their families and from the plantations, which were in many cases the only homes they had ever known. Powell's petition also reveals, however, the tenacity with which blacks struggled to preserve the family unit.

The Humble Petition of Margareta Powell to his Excellency the Governor of the State of Maryland

Show that your Honor humble petitioner being formerly the property of a certain late John Campbell lastly living near the Fork of Potocktion near Mr. Henry Ridgley's in the year 1764. My master John Campbell set me free and for to certify the same, I have enclosed a certificate from the gentleman whom my master employed to enter me upon the Records. At the decease of my master he left me part of 200 acres of land and part of the moveable which was left by him for support of myself and my children whom my master had set free altogether for the space of three years before my master decease. My children were free dealers throughout the neighborhood, those that were of age have taken the oath of fidelity and have entered into the service of their country and one of them having a furlong to come to see me. They who have disinherited me have taken and sold him for life time and if the other should come from the camp they threaten to do the same to him—and all the rest of my children and grandchildren throughout the neighborhood. They have sold and have stripped me of everything I had and burned me out of my house and I being old and infirm and unable to help myself I most humbly implore your honor would look into the affair and help the wronged and afflicted and I shall be in duty bound to pray and thank your excellency.
Margareta Powell

The man who claims this right from me and my children is one John Ashton, a Priest—he sold my child to a certain Thomas Snowden residing in the same neighborhood and he has sold them to others about the neighborhood Fork of Potocktion.
Ann Arundal County

MOTHERS AND CHILDREN

The shift from the authoritarian, patriarchal family to the more egalitarian, affectionate family was accompanied by significant alterations in child-bearing and child-rearing practices. Change was gradual, often imperceptible, and perhaps affected principally well-to-do white families living in urban centers. One of the most dramatic changes

was the decline of marital fertility, the apparent result of the cooperation of husbands and wives in the prevention of pregnancy. As a result
both of the increasing privitization of family life and of medical advances, particularly the development of obstetrics, the rituals of childbirth were also transformed, first in urban centers and much later in
rural areas. Among upper- and middle-class families, children became
the center of emotional focus, with indulgence rather than discipline
being the key to the development of self-reliant, independent children.
Despite the existence of serious impediments both to slave morality and
to family stability, by their early twenties most slave women, like most
white women, were married and settled into stable family relations.

Childbearing

The Diary of Colonel Landon Carter, 1770[11]

The contraceptive effects of lactation were long known and understood, both by American Indian women and by their colonial counterparts. As a result of the improved status of women within the family
and the decline of the notion that the pains of childbirth were divinely
ordained, many couples in post-Revolutionary America relied increasingly on prolonged lactation or other primitive methods of contracep-
tion to limit family size. Colonel Landon Carter's objections to maternal
breast-feeding by his daughter-in-law of her child Fanny were based
on the fear that she would communicate her own illness to the child.
Some husbands complained, however, because medical theory opposed
intercourse with a nursing mother.

14 Sunday
    My son who would not go to Mr. Beverley's, because after his saying I
pretended to be serving him, but yet never did it, I put him in mind that he
was even then going in my petty auger. I say he ordered his horses to meet
him this morning at Randal's; but [who] was to carry them? My boy Ben and
upon one of my horses. So that this passionate fool is every day obliged to be
beholden for the very thing he denies.
    Mrs. Carter taken ill yesterday and was to be seen so before, though she
would not own it. And the poor little baby Fanny is every time to share her
Mama's disorder by sucking her, and this because she should not breed too
fast. Poor children! Are you to be sacrificed for a parent's pleasure?
    I have been a parent and thought it murder and therefore hired nurses or
put them out.

15 Monday
    Mrs. Carter and little Fanny very ill and [y]et this child is to continue to
suck the poison; she can't live, it is said, without the baby and it is certain
she can't live with it. Of course, the death of the child is inevitable from such

an absurd way of reasoning: I hope my Lord and my God [faded] clear of this death. I would [faded] under.

Once more we go about our fodder. Our bulks of tobacco all to this day's striking are stripped out into large bundles.

20 Saturday

I fancy our good weather will leave us soon. It grew cloudy in the evening yesterday, mizled a little at night with the wind at South by East and quickly changed to Northeast and North and continued cloudy all night, and is now cloudy.

Yesterday the two wenches that went to pick the Fork cotton brought home about 40 pounds in the seeds.

Last night, I thank god, little Fanny missed her terrible ague; it was thought she had a fever; but it is common for the flesh to feel warm on the period of the ague when it leaves them, especially if that is obtained by the bark, which I fancy this was. Note: the day before the child only took 3 doses of 6 grains each with rhubarb in them and yesterday 3 doses of 10 grains each without rhubarb; and if my advice is followed she shall take 2 doses this day with a small quantity of rhubarb, this for 2 days and then some drops of Elixir Proprietatis to prevent any ill effects of the bark and carry off what remains of the bile: but unless they wean her, still sucking from a morbid breast will in spite of fate bring on a return. Poor baby.

I cannot help taking notice of many writers ridiculing the general complaints of mankind as to the weather, and charging it as an uneasy disposition; but I think the contrary, and that is rather a greater sensibility of the rod that may be used, and, of course, it must argue a submission to it with a due concern, while he who discovers no emotion at it shows either a want of due concern, or a stupid inconsiderateness of what he may suffer. But let it not be argued from hence, that I am for indulging others desponding in an outrageous anxiety.

At last poor Fanny attended with a violent phlegmy cough and a fever with it; how she got it is not known; she took another vomit this morning first, and brought off abundance of tough phlegm.

Elizabeth Drinker's Journal, 1799[12]

The dramatic decline in family size after 1780 was accompanied by changes in the rituals of childbirth. The use of forceps in obstetrical practice after 1752 and the development of obstetrics as a branch of medicine changed the lying-in experience of well-to-do women in large cities, such as New York and Philadelphia. In place of the female midwife, the male physician, trained in Europe or later in North American medical schools, now presided over the delivery process. Elizabeth Drinker's account of the birth of her daughter Sally Downing's sixth child gives unusual detail about medical practices and social customs surrounding birth in the late eighteenth century. In ordering his patient bled and in his recommendation of a forceps delivery, Dr. William Shippen, a pioneer in obstetrical medicine, was applying the newest ideas in medical care to ensure a safe and fast delivery without unnecessary pain to the mother.

October 23, 1799

'My poor dear Sally was taken unwell last night, Dan came for us early this morn. Sister is gone here—I stay to see Dr. Kuhn when he visits William . . . I went—found Dr. Shippen half asleep in the back parlor by himself—I questioned him relative to Sally's situation, he said she was in the old way, and he thinks she dont require bleeding by her pulse—I went upstairs, Sister and nurse were in the front chamber looking at the funeral of Zachary Collins' wife, Christopher Marshall's daughter who died in the country of a consumption. J. Downings front windows look into friends burying ground, being opposite to it—soon after came the procession of carriages with the body of John Wharton, he also died out of town—went into Sally's chamber. She is in pain at times, forerunning pains of a lingering labor, a little low spirited, poor dear child—This day is 38 years since I was in agonies bringing her into this world of troubles: she told me with tears that this was her birthday, I endeavored to talk her into better spirits, told her that, the time of her birth was over by some hours, she was now in her 39th year, and that this might possibly be the last trial of this sort, if she could suckle her baby for 2 years to come, as she had several times done heretofore &c. . . . I went again in that afternoon . . . found no change had taken place: Sally in almost continual pain, I came home again in the evening . . . 'twas near 11:00 when I got there—Sally was all night in great distress, the pain never quite off, sometimes on the bed, but most of the night in the easy chair as it is called—between two and 3:00 in the morning Dr. Shippen desired Jacob to call up a John Perry, who lives near them, to open a vein, although it is an operation she very much dreads, she gave up to it without saying a word: he performed with great care and dexterity as I thought, he took twelve or 14 ounces. Sally had two smart, or rather hard pains while the bleeder was there, he is a married man; She has taken 80 or 90 drops liquid ladanum during the day and night, but has not had many minutes of sleep for 48 hours—the Doctor says the child is wedged on or near the shear bone and he cannot get at it, to alter the position of its head, I came home between 7 and 8 in the morning of the—24th after breakfast, and giving orders for dinner &c. W.D. upstairs, I went again to Sally, the Doctor had given her an opium pill three grains he said, in order to ease her pain, or to bring it on more violently: neither appeared to happen—in the afternoon the Doctor said, the child must be brought forward—he went out, which he had not done before, that he was going for instruments occurred to me but I was afraid to ask him, least he should answer in the affirmative—towards evening I came home as usual, and after seeing all things in order, was getting ready to depart, when little Dan entered, the sight of him fluttered me, yet I had a secret hope that it was over, when Dan told us that his Mistress had a fine boy and was as well as could be expected . . . I was thankful, that I happened to be absent at the time, though I intended otherwise, Dr. Shippen told me that he thought he should have had occasion for instruments, which said he I have in my pocket, clapping his hand on his side, when I heard them rattle, but sometime after you went away, I found matters were changed for the better.

The child, said he, is a very large one for Sally—It is a very fine lusty fat boy .... The Doctor was very kind and attentive during the whole afflicting scene, was there two nights and 2 days and slept very little—'

Childbearing and Slave Women, 1770[13]

The care and attention slave women received during pregnancy was determined by the master. Because the natural increase of slaves was economically desirable, many owners lightened the work load or cut it in half during the month before and the month after childbirth. Many did not. Although Landon Carter, the great Virginia planter, was a relatively humane master, he obviously subscribed to the commonly held assumption that black women, being physically stronger, needed less consideration than their white counterparts.

22 Thursday

Colonel Fauntleroy's feast day where I suppose my family must go.

We have heaped our dung at Mangorike, the mud house and the barn. Those people are finishing the hoeing their new corn field but up here Dolman though 3 days at it has not finished heaping the dung in the cow yard quite and has the tobacco house and sheep house to do.

Guy came home yesterday and had his correction for run away in sight of the people. The 2 Sarahs came up yesterday pretending to be violent ill with pains in their sides. They look very well, had no fever, and I ordered them down to their work upon pain of a whipping. They went, worked very well with no grunting about pain but one of them, to wit Manuel's Sarah, taking the advantage of Lawson's ride to the fork, swore she would not work any longer and run away and is still out. There is a curiosity in this creature. She worked none last year pretending to be with child and this she was full 11 months before she was brought to bed. She has now the same pretence and thinks to pursue the same course but as I have full warning of her deceit, if I live, I will break her of that trick. I had two before of this turn. Wilmot of the fork whenever she was with child always pretended to be too heavy to work and it cost me 12 months before I broke her. Criss of Mangorike fell into the same scheme and really carried it to a great length for at last she could not be dragged out. However by carrying a horse with traces the lady took to her feet run away and when caught by a severe whipping has been a good slave ever since only a cursed thief in making her children milk my cows in the night.

Childrearing

David Zeisberger's Account of Indian Childrearing Practices, 1779[14]

As a result of extended contact with white culture, Indian mothers had, by the eighteenth century, abandoned the use of the cradleboard.

In most other aspects of childrearing, however, Indian practice remained largely unchanged: Indian mothers continued to limit the size of their families through prolonged lactation, to give birth alone, and to lavish love and attention on their offspring.

The Indian women are in general of a very strong bodily constitution. There are generally clever and experienced women enough who are able to give assistance and advice in time of labor: generally, women will remain in the house at this time. Some go into the woods by themselves and bring their children to the house when they have seen the light of day. Most nurses nurse their children until they are two or more years old. During this time many husbands have concubines, though not in the house.

If it is left to the mother to give the child a name, she uses little ceremony and calls it after some peculiar mark or character in it, for instance the Beautiful, the Good Child, the Great Eye, sometimes giving it a name of unsavory meaning. If the father gives the child a name he pretends that it has been suggested to him in a dream. The name is given at a sacrifice on which occasion the Indian brings to some aged person, who performs the offering, a string of wampum, and tells him that he wishes his child's name to be named thus and so. During the sacrifice some other person sings a song in Indian fashion at a public gathering and makes known the child's name. This is called praying over the child. The same ceremony is performed when an adult person receives a name, even although he may already have been named. It is not common to call an adult by his name, for they are ashamed of their own names. If the attention of any one is to be attracted it is done in some other fashion than by the use of the name. In case of children, the names are used. In assemblies and in discourses they do not use the name of any one who is present, though absent persons are referred to by their names.

The children have entirely their own will and never do anything by compulsion. Told to do something they do not care about, the children let it go by default and are not reprimanded for it. Yet many well bred children are found among them who pay great attention and respect to parents and do things to please them. They are courteous, even to strangers. They respond to mild treatment. The contrary generally produces bitterness, hatred and contempt. The women are frequently guilty of thus raising their children to anger, for the women are often ill-tempered. By way of punishment, they will pour water on the children or thrust them into the water. The parents are careful not to beat their children, lest the children might remember it and revenge themselves on some future occasion. Instances are not wanting where children when grown have reproached their parents for corporal punishment received in youth and have threatened to return the indignity....

Families have from four to six children. More than this number is unusual. Birth of twins is rarely heard of. In many cases children who have become motherless after birth have been reared by careful old women. Sometimes children are given to such women. Then they spare no pains in rearing them. Soup made of Indian corn, pounded very fine, is given by them to infants of tender age, that may have come into their possession. Ordinarily, orphans even if they have lost but the mother, meet with hard experience and often suffer want. Children who have been given or bequeathed, on the contrary, are almost without exception well cared for.

Phillis Wheatley, "On the Death of a Young Lady," n.d.[15]

The paucity of records makes it virtually impossible to learn much about the intimacies of black families before 1800. But the elegies of the black poet Phillis Wheatley—who lost three children in six years— suggests the affectionate nature of the parent-child relationship. Unlike Ann Bradstreet's elegies for infants, which ignore the child's parents, Wheatley's elegies emphasize the mourning of both father and mother.

ON THE DEATH OF A YOUNG LADY
OF FIVE YEARS OF AGE

From dark abodes to fair etherial light
The enraptured innocent has wing'd her flight,
On the kind bosom of eternal love
She finds unknown beatitude above.

This known, the parents, nor her loss deplore,
She feel the iron hand of pain no more;
The dispensations of unerring grace,
Should turn your sorrows into grateful praise;
Let then no tears for her henceforward flow,
No more distressed in our dark vale below.

Her morning sun, which rose divinely bright
Was quickly mantled with the gloom of night;
But hear in heavn's blest bow'rs your Nancy fair,
And learn to imitate her language there.
"Thou, lord, whom I behold with glory crowned,
"By what sweet name, and in what tuneful sound
"Wilt thou be praised? Seraphic pow'rs are faint
"Infinite love and majesty to point
"To thee let all their grateful voices raise
"And saint and angels join their songs of 'praise.' "

Perfect in bliss she from her heavenly home
Looks down, and smiling beckons you to come;
Why then, fond parents, why these fruitless groans?
Restrain your tears, and cease your plaintive moans.
Freed from a world of sin, and snares, and pain,
Why would you wish your daughter bad again?
No—bow resigned. Let hope your grief control,
And check the rising tumult of the soul.
Calm in the prosperous, and adverse day,

Adore the God who gives and takes away;
Eye him in all, his holy name revere,
Upright your actions, and your hearts sincere,
Till having sailed through life's tempestuous sea,
And from its rocks, and boisterous billows free
Yourselves, safe landed on the shore
Shall join your happy babe to part no more.

Benjamin Rush, Thoughts upon Female Education, 1787[16]

The development of the intimate, affectionate family was characterized by a change in attitudes toward children. Under the influence of British physicians and educators, American educators began to stress the importance of more gentle nurturing of children. The didactic literature of the post-Revolutionary period, which appealed principally to well-to-do Americans, also emphasized the relationship between child-rearing practices and the inculcation of republican principles, such as virtue and independence, self-reliance, and restraint. Benjamin Rush, a Philadelphia physician and educator, was among the first to call attention to the importance of nurturing children within the home. His innovative and influential tract *Thoughts upon Female Education* advanced the idea that American women, as republican mothers, had a fundamental role to play in the molding of future citizens. Although Rush did not challenge the conventional wisdom that a woman's place was in the home, the effect of his argument was to enhance the significance of what she did in the home. The growth of female education and the political socialization of women were the ultimate results.

Gentlemen:

I have yielded with diffidence to the solicitations of the Principal of the Academy, in undertaking to express my regard for the prosperity of this seminary of learning by submitting to your candor a few thoughts upon female education.

The first remark that I shall make upon this subject is that female education should be accommodated to the state of society, manners, and government of the country in which it is conducted.

This remark leads me at once to add that the education of young ladies in this country should be conducted upon principles very different from what it is in Great Britain and in some respects different from what it was when we were a part of a monarchical empire.

There are serveral circumstances in the situation, employments, and duties of women in America which require a peculiar mode of education.

I. The early marriages of our women, by contracting the time allowed for education, renders it necessary to contract its plan and to confine it chiefly to the more useful branches of literature.

II. The state of property in America renders it necessary for the greatest part of our citizens to employ themselves in different occupations for the advancement of their fortunes. This cannot be done without the assistance of the female members of the community. They must be the stewards and guardians of their husband's property. That education, therefore, will be most proper for our women which teaches them to discharge the duties of those offices with the most success and reputation.

III. From the numerous avocations to which a professional life exposes gentlemen in America from their families, a principal share of the instruction of children naturally devolves upon the women. It becomes us therefore to prepare them, by a suitable education, for the discharge of this most important duty of mothers.

IV. The equal share that every citizen has in the liberty and the possible share he may have in the government of our country make it necessary that our ladies should be qualified to a certain degree, by a peculiar and suitable education, to concur in instructing their sons in the principles of liberty and government.

V. In Great Britain the business of servants is a regular occupation, but in America this humble station is the usual retreat of unexpected indigence; hence the servants in this country possess less knowledge and subordination than are required from them; and hence our ladies are obliged to attend more to the private affairs of their families than ladies generally do of the same rank in Great Britain. "They are good servants," said an American lady of distinguished merit in a letter to a favorite daughter, "who will do well with good looking after." This circumstance should have great influence upon the nature and extent of female education in America.

The branches of literature most essential for a young lady in this country appear to be:

I. A knowledge of the English language. She should not only read but speak and spell it correctly. And to enable her to do this, she should be taught the English grammar and be frequently examined in applying its rules in common conversation.

II. Pleasure and interest conspire to make the writing of a fair and legible hand a necessary branch of female education. For this purpose she should be taught not only to shape every letter properly but to pay the strictest regard to points and capitals....

III. Some knowledge of figures and bookkeeping is absolutely necessary to qualify a young lady for the duties which await her in this country. There are certain occupations in which she may assist her husband with this knowledge, and should she survive him and agreeably to the custom of our country be the executrix of his will, she cannot fail of deriving immense advantages from it.

IV. An acquaintance with geography and some instruction in chronology will enable a young lady to read history, biography, and travels, with advantage, and thereby qualify her not only for a general intercourse with the world but to be an agreeable companion for a sensible man. To these branches of knowledge may be added, in some instances, a general acquaintance with the first principles of astronomy and natural philosophy, particularly with such parts of them as are calculated to prevent superstition, by explaining the causes or obviating the effects of natural evil.

V. Vocal music should never be neglected in the education of a young lady in this country. Besides preparing her to join in that part of public worship which consists in psalmody, it will enable her to soothe the care of domestic life. The distress and vexation of a husband, the noise of a nursery, and even the sorrows that will sometimes intrude into her own bosom may all be relieved by a song, where sound and sentiment unite to act upon the mind....

VI. Dancing is by no means an improper branch of education for an American lady. It promotes health and renders the figure and motions of the body easy and agreeable. I anticipate the time when the resources of conversation shall be so far multiplied that the amusement of dancing shall be wholly confined to children. But in our present state of society and knowledge, I conceive it to be an agreeable substitute for the ignoble pleasures of drinking and gaming in our assemblies of grown people.

VII. The attention of our young ladies should be directed as soon as they are prepared for it to the reading of history, travels, poetry, and moral essays. These studies are accommodated, in a peculiar manner, to the present state of society in America, and when a relish is excited for them in early life, they subdue that passion for reading novels which so generally prevail among the fair sex....

VIII. It will be necessary to connect all these branches of education with regular instruction in the Christian religion. For this purpose the principles of the different sects of Christians should be taught and explained, and our pupils should early be furnished with some of the most simple arguments in favor of the truth of Christianity. A portion of the Bible (of late improperly banished from our schools) should be read by them every day and such questions should be asked, after reading it, as are calculated to imprint upon their minds the interesting stories contained in it.

Rousseau has asserted that the great secret of education consists in "wasting the time of children profitably." There is some truth in this observation. I believe that we often impair their health and weaken their capacities by imposing studies upon them which are not proportioned to their years. But this objection does not apply to religious instruction. There are certain simple propositions in the Christian religion that are suited in a peculiar manner to the infant state of reason and moral sensibility. A clergyman of long experience in the instruction of youth informed me that he always found children acquired religious knowledge more easily than knowledge upon other subjects, and that young girls acquired this kind of knowledge more readily than boys. The female breast is the natural soil of Christianity, and while our women are taught to believe its doctrines and obey its precepts, the wit of Voltaire and the style of Bolingbroke will never be able to destroy its influence upon our citizens.

IX. If the measures that have been recommended for inspiring our pupils with a sense of religious and moral obligation be adopted, the government of them will be easy and agreeable. I shall only remark under this head that strictness of discipline will always render severity unnecessary and that there will be the most instruction in that school where there is the most order....

I cannot dismiss the subject of female education without remarking that the city of Philadelphia first saw a number of gentlemen associated for the purpose of directing the education of young ladies. By means of this plan the power of teachers is regulated and restrained and the objects of education are extended. By the separation of the sexes in the unformed state of their manners, female delicacy is cherished and preserved. Here the young ladies may enjoy all the literary advantages of a boarding school and at the same time live under the protection of their parents. Here emulation may be excited without jealousy, ambition without envy, and competition without strife.

The attempt to establish this new mode of education for young ladies was an experiment, and the success of it has answered our expectations. Too much praise cannot be given to our principal and his assistants, for the abilities and fidelity with which they have carried the plan into execution. The proficiency which the young ladies have discovered in reading, writing, spelling, arithmetic, grammar, geography, music, and their different catechisms since the last examination is a less equivocal mark of the merits of our teachers than anything I am able to express in their favor.

But the reputation of the academy must be suspended till the public are convinced by the future conduct and character of our pupils of the advantages of the institution. To you, therefore, YOUNG LADIES, an important problem is committed for solution; and that is, whether our present plan of education be a wise one and whether it be calculated to prepare you for the duties of social and domestic life. I know that the elevation of the female mind, by means of moral, physical, and religious truth, is considered by some men as unfriendly to the domestic character of a woman. But this is the prejudice of little minds and springs from the same spirit which opposes the general diffusion of knowledge among the citizens of our republics. If men believe that ignorance is favorable to the government of the female sex, they are certainly deceived, for a weak and ignorant woman will always be governed with the greatest difficulty.

I have somtimes been led to ascribe the invention of ridiculous and expensive fashions in female dress entirely to the gentlemen in order to divert the ladies from improving their minds and thereby to secure a more arbitrary and unlimited authority over them. It will be in your power, ladies, to correct the mistakes and practice of our sex upon these subjects by demonstrating that the female temper can only be governed by reason and that the cultivation of reason in women is alike friendly to the order of nature and to private as well as public happiness.

WIDOWHOOD

Demographic shifts affected marriage patterns in a variety of different ways. The more equal sex ratio in the Chesapeake, the westward migration of young men from New England, and the relative longevity of women as compared to men all created fewer opportunities for women to marry, with the result that some women did not marry at all and widows remarried less frequently. Accompanying these demographic changes was a redistribution of wealth, caused principally by the economic dislocations produced by the Seven Years War and by spreading commercialization. The results, including the accumulation of great fortunes and the growth of poverty, were especially apparent in urban areas after the 1750s. Among the most impoverished members of the growing body of the poor were widows and orphaned children, and the aged without relatives to care for them.

Margaret Hill Morris, Journal, 1766, 1780[17]

Although husbands were required by law to provide for their widows, raising children alone could be an expensive and difficult task, even for prominent widows like Margaret Morris. In 1758 Margaret Hill married William Morris, Jr., a moderately successful drygoods merchant from Philadelphia, whose family traced its roots to the founding of Pennsylvania. The sudden death of William Morris in 1766 left the young mother with four children, all under the age of seven. In 1770 she took her family to Burlington, New Jersey, which during the Revolutionary War was the object of contending armies. The widow Morris, a devout Quaker, used the medical skills she had acquired from her physician father, Dr. Richard Hill, to relieve the sufferings of soldiers from both sides, as this excerpt from her journal reveals. In 1780, to supplement her small income, she opened a shop to retail medicine. When that failed she began practicing medicine in Burlington, aided no doubt by the reputation she had earned as a skillful physician during the war.

Philadelphia, May 21, 1766
On this melancholy day I left the once sweet and delightful habitation where I enjoyed an uninterrupted happiness for seven years and seven months, and removed with my dear little orphans to our lonely dwelling in A.B.'s house, and hope and pray that the good hand who has led me hitherto will not leave me now in my deep distress, but that through his grace I may be enabled so to conduct with regard to the dear children now more particularly committed to my care....

MARGARET HILL MORRIS TO HER SISTER, 1780

I have been fearful my beloved sister has thought me forgetful or unkind in not writing to her for so long a time; as to the first, I can truly say it has not been the case, for thou art present to my mind both sleeping and waking, with strong desires for thy preservation and perseverance in the right way; which though at first it may appear to be a straight and narrow one, will certainly lead to a place of broad rivers and streams, where the travellers of hope will be sweetly refreshed and rewarded for all the toils of a painful journey. I write to my own feelings at the time, for in looking forward to the end of a worrisome journey, I seem to think it will be as I have expressed it above, though I acknowledge I do not believe myself entitled to such a reward....

I must not conclude my letter without thanking dear brother Charles for the seasonable supply he sent me, without which I could not possibly have procured the necessary provisions for my family, as my Richard had straitened himself in buying a mill, and wrote he could not supply me as usual, which made me cast about in my mind how I might dispose of a small part of what brother C. sent me, so as to bring me in a little matter, and I concluded to buy a few medicines and retail them at a moderate price, and have actually sent a list to Speakman, which I expect by next boat. There is not a dose of physic to be got in this town without coming to me for it, and I have long supplied many gratuitously. I feel quite alert at the thoughts of doing something that may set me a little step above absolute dependence; the Doctor in our town will not sell any medicines, except to his own patients, so that I've no doubt of having custom enough, and all my friends here approve of my making the trial; if it succeeds, I shall add to my shop, by a little at a time, till I get a good assortment. T'is my first attempt at business, as I may say, and as I do not often engage in anything on which I dare not ask a blessing, so I presume to hope for one on my present undertaking. Will thee believe me when I tell thee, after scribbling half a sheet, that I've got a sore thumb, with the nail half off? My dear S.D. is well, and joins in much love.

Petition of Mary Cox to Governor Thomas Johnson, 1779[18]

In an effort to cope with the growing problem of indigency, many American communities began in the 1750s to abandon the familial system of relief in favor of institutional care, which was expected to both reduce the poor rates and check the growth of poverty. Their efforts were inadequate and by the eve of the Revolution most cities had large numbers of impoverished people, a disproportionately large percentage of them women. The Revolutionary War greatly exacerbated the problem of female indigency. Casualties suffered in the war exceeded those of all American wars since, excepting only the Civil War, as a percentage of the adult male population. With no source of income, without families to care for them, many widows left destitute by the war were forced to petition for relief. When they could get no assistance from the new national government, many widows like Mary Cox turned to the states for help. As the widow of an officer, Mrs. Cox had a better chance than the widows of enlisted men of securing a small pension through pension legislation.

I am the unhappy widow of Major James Cox who fell in his country's cause at German Town on 4 October 1777. By industry we lived comfortably. His spare cash he laid out in lands from which now I can reap no benefit. His own cash he left with me did not exceed £50 and the public money which he had to pay off his company was lost at his death which I have since refunded. I have five small children to maintain. I expected the benefit of the law in that case provided. Consequently six months after my husband's death I applied to the Orphan's Court. They put me off till the next session (?) I applied again [and] they granted me half pay for eight months in which time I sold all my spare furniture and part of my stock raised a little cash and went to shop-keeping. I found I could not keep my stock good which I began with; I again applied to the Court their reply was you are making money fast and we don't think you are entitled to the benefit of that law. Sir, it is truly distressing to a mind not entirely depraved to beg and to dig I am not ashamed though my natural strength will not admit of it.

Now sir, as you are the guardian of this state and more especially of the widow and fatherless I will expect a few lines from you informing me whether I may expect the benefit of the law or not—I have three sons and two daughters, all promising children, would be glad they might be properly educated and instructed to get a living in a genteel way which cannot be the case without assistance. Now Sir when you consider the irreparable loss I have sustained by the death of the best of husbands, the weak infirm state of my body and numerous helpless family to provide for and the amusing prices of the neces-saries of life, I say when you consider these things I doubt not but you will do everything in your power to alievate such distresses and as in duty bound I will for your welfare ever pray.

Mary Cox

NOTES

1. Leo Hershkowitz, ed. *Letters of the Franks Family, 1733–1748* (Waltham, Massachusetts, 1968), pp. 116–22. Reprinted with permission of the American Jewish Historical Society, Waltham, Mass.

2. Sarah Hanschurst Papers, 1762, Library of Congress, Washington, D.C.

3. "Randolph and Tucker Letters," *Virginia Magazine of History and Bi-ography* XLII (No. 1, 1934), pp. 49–50.

4. Thomas Anburey, *Travels Through the Interior Parts of America*, 2 vols. (London, 1789), II, pp. 385–86.

5. David Zeisberger, *History of the Northern American Indians*, eds. Archer Butler Hulbert and William Nathaniel Schwarze (Columbus, Ohio, 1910), pp. 77–80.

6. Robert Barclay, *A Catechism and Confession of Faith* (Philadelphia, 1788), pp. 83–84.

7. Journal of Elizabeth Foote (Mrs. Lunde) Washington, 1779–1796, in Washington Family Papers, 1522–1915, Library of Congress, Washington, D.C.

8. Susanna Rowson, *Miscellaneous Poems* (Boston, 1804), pp. 105–8, 114–15.

9. Massachusetts Historical Society, *Collections*, 5th ser., 111 (1877), pp. 432–33.

10. Maryland State Papers, *Blue Book* IV, 10, Maryland Hall of Records, Annapolis, Md. Reprinted with the permission of the Maryland State Archives.

11. Jack P. Greene, ed. *The Diary of Colonel Landon Carter of Sabine Hall, 1752–1778*, 2 vols. (Charlottesville, 1965), I, pp. 511, 512, 515. Reprinted with permission of the University of Virginia Press.

12. Cecil Kent Drinker, *Not So Long Ago: A Chronicle of Medicine and Doctors in Colonial Philadelphia* (New York: 1937), pp. 59–62.

13. Greene, ed., *The Diary of Colonel Landon Carter*, I, pp. 371–72. Reprinted with the permission of the University of Virginia Press.

14. Zeisberger, *History of the Northern Indians*, pp. 80–81.

15. Julian D. Mason, Jr., ed., *The Poems of Phillis Wheatley* (Chapel Hill, 1966), pp. 10–11. Reprinted with the permission of the University of North Carolina Press.

16. Frederick Rudolph, ed. *Essays on Education in the Early Republic* (Cambridge, Mass., 1965) pp. 27–40.

17. John Jay Smith, ed., *Letters to Dr. Richard Hill and His Children* (Philadelphia, 1854), pp. 353, 414–16.

18. Maryland State Papers, *The Red Books*, XXV, p. 80.

BIBLIOGRAPHY

Cott, Nancy F. *The Bonds of Womanhood: "Woman's Sphere" in New England, 1780–1835.* New Haven, Conn., 1977.

Gutman, Herbert G. *The Black Family in Slavery and Freedom, 1750–1925.* New York, 1978.

Johnson, Michael P. "Planters and Patriarchy: Charleston, 1800–1860." *Journal of Southern History* XLVI (1980):45–72.

Jordan, Winthrop D. "Familial Politics: Thomas Paine and the Killing of the King, 1776." *Journal of American History* LX (1973):294–308.

Kerber, Linda K. *Women of the Republic: Intellect and Ideology in Revolutionary America.* Chapel Hill, N.C., 1980.

Keyssar, Alexander. "Widowhood in Eighteenth-Century Massachusetts: A Problem in the History of the Family." *Perspectives in American History* VIII (1974):83–119.

Kulikoff, Allan. "A 'Prolifick' People: Black Population Growth in the Chesapeake Colonies, 1700–1790." *Southern Studies* XVI (1977):391–414.

————. "The Origins of Afro-American Society in Tidewater Maryland and Virginia, 1700 to 1790." *William and Mary Quarterly*, 3d ser., 35 (1978):226–59.

Morgan, Edmund. *Virginians at Home: Family Life in the Eighteenth Century.* Williamsburg, Va, 1952.

Norton, Mary Beth. *Liberty's Daughters: The Revolutionary Experience of American Women, 1750–1800.* Boston, 1980.

Reinier, Jacqueline S. "Rearing the Republican Child: Attitudes and Practices in Post-Revolutionary Philadelphia." *William and Mary Quarterly*, 3d ser., 39 (1982):150–63.

Smith, Daniel Blake. *Inside the Great House: Family Life in Eighteenth-Century Chesapeake Society.* Ithaca, N.Y., 1980.

Wells, Robert V. "Family Size and Fertility Control in Eighteenth-Century America: A Study of Quaker Families." *Population Studies* XXV (1971):73–82.

Wilson, Joan Hoff. "The Illusion of Change: Women in the American Revolution." Alfred F. Young, ed., *The American Revolution: Explorations in the History of American Radicalism.* De Kalb, Ill., 1976, 383–445.

6 WOMEN AND WORK, 1700–1815

Significant economic changes took place throughout the eighteenth century, including the development of a market economy and the growth of cities and a factory system. The colonists had always sold or bartered the surplus products of their fields and households, but, especially in the northeast, there was an acceleration of the trend to a commercialized economy in which goods and services were produced not for use by one's own family, but for sale to others. This commercialization brought with it a specialization of economic functions so that the versatility of the male or female worker on the colonial farm was gradually supplanted by the ability to do only one job well and for pay.

Accompanying and fostering these developments were the thriving cities which grew up in locations of commercial importance, particularly seaports since much of colonial trade was carried on with Europe, especially England. In other cities of the northeast where water power was available, the earliest manufactories and small factories were founded. Their growth was further stimulated by the desire for independence from the trade restrictions imposed by England. These institutions foreshadowed the dramatic industrialization of the nineteenth century.

Despite the altering economy, most women continued to play their economic roles in an agrarian setting. As the population moved West, especially after the American Revolution when British restraints were removed from the lands west of the Appalachians, the primitive economic conditions of the seventeenth century were reproduced. Huswifery was as crucial as ever for the survival of the family and community. Considering the importance and the relative scarcity of women on the frontier, the famous historian Frederick Jackson Turner claimed that the West was the cradle of equality for women, pointing to the early enfranchisement of women by western states in the late nineteenth century. However, according to Julie Roy Jeffries, women took to the frontier traditional customs and ideas about female roles which they had acquired in the more settled regions. Whether these customs and ideas were conducive to sexual equality is an unresolved issue.

In the South, slavery became more deeply entrenched as the economy became more dependent on large-scale commercial farming, especially cotton. Indentured servitude was replaced by slavery in the South during the eighteenth century and, more slowly, by free labor in the North.

The economic transformations of the period did change the lives of many women, although historians disagree about the extent of these changes and whether they were for better or for worse. The increasing specialization and commercialization during the late eighteenth century may have meant for some urban women a diminished importance for the household and its housewife—"Adam's Rib," as Mary Ryan has suggested. Moreoever, the specialization of the economy was paralled by a growing specialization of male and female economic functions, a more rigid delineation of what was "women's work." For example, medicine, long a woman's province, became more professional and simultaneously less female-dominated.

The growth of a capitalized, semi-industrial economy also sharpened class distinctions, as the economic and social gap between the lifestyles of the rich and poor widened. The leisured "lady" emerged within the colonial upper class in northern cities and on some southern plantations, but many more women, deprived of land and useful urban skills, became public charges, the recipients of grudging and stingy charity from local male public officials and of the solicitous attentions of benevolent upper-class women.

On the other hand, these same economic changes may have brought a measure of economic independence to other women as their work moved out of the familial context and into the paid (although underpaid) labor force, as Linda Kerber has maintained. Although it must be noted that these commercial ventures were generally extensions into the marketplace of work that women had traditionally done in the home, an economy in flux and the social and ideological disruptions caused by the more or less constant warfare of the eighteenth century did allow a handful of women to play very untraditional roles, both within and outside the home.

ON THE FRONTIER AND FARM

Except for the solitary trappers and woodsmen of legend, most men who followed the lure of the West across sea or land traveled with their wives and families. Women's labor was necessary as it had been in the early colonies, and in the small settlements and farms of the frontier, their work was done within the household.

Although the southern plantation household was also the primary economic unit, here there was little sexual division of labor between slave men and women. Both worked in the fields and less often as house servants. Male slaves also had occasional opportunities to learn a craft or skill; female slaves almost never did.

Frontier

To the New World, 1805[1]

This is the passenger list of the ship Margaret, which landed in Philadelphia in August, 1805. On board were followers of the German religious leader George Rapp. They had crossed the Atlantic to join a religious community which he planned to establish at Harmonie, Pennsylvania. Later the community moved farther west to found New Harmony, Indiana, which later still became the site of a more famous utopian experiment directed by Robert Owen. These Germans, like the Puritans, traveled in families. The descriptive entries reveal the size of these families, the age differences between spouses and between siblings, and the men's occupations. Note how few men and women arrived in the wilderness alone. What do the naming patterns suggest about the relationships between children and parents?

Report of alien passengers on board the ship Margaret:
Jacob Geyger, 36, farmer, brown and tall;
   Elizabeth Geyger, 34
J. A. Librant, tanner, light, ordinary;
   Rosina Librant, 34; Andras Librant, 12; Frederica Librant, 9; Ludwig Librant, 6; Jacob Librant, 3; Edward Librant, 2 months.
Solomon Woolf, 35, farmer, ordinary;
   Elizabeth, 30; George 9; Johannas, 3; Magdalena, 1 1/2; Solomon, 6 months.
Michael Libely, 43, farmer, ordinary;
   Maria, 45, wife and children, Michael, 19; Joseph, 17; Christian, 8; Maria, 6; Louisa, 3.
Casper Byrer, 39, farmer, ordinary;
   Rosina, 39; Frederick, 13; Gotlope, 2 1/2; Johannas, 9 months.
Joseph Geyger, 32, farmer, 6 feet 6 inches;
   Anna, 30.
Margaret Desting, 17, servant maid, ordinary.
Johann Senable, 29, shoemaker, very light complexion;
   Regina, 22; Frederick, 9 months.
Johann G. Specht, 44, wine gardener, low stature with hump on his back;
   Margaret, 48; K. Margaret, 20; Catherine, 18; Gottlieb, 16; David, 12; Abraham, 5.

Michael Binenger, 67, house carpenter, ordinary and grey;
   Sabina, 55; Anna Maria, 28; Frederica, 25; Sabine, 18.
Adam Librant, 19, stone mason, light complexion.
Paul Frank, 45, farmer, low stature, old and dark;
   Barbara, 42; Regina Barbara, 18; John George, 12; Frederich, 5; Avelhart,
   3; Froneca, 2; Christina, 9 months.
George Miller, 25, butcher, tall and light.
Frederich Miller, 13, servant boy, light complexion.
George F. Frank, 45, farmer, wine dresser, ordinary stature, dark;
   Margaret, 38; Feronaca, 12; Christina, 10; G. Frederich, 6; Elizabeth, 3 1/2;
   Christianen, 2.
Jacob Lible, 25, farmer, light complexion;
   Christina, 21; Johannas, 2.
Christopher Bower, 35, farmer, light complexion.

To the New West, 1810[2]

Margaret Van Horn Dwight was twenty years old when she left New
Haven, Connecticut, to visit cousins in Youngstown, Ohio. The culture
shock that she experienced along the way was probably typical of such
city-bred, gently-raised young ladies as Margaret, who were unfamiliar
with the rigors of frontier life such as her mother and grandmother
had probably experienced. Margaret's descriptions of the women she
met are useful, although colored by her own ideas of what women
should look like and do. In 1821 she married William Bell and later
bore thirteen children on the newly settled frontier.

                          October 22, Monday, Cook's Inn
                          County West Chester [Pennsylvania]
   I will never go to Connecticut [Ohio] with a deacon again, for we put up at
every byeplace in the country to save expense. It is very grating to my pride
to go into a tavern and furnish and cook my own provision—to ride in a wagon,
etc., etc., but that I can possibly get along with, but to be obliged to pass the
night in such a place as we are now in, just because it is a little cheaper, is
more than I am willing to do. I should even rather drink clear rum out of the
wooden bottle after the deacon has drank and wiped it over with his hand,
than to stay here another night. The house is very small and very dirty. It
serves for a tavern, a store, and I should imagine, hog's pen, stable, and everything else.

                               Sunday Eve—Sundown
   I can wait no longer to write you, for I have a great deal to say. I should not
have thought it possible to pass a Sabbath in our country among such a dissolute vicious set of wretches as we are now among. I believe at least fifty
dutchmen [Germans] have been here today to smoke, drink, swear, pitch cents,
almost dance, laugh, and talk dutch and stare at us. They come in, in droves,
young and old, black and white, women and children. It is dreadful to see so

many people that you cannot speak to or understand. Just as we set down to tea, in came a dozen or two of women, each with a child in her arms and stood round the room. As they said nothing, I concluded they came to see us Yankees, as they would a learned pig. The women dress in striped linsey woolsey petticoats and short gowns not six inches in length. They look very strangely.

Monday morn

We have now I think met with as bad as can befall us. Never, never did I pass such a night. We could get no bed and for a long time expected to be obliged to set up all night, but we could get no room nor fire to stay by, and the landlady was so kind as to give up her bed to us. So Mrs. W. and Susan went to bed there, while I went to bed with Mrs. Jackson in another room. I took off my frock and boots, and had scarcely lain down, when one of the wretches [wagoneers staying in the same inn] came into the room and lay down by me on the outside of the bed. I was frightened almost to death and clung to Mrs. Jackson, who did not appear to mind it, and I lay for quarter of an hour crying and scolding and trembling, begging of him to leave me. At last, when persuaded I was in earnest, he begged of me not to take it amiss, as he intended no harm and only wished to become acquainted with me. A good-for-nothing brute, I wonder what he supposed I was. I don't know of any thought, word, or action of mine that could give him reason to suppose I would authorise such abominable insolence. The man and his wife who are here and their family, John Jackson and his wife, and Mrs. Jackson, were all in the room.

November 24, Friday morn
Turtle Creek, Penn.

One misfortune follows another, and I fear we shall never reach our journey's end. Yesterday we came about three miles. After coming down an awful hill, we were obliged to cross a creek, but before we quite came to it, the horses got mired, and we expected every moment that one of them would die, but Erastus held his head out of water, while Mr. W. was attempting to unharness them, and Mrs. W. and Susan were on the bank, calling for help. I sat by, to see the horse breathe his last, but was happily disappointed in my expectation. No assistance could be got until Mr. W. waded through the water, and then two men with three horses came over. We came to this inn, and Mr. W. thought it best to stay till this morning. We got into the slough of Despond yesterday and are now at the foot of the hill Difficulty, which is half a mile long. One wagon is already fast in the mud on it, and Mr. W. is afraid to attempt it himself. I think I will winter here.

Thursday eve

Ten miles as usual has been our day's ride. I have not walked my nine miles, but I walked as much as I could. We are in a comfortable house before an excellent fire. It is snowing very fast.

Sunday, p.m., Warren,
after so long a time

We reached Cousin Joseph Woodbridge's about the middle of the eve. They got us a good supper and gave us a bed. Mrs. W. is a very pretty woman (I mean pleasing). They have three children and appear to be very well off and happy. They live in a very comfortable log house, pleasantly situated. A cousin in this country is not to be slighted, I assure you. I would give more for one in this country, than for twenty in old Connecticut. The town is pleasanter than I expected, the house better and the children as fine. My very best love to everybody.

Most affectionately yours,
MVD

Farm

In George Washington's Fields, 1788[3]

Like most of the leaders of the American Revolution, Washington was a slave owner. His description of slave work during the winter months reveals the minimal division of labor between males and females and the backbreaking labor done by both.

1788 January

January 1st

Mr. Lee returned to Alexandria after breakfast, as Mrs. Stuart did from Mr. Lund Washington's. I remained at home this day also.

Wednesday, 2d

Colo. Humphreys and myself accompanied Mr. Paradise and his lady to Alexandria. Dined with Mr. Charles Lee and returned in the Evening—leaving Mr. and Mrs. Paradise there.

Thursday, 3d

Visited the plantations at the Ferry, Dogue Run, and Muddy Hole.

At the first the women were taking up and thinning the trees in the swamp which they had before grubbed. The men were getting stakes and trunnels for fencing and making racks to feed the creatures in. Began yesterday and would about finish today sowing the New Meadow at this (which was too thin of timothy) with a quart of timothy seed to the acre.

At French's they were putting up racks to feed the cattle in. One man was getting stakes for fencing.

At Dogue Run, the women began to hoe the swamp they had grubbed in order to prepare it for sowing in the spring with grain and grass seeds. The men were cutting the tops of the trees which had been fallen for rails into coal-wood.

At Muddy Hole, the women after having threshed out the peas, went about the fencing, two men getting stakes, etc., for it.

Friday, 4th

Ride to all the plantations.

In the Neck the men were getting posts and rails; the women were threshing oats.

At Muddy Hole, the men were getting rails and the women making fences.

At Dogue Run, the men were cutting coal-wood and the women hoeing swamp as yesterday.

At French's the men were cutting and mauling fence stakes and the women levelling old ditches and grubbing.

At the Ferry, the men were getting stakes, making racks, etc., and the women thinning trees in the swamp.

Monday, 7th

Visited the plantations at Dogue Run and French's. At the first the women (though the ground was too hard to hoe) were grubbing and otherwise preparing the swamp for meadow. The men were cutting as usual.

At French's (except Abram who was cutting stakes) the rest were threshing out peas.

Set the women belonging to the Ferry and to Muddy Hole to grubbing the woods in front of the house, adjoining the last year's corn.

Polly Kirtland's Cookbook, 1804[4]

Polly Kirtland came with her husband Turhand Kirtland to the Western Reserve of Ohio from Connecticut. Her husband was an agent for the Connecticut Land Company and later a state senator and judge in Ohio. His wife cared for the home and children. Her numerous chores included the preparation of food, and these extracts from her recipe book, brought with her from her New England home, reveal the rigors of both cooking and eating.

Loaf Cake

12 lbs. flour
 4 lbs. butter
 4 lbs. sugar
 4 lbs. currants
20 eggs
 1 oz. mace
 1 oz. cloves
 1 qt. wine
 1 qt. milk
 1 pt. yeast

Beef How Salted

To 1 Barrel
Powder 4 qts. salt
8 oz. salt-petre and 5 lbs. brown sugar.

Let the salt be well rubbed into the pieces of meat, pack them close in a barrel, and sprinkle the salt petre and sugar evenly between the layers. No water is to be applied. The juice of the meat will form a sufficient quantity of brine to keep sweet through the summer.

FROM THE NEW ENGLAND FARMER AUGUST 3, 1792
APPLES HOW SAVED

Gather them about noon on the day of the full moon in the latter part of September or beginning of October. Spread them in chamber till about the last of November, then put them in boxes in the cellar out of the way of frost but as cool a part as any, and they will keep till the last of May and not one in fifty rot.

IN THE CITY

In 1790 the United States had only a dozen cities, places with a population of over 2,500. Tiny by today's standards, these cities were still dirty, crowded, unsanitary, and often disagreeable places to live. Nevertheless, as the flow of citizens into them testifies, urban areas offered greater possibilities for jobs, education, and simply social intercourse. Urban dwellers, however, often could not as easily grow their own food or engage in home manufactures as could farm families, primarily because of the economic specialization that demanded that energies be concentrated on one, rather than several, tasks. This created a demand for the skills and talents of a wide variety of female workers: midwives, milliners, tavern-keepers, seamstresses, prostitutes, domestic servants, and retailers of dry goods and foods. Early manufacturing establishments also provided jobs for women, primarily in the textile industry as the manufacture of cloth had been long associated with female labor.

In sharp distinction, some few women all but lost their economically productive roles. Wealth and social status made household labor for them unnecessary; urban living allowed them to purchase whatever their own servants could not make. Other well-to-do women formed charitable associations and institutions, for during this same period the numbers of poor and dependent increased—victims rather than the beneficiaries of the urban market economy.

The Sold and the Sellers

Slaves in Boston, 1727[5]

Slavery never played the important role in the northern colonies that it did in the South, but slaves were purchased for household service and for other skilled and unskilled tasks in the northern cities. This account book is from the sloop Katherine which carried slaves to Bos-

ACCOUNTS OF THE KATHERINE, 1727

Per Contra		Cr.		
		£	s	d
By Joseph Plasted	1 boy	75	0	0
By William Thomas	1 ditto	75	0	0
By John Stanford	1 man	75	0	0
By Capt. Macarty	1 boy	80	0	0
By Thomas Jackson	1 girl	80	0	0
By Joseph White Esq.	1 boy	62	0	0
By William Mallus	1 woman	80	0	0
By Mathew Bond	1 boy	60	0	0
By Samuel Weekes	1 ditto	80	0	0
By Jonathan Brown	1 ditto	60	0	0
By Captain Jonathan Pittes	1 woman	80	0	0
By Captain Jonathan Webster	1 ditto	70	0	0
By Joseph Cowell	1 girl	65	0	0
By Herbert Newton	1 boy	65	0	0
By Edward Luttwich	1 man	75	0	0
By George Cambles	1 girl	30	0	0
By Nathaniel Weles	1 boy	75	0	0
By Mary Gilbart	1 ditto	75	0	0
By James Pecker	1 boy	60	0	0
By Gideon Ball	1 girl	60	0	0
By Nathanael Emes	1 girl	50	0	0
By James Fordike	1 girl	47	0	0
By Daniel Goff	1 girl	59	0	0
By Francis Plasted	1 boy	45	0	0
By John Stover	1 girl	70	0	0

ton. What factors determined the price of slaves? Who could afford to buy them?

The New England Courant, 1722[6]

The following advertisements for the goods and services of enterprising women indicate the number and kinds of commercial opportunities in the growing cities. As we would expect, most opportunities involved conventional women's work, but occasionally women stretched the boundaries of what was appropriately feminine in this new economic setting.

Any person that wants a wet nurse into the house may hear of one by enquiring of the printer hereof.

All persons indebted to the estate of Mr. Richard Pullen, late of Boston, Innholder, deceased, are hereby desired and required forthwith to pay in their respective debts unto Mrs. Ellinor Pullen, Widow, Administratrix to said estate, as they would avoid further trouble. And all persons to whom the said estate is indebted, are hereby notified to bring in their several claims unto the said Administratrix, in order to their being paid.

Pennsylvania Gazette, 1742[7]

Some women sought their fortunes in the city; others sought to salvage them. These women were taking advantage of the urban population's needs and desires.

The household goods of William West, mariner (who was taken by the Spaniards about two years hence) being distrained for ten pounds, ten shillings rent, and to be sold on the 15th instant, at the house of Second Street, where John Songburst formerly lived. The charitable and considerate are requested by the indigent wife of the said West, to come and bid for the said goods, to prevent their being sold at an under-value.

TO BE SOLD

By Mary Oswald at the house of Mr. Joseph Turner and by William Wallace at the Sugar House, Sugar Baker, choice double and single refined loaf sugar, sugar candy, molasses, green and bohea tea.

Virginia Gazette, 1768[8]

Women placed a very small proportion of the advertisements in colonial papers but were not reticent about the virtues of what they did have for sale. This is particularly true of Catherine Rathell, whose notice appears below. Of special interest are the inferences that can be drawn about male and female fashions and about the lifestyles and socioeconomic status of Rathell's clientele.

Just imported from London and selling by the subscriber, at a low advance for ready money only, the following articles, viz.

Flowered satin and spotted mode cardinals and cloaks; hats and bonnets; gauze and lace; plain, striped, and book muslins; fine thick cambrics and clear lawns; bordered handkerchiefs; a large and fashionable assortment of ribbons, caps, egrets, plumes, feathers and fillets; exceeding fine lappet beads; a neat assortment of garnet, paste, and other rings; shoe, knee, and stock buckles; silver mounted Morocco pocket books with instruments, and some very complete and secure with two locks; housewives for ladies with instruments; satin caps of all sizes, white, black, and colored silk hose; fine India cotton [hose] and worsted [hose], boys' and girls' worsted [hose]; Disbury's best shoes and pumps for gentlemen; red, blue, and yellow slippers for [gentlemen]; Disbury's best and neatest black and white satin and callimanco pumps.

For ladies, a very neat and genteel assortment of wedding, mourning and second mourning, and children's shoes of all sizes, artificial hair pins, breast flowers equal in beauty to any ever imported, and so near resembles nature, that the nicest eye can hardly distinguish the difference; colored and white silk French kid, lamb gloves and mitts for ladies, girls, and children; buck, doe, kid lamb and white gloves for gentlemen; black silk bags and roses for [gentlemen]; blond, silk, and cotton thread for working; sewing silks of all sorts and paper pins; needles sorted; fine plaited stocks and stock tapes; quilted petticoats and red cardinals, garlands, and trimmings; walking sticks, canes, with many other items too numerous to mention.

As the above goods are fashionable, new and good, she hopes to meet with encouragement, which shall be most thankfully acknowledged by

Catherine Rathell

At the same place, LODGINGS FOR SIX GENTLEMEN.

Polly Miller, Brothel-Keeper, 1814[9]

The growth of prostitution in American cities is another illustration of economic specialization and commercialization. At the same time, however, prostitution is an example of women earning money in a traditionally female way since women have always exchanged their bodies for money or security. This eulogy suggests a certain amount of tongue-in-cheek acceptance of this female entrepreneur.

Closed her mortal pilgrimage on the 1st instant at the Great Bridge, Mrs. Mary Jones, formerly Miss Polly Miller, aged 73. While characters far less distinguished than the subject of this communication, who have crawled on through life without giving rise to a solitary incident worthy the notice of the biographer or anecdotarian, have been complimented with flaunting panegyrics, it would be the very acme of injustice, the quintessence of ingratitude, to consign the memory of this heroine to "dull forgetfulness," without one scratch of the pen to perpetuate her name and record her extraordinary merit and good qualities. Good nature, and a disposition to accommodate mankind, no doubt, led her, at an early period of her life, to open a house of entertainment, which she continued to keep until death. Her services in behalf of her country, during the struggle for independence, deserve the highest strains of eulogy. For having naturally a love of freedom and abhorrence of all restraint whatever, she took a decided stand on the side of her country. The bustle of war having penetrated as far as the Great Bridge, she had often an opportunity of ministering to the wants of her countrymen in arms, and affording them aid and comfort whenever an exigency required. The defeat of the British, who were sent to dislodge the Americans from their post at the Great Bridge, and the fall of their leader, the gallant Captain Fordyce, are circumstances well known. On this occasion our heroine was not inactive; she ordered refreshments for the soldiers after the battle and took charge of the wounded men, whose wounds she dressed and attended to until they were cured. Indeed, it is asserted, that she saved the lives of more than half a dozen, who certainly would have died in the hands of the regular physicians. Her generosity and patriotism acquired her great celebrity so that her house soon became the resort of all who traveled that way, and she found herself in a little time, perfectly independent of the world. But wealth was not her object. It was sacrificing one's life, she thought, if the pursuits of business would not admit of a few moments for dalliance, and she was extremely happy in making her business subservient to her inclinations. Thus passed on her days, "merrily and cheerfully"; old age, it is true, deprived her cheeks of their roses, but it did not impair the vigor of her mind and her constitution.

And may those who remember her frailties, never forget her amiable qualities. She was upright in her dealings, and she was charitable and humane to the poor and afflicted, who never sought her bounty or assistance in vain, which is more than can be said of millions who boast a purer fame.

Women in Manufacturing

Textile Mills in Boston, 1789[10]

Textile mills were the first American factories, and women and children the first factory workers. Promoters of manufacturing such as Alexander Hamilton also believed that women could be more usefully employed outside than inside the home, reflecting perhaps the reality that women's domestic work was of less economic value than formerly. George Washington's observations about female workers in this small factory in Boston noted the hours and working conditions. Notice the evidence of the growing class stratification of the period.

Wednesday, 28th
Went after an early breakfast, to visit the duck [cloth] manufacture, which appeared to be carrying on with spirit, and is in a prosperous way. They have manufactured 32 pieces of duck of 30 or 40 yards each in a week and expect in a short time to increase it. They have 28 looms at work, and 14 girls spinning with both hands (the flax being fastened to their waist). Children (girls) turn the wheels for them, and with this assistance each spinner can turn out 14 lbs. of thread a day when they stick to it, but as they are paid by the piece for work they do, there is no other restraint upon them but to come at 8 o'clock in the morning and return at 6 in the evening. They are the daughters of decayed families, and are girls of character. None other are admitted.

After my return I dined in a large company at Mr. Bowdoin's and went to the Assembly in the evening, where (it is said) there were upwards of 100 ladies. Their appearance was elegant, and many of them very handsome. The room is small but neat and well ornamented.

The Factory Girl, by "A Lady," 1814[11]

This novel, whose author was Sarah Savage (1784–1837), reflects the prevalent ambiguities about women working outside the home, particularly in the new environment of the factory. "A lady" was not supposed to be economically productive, according to developing ideas about women's roles. On the other hand, the factory girl heroine of the novel, Mary, is forced into the factory by economic necessity and in all ways is a model nineteenth-century woman, domestic, pure, and especially pious. She marries happily in the end but actually supports herself and her grandmother most successfully as a school teacher prior to her marriage. Mary's character and motivation are clearly established in these opening passages of the novel. Note also the author's choice of a pen name.

"I will go this morning, if you think it best, and hear what Mr. Crawford will say to me," said Mary, as she stood washing cups and saucers after breakfast.

"I don't know what to say to it, dear," replied Mrs. Burnam [Mary's grandmother], "for this is your birthday, and I have all along promised you that when you were eighteen, you should have my consent to try to earn something. Yet when the time comes, my heart misgives me. It will indeed be a sad day to me when you go into the factory, for I shall be thinking all the time what your poor father would say, were he alive, to have you get your bread in such a manner, but not what he would love you the better for being industrious, and so dutiful to your grandmother. For I know it is not to get fine clothes for yourself, but comforts for me, that makes you so desirous to go out to work, but I don't think he would consent. Oh, no, I am sure that he would not consent to your being with people who were not good and serious. I never shall forget what he said to me on his dying bed: 'My dear mother,' said he, 'with all my hard labor, I shan't be able to leave you and my poor little girl, very well in the world, for though you own this little snug house, and the clever bit of land about it, and have got along in times past, yet when I am gone, you will find a difference. Though you will have to work hard to get along, I know you will contrive to spare time to teach Mary (as you did me) to read the Bible and to talk to her about what it contains. When Mary is grown up, she will, I am sure, want to return some of your goodness (for the knowledge of the Bible, that you will give her, will make her dutiful) and if she should incline to show her gratitude by earning something for you, you will be careful, dear Mother, that she does not work for any one, or with anybody who is not good, for then she may forget her Bible, and your advice, and go astray after all.' "

"How can I, my child, after this that your father said to me," cried Mrs. Burnam, "allow you to leave me?"

"I would not, dear grandmother," said Mary, "do anything for the world to make you uneasy; or any thing you think my father would dislike, were he alive, but I cannot think even he would have any objections to my working in the factory. The young people there are much better than you suppose."

Mary had set up the little breakfast table, and waited nearly two hours before Mrs. Burnam granted her reluctant consent to the solicitations of her grand-daughter, who, the moment she received it, hastened to Mr. Crawford, the superintendent of the cotton factory in the neighborhood to whom she offered her services, which were readily accepted, and on some abatement of wages, he complied with her request of having the privilege to leave the factory at sunset; the infirmities of her grandmother rendering her attentions necessary in the evening. The lightness of her heart was only rivaled by her steps as she returned home filled with anticipation of future pleasure, from having it in her power to procure for her grandmother the comforts which declining life had made peculiarly needful. The glow of filial benevolence kept her unusually cheerful through the day, and it was not till she united with her grandmother at night, in petitions for divine protection, amidst the temptations and difficulties to which she might be exposed, that she remembered that there was any labor, or there were any privations, attending her new situation.

Women in Medicine

Midwives, 1762[12]

Ezra Stiles (1727–1795), a traveling Congregational minister who later became president of Yale College, remarked upon the large number of babies which this Newport, Rhode Island midwife had delivered, indicating the possibilities for money-making in the cities as well as the size of colonial families. Midwifery had traditionally been a woman's occupation, but by the end of the eighteenth century, the upper class began to rely upon male doctors who specialized in obstetrics. Male practitioners would eventually crowd female midwives out of the field, though middle class women used them until the mid-nineteenth century and European immigrants into the twentieth.

July 22, 1762

Mrs. Turner of Newport, midwife, showed me her list of women she had delivered from January 8, 1745/6, to July 22, 1762, mostly in Newport, perhaps 30 off the Island in the whole term. I counted the list and found deliveries, white, in the year:

1746	95	1754	146
1747	102	1755	160
1748	116	1756	152
1749	136	1757	160
1750	136	1758	191
1751	152	1759	171
1752	133	1760	178
1753	161	1761	206
		To July 22, 1762	103
			2498

In this term she delivered 284 Negroes. Died in Newport, A.D. 1760, whites 175, of which 41 were infants.

No allowance is made for twins. It is judged that she delivers three quarters of the women in town.

The New York Lying-in Hospital, 1799[13]

Like most charitable institutions, this hospital had a male board of governors which handled its financial and legal affairs. It also had a medical staff of four male doctors. Yet women played important roles as volunteers on the visiting committee which oversaw the daily operations of the hospital, as paid resident matrons and nurses, and as medical students. The establishment of training hospitals such as these indicates the growing professionalization of medicine which would in the next century almost force women out of medicine, except as nurses. Since most women had their babies at home until the 1920s, the patients in these early maternity hospitals were usually poor women upon whom the doctors could practice their obstetric skills.

LAWS, RULES, AND REGULATIONS

One or more female pupils shall be admitted on the recommendation of the physicians, for the purpose of receiving instruction in the art of midwifery, to remain in the house during the pleasure of the Governors, and at the time of her or their admission, to pay into the hands of the Treasurer such a sum as the Governors may consider a sufficient compensation to defray the expenses of her or their support, as incurred by the house.

DUTIES OF THE MATRON

With the directions of the Visiting Committee, she is to purchase wood, provisions, and all other stores, except medicines, for the Hospital.

To take charge of all stores, wines, spirits, sugar, molasses, linen, blanketing, household furniture, and all other necessaries for the Hospital.

To visit the sick twice every day, at least, and see that they are properly attended by the nurses and servants employed in the house.

She shall oversee all the patients and servants; take care that the different chambers, beds, bedding, linen, clothing, etc., be clean, and to that end, all the patients and servants shall be obedient to her direction.

To be present at the delivery of all the patients, and to have in readiness everything necessary for the comfort of mother and child.

RULES RESPECTING PATIENTS

Application for admission into the Hospital must be made in the first instance to any one of the subscribers or physicians, who, if they think proper, will give recommendation [for admission].

No patient having the venereal disease shall be admitted to the Hospital except under extraordinary circumstances.

No unmarried woman shall be admitted as a pauper, except under extraordinary circumstances.

That no patient remain in the house longer than 4 weeks before delivery [or] 4 weeks after delivery except in case of sickness.

That such patients as are able shall assist in nursing others, in washing and cleaning the rooms, and such other services as the matron may require.

Poor and Dependent Women

Danvers, Massachusetts, 1767[14]

Colonial law provided that the local political institutions must care for those who could not care for themselves with tax monies provided by the local citizenry. For this reason communities tried to exclude persons who might become public responsibilities and to distribute as few public funds as possible to discourage continued dependence on public charity. This tradition has survived to the present although the responsibility for the care of dependents is no longer borne exclusively by local government. Some of the seventeenth-century poor were simply given the necessities of life, which was called "outdoor relief"; others who were less able to care for themselves were kept in public institutions like the alms-house in Boston described by Cotton Mather in 1691. In small towns like Danvers, however, the poor were kept in private homes, chosen on the basis of the lowest bid. Notice the age and gender of these dependent people and the possessions which defined their poverty. What factors might explain the different rates paid to the householders who took in these people?

An account of the poor that was put out April 13, 1767, and the places where and with what the persons were to have for keeping them:

Elizabeth Moar, a poor child, to Israel Chever for one year to keep from the 13th of April, 1767, at £ 6,18,8.

Samuel Boyce, one of the poor, to John Waters one year at £ 2,0,0.

Hannah Haibord, one of the poor, to John Waters, from the 20th of March, 1767, to next March, at £ 6,13,4.

Margaret Royal, one of the poor, to Samuel Putnam one year to keep from the 13th of April, 1767, at £ 5,10,11.

Sarah Croel, a poor child, to Jonathan Tarbell for one year from the 13th of April, 1767, at £ 6,11,9.

Jean Woieat, one of the poor, to Ezra Batchelder one year to keep from April 13th, 1767, at £ 5,10,11.

Bridget Weabe, one of the poor, to Elisha Flint to keep one year from the 13th of April, 1767, at £ 6,18,8.

Thomas Neallson, one of the poor, to Elisha Flint to keep one year from the 2d day of June, 1767, to £ 8,8,0.

Isaac Peeas, one of the poor, to David Putnam to keep one year from the 2d day of June, 1767, at £ 6,18,8.

Joseph Vearey, one of the poor, to Elisha Flint, to keep one year from the 2d day of June, 1767, at £ 6,18,8.

An inventory of what the poor of the town has this present year, March 2, 1767, and taken by the Overseers of the Poor at Danvers:

Sarah Veary, age 75 years, hath one good feather bed, one bolster, one pillow, one pillow case, one coverlet, one blanket and sheet, and very comfortably for wearing apparel.

Thomas Nelson, age 98 years, no bed or bedding, but comfortably off for clothes, except shoes.

Joseph Veary, age 66, no bed or bedding, but comfortably off for clothes except britches and shoes.

Elizabeth Moar, age 2 years.

Samuel Boyce, age 47 years, hath an under bed, feather bed, and 2 rugs.

Hannah Haibord, age 87 years, hath a good feather bed and other household stuff and well clothed.

Margaret Royal, age 65 years.

Bridget Weabe, age 98 years.

Isaac Peeas, age 69 years, with a bed and bedding.

William Henfield, age 80 years, and his wife, age 68 years, hath beds, bedding, clothing and household goods and wearing apparel.

Caleb Wolles, age 64 years, and his wife, age 68 years, hath no bed, nor bed clothes and very poorly for clothing.

Abigail March, age 87 years, hath a feather bed, bolster and rug and clothing.

Kingston Parish, Virginia, 1756[15]

In the southern colonies, the local parish and its vestry or government board of laymen cared for the dependent. During the eighteenth century, the number of women who became recipients of public charity increased due to the rapid and dramatic economic changes and social disruption which shook women loose from their families and often left them poverty-stricken. In this Virginia parish, however, women also provided charity for others and got paid for it. Pay was in the designated amounts of tobacco, which was accepted as currency in Virginia at this time. What similarities or differences are there between these dependents and those in Danvers?

AT A VESTRY HELD FOR KINGSTON PARISH
IN THE YEAR OF OUR LORD, 1756

Present: The Reverend Mr. John Dixon, minister;
   Mr. Charles Blacknall, Captain Gwyn, church wardens;
   Mr. William Tabb, Mr. Charles Debnam, Captain Kemp Plummer,
   Mr. John Hayes.

Ordered that tobacco be levied as follows:

To the Reverend Mr. Dixon, Minister	1600 & cask
To Thomas Dawson, clerk	1200 & cask
To John Davis, clerk of vestry	1700 & cask
To Ann Pallister, sexton	400
To Mary Gordan, sexton	400
To Captain John Clayton, clerk of the county	454
To Mr. Charles Tomkies, sheriff	72
To Elizabeth Evans and two children	800
To Ann Pallister for keeping two children 3 months	150
To Elizabeth Baker for keeping Jane Hundley	400
To Averilla Bridge	400
To Elenor Huts	500
To John Bridge	400
To Lucy Summers	300
To George Hudgen for keeping a child	700
To Deborah Edwards for keeping Christian Owen	400
To Elizabeth Bridge	300
To Sarah Merchant for keeping her mother	500
To Thomas Jarrett for keeping his father	400
To Lewis Peed for keeping Onner Powers	1000
To John Hudgen for keeping the child of Ash Berries	583
To Thomas Forrest for keeping the said child for two months	117
To Richard Davis for clearing the new church yard	100
To Hannah Fordom, widow	300
To Robert Bridge	300
To George Mullens for taking Thomas Longest, a child of Mary Longest, to be bound to him	800
To Izbel Parrett, widow	300

Upper-class Women

Nancy Shippen, the Urban "Lady," 1783[16]

Nancy Shippen was born in 1763, daughter of a distinguished and wealthy Philadelphia family. Her personal letters and memoirs record a flirtatious youth; she entertained both British and American soldiers during the Revolution. This journal, however, was begun in 1783 after she had left her husband, the aristocratic philanderer Henry B. Livingston, whom she had married at eighteen. She returned to her parents' home with her two-year-old daughter, whom her husband later reclaimed. The journal entries illustrate the life of a fashionable "lady" with no significant work to do.

JOURNAL

April 10th

After breakfast rode out with Lord Worthy [her father]. Had a conversation about Lord B. [her husband] and dear Leander [an admirer]. His sentiments corresponding with mine made me extremely happy—Would to God it was a happiness that would last—but the die is cast—and my life must be miserable! Lord Worthy sees the consequences of my unhappy choice too late. It is well for me he sees it at all.

April 11

Saw Leander—spoke to him—he praised my sweet child—good man!

April 15

Dressed my darling baby, kissed her; and for some minutes was happy— received a message from Miss B____and Miss M____—returned an answer— would be happy to see them—how insipid the company of formal acquaintances! Miss B. is handsome and well bred—but unentertaining. Miss M. agreeable. We chatted—sung—walked in the garden—the afternoon more agreeable than I expected.

April 16

Worked at my needle in the morning as usual, and read. In the afternoon visited Mrs. Bland—found a great deal of company—a great part of it insignificant and trifling.

April 17

This morning went to St. Paul's Church, where I heard a lively discourse preached by Mr. Magan—In the afternoon had company.

April 18

This day I spent entirely alone, enjoying my own meditations—they were not unpleasant—I feel calm and composed, and please myself with the reflection of having conformed to the will of my parents in the most important action of my life—O! May I reap the benefit of it! I'm sure I shall! I have the sweetest child that ever was born—in her I shall be most blest.

April 27

Heard from Lord B.—obdurate man! He still continues to persecute me with his reproaches—God knows that I do not deserve them. How miserable should I be if it was not for my dear child. Would to Heaven he could but see it perhaps it would soften him and make him relent.

May 4

Felt dull and stupid all day. Mr. Washington drank tea with me in the afternoon. We sang, laughed, and played at chess. Upon the whole spent the evening very merrily—Lady Worthy and young Worthy of the party.

May 14

Detained all last evening by company, and today I am engaged to go out of town with Lady Worthy and Mrs. Bland and Mr. Washington and spend the day at Chaillot. We shall spend a very rural day—8 in the evening—just come home—undressed and played with Peggy, and sit down now to write. It was one of the most agreeable jaunts I ever had in my life. The day fine, the company agreeable, and the best rural dinner I ever ate. We walked by the River Delaware—we sang—we rambled about the woods; played at chess—in short, the variety of the scene, and the sociability that prevailed throughout the company served to make it a delightful day. I am now sleepy and my darling baby cries for her bedfellow.

Ladies Society for the Relief of Poor Widows with Small Children, 1799[17]

Not all wealthy women were content with a leisurely life of repining like that of Nancy Shippen. Some, prompted by the Christian tradition of charity, by a desire to curb the potential disorderliness of the lower class, or perhaps simply by a need to get out of the house, formed private charities such as this one to supplement meager public efforts to aid the poor. The women who volunteered to visit the poor in their homes established the tradition of "friendly visiting" used by nineteenth-century charity workers and today by social caseworkers. Why are the recipients of this charity regarded as having "peculiar claims on the public beneficence?" What do the stringent conditions attached to this charity say about these women's attitudes about poverty and about their own motives? Notice the similarities between this society and the New York Lying-in Hospital, also a charitable operation.

Among the many humane institutions in this city, there is none for the particular assistance of a large class of sufferers, who have peculiar claims on the public beneficence, viz, POOR WIDOWS WITH SMALL CHILDREN.

Commiserating [with] their situation and persuaded that none can be relieved with happier effect, a number of ladies have formed for their exclusive aid, a Society for the Relief of Poor Widows with Small Children.

Every Manager shall insert in a book kept for the purpose the names, places of abode, and circumstances of the widows whom she relieves together with the names and ages of their children, and the kind and amount of the relief granted to each family. This book must be presented at every meeting of the Managers.

Every Manager shall endeavour to find schools for the children on her books, and places in sober virtuous families for such of them as shall be put into service.

No exceptions shall be made to this rule but for reasons approved by the Board.

The Managers shall exert themselves to create and maintain habits of industry among their applicants, by furnishing them, as far as possible, with suitable employment.

Relief shall not be granted to any applicants till they be visited at their dwellings by one of the Managers, and particular inquiry made into their character and circumstances. Immorality excludes them from the patronage of the Society.

No applicant, unless in very particular cases, shall be relieved who refuses to put out to service or to trades, such of her children as are fit; and to place the younger ones of a proper age, at a Charity School.

Relief shall be given in necessaries and never in money, but by a vote of the Board.

Black and White Women Together, 1797[18]

Because of its Quaker population, Pennsylvania, particularly Philadelphia, became an early center for activities on behalf of slaves and freed blacks. White women were active in founding colonial schools, and the schools described here reflect not only an interest in education but an attempt at interracial cooperation. Teaching would become the profession most open to women of both races. Compare the goals of these women with the goals of the Ladies Society for the Relief of Poor Widows with Small Children.

Early in the year 1793 the Committee of the [Pennsylvania] Abolition Society, for improving the condition of free blacks, purchased on a ground rent of fifteen pounds per annum, a lot of ground situated on the north side of Cherry Street, on which they soon after placed a frame building and opened a free school for the instruction of children of color of both sexes; in this school are taught spelling, reading, and needlework. Eleanor Harris, a black woman, being judged well qualified, has been employed as their teacher since the opening of the school. Her salary is one hundred dollars per annum; she is provided with a dwelling in the house and with fire wood. The children are furnished with the necessary school books. The expenses of the school are defrayed out of the particular funds of this committee, raised by donations, legacies, and annual subscriptions. The school is regularly visited every month by the committee of education. The number of scholars who generally attend is thirty.

In the year 1771 two schools for the instruction of black children, male and female, were instituted by the Society of Friends, on a lot of grounds belonging to them in Willing alley. A house was built, and the school supported by voluntary contributions from the members of that society. The teachers live in the house rent-free, and are provided with firewood—no children of color whether slaves or others are refused admittance to the school. The average number in each school is about forty scholars.

In the year 1795 a number of young women of this city formed a society for the purpose of teaching black women and girls reading and writing. They have procured a school room, give their personal attendance as teachers alternately, provide fire wood, and for those who are not able to procure them, books and stationery. The expense is defrayed by voluntary contributions. The school is held in the evening during the fall and winter months. The average number of scholars who attend is thirty.

Exceptional Women

The economic and political changes of this period, the migration into cities and frontier settlements, the ethnic diversity, and the dispersion of the population allowed for flexibility in women's work and lifestyles. The mistress of the southern plantation, for example, had always had important managerial functions within the limits of her role as wife and second-in-command. Husbands absent for political, military, or business reasons, however, allowed their wives or their daughters, like Eliza Lucas Pinckney, a great deal of latitude in their conduct of the family farm. The independence and competence of Abigail Adams, whose husband John was perenially absent serving his country during and after the Revolution, have been often noted; she was only one of thousands of women left to manage alone during those years.

The women who actually served on the front lines during the Revolution were primarily camp followers or the wives of soldiers, who traveled with the patriot armies because they had no other means of support. The disruptions of wartime, however, often weakened social custom, allowing the most energetic women, like Deborah Sampson Gannet, to slip unnoticed into male roles.

The Revolution also loosened the chains of slavery for some blacks. Slaves fought on the patriot side (and for the British as well) in exchange for freedom. Gradual emancipation by some northern states also helped to swell the free black population, allowing black women, as well as men, to play independent economic roles, like the teachers in Philadelphia, or like Jemima Hunt.

Eliza Lucas Pinckney[19]

Eliza Lucas Pinckney (1722–1793) was left in charge of her father's large South Carolina estate when she was seventeen years old, while he served in the British army in the West Indies. She was fascinated with horticulture and developed, through painstaking effort, a strain of indigo which became the staple export of her colony. Her husband's death in 1758, shortly after her marriage, left her again manager of several estates at which she was again successful. Her letters, written while she was still single, show how busy and productive a wealthy southern lady might be.

Dear Miss B[artlett],

Why, my dear Miss B, will you so often repeat your desire to know how I trifle away my time in our retirement in my father's absence? Could it afford you advantage or pleasure I should not have hesitated, but as you can expect neither from it I would have been excused. However, to show you my readiness in obeying your commands, here it is.

In general then, I rise at five o'clock in the morning, read till seven, then take a walk in the garden or field, see that the servants are at their respective business, then to breakfast. The first hour after breakfast is spent at my music, the next is constantly employed in recollecting something I have learned least for want of practice it should be quite lost, such as French and shorthand. After that I devote the rest of the time till I dress for dinner to our little Polly and two black girls whom I teach to read, and if I have my papa's approbation (my Mama's I have got) I intend [them] for school mistresses for the rest of the Negro children—another scheme, you see. But to proceed, the first hour after dinner as the first after breakfast, at music, the rest of the afternoon in needlework till candle light, and from that time to bedtime, read or write. Mondays my music master is here. Tuesdays my friend Mrs. Chardon (about 3 mile distant) and I are constantly engaged to each other, she at our house one Tuesday—I at hers the next and it is one of the happiest days I spend. Thursday, the whole day except what the necessary affairs of the family take up is spent in writing, either on the business of the plantations, or letters to my friends. Every other Friday, if no company, we go a-visiting so that I go abroad once a week and no oftener.

O! I had like to forgot the last thing I have done in a great while. I have planted a large fig orchard with design to dry and export them. I have reckoned my expense and the profits to arise from these figs, but was I to tell you how great an estate I am to make this way, and how 'tis to be laid out you would think me far gone in romance. Your good uncle, I know, has long thought I have a fertile brain at scheming. I only confirm him in his opinion, but I own I love the vegetable world extremely. I think it an innocent and useful amusement. Pray tell him, if he laughs much at my project, I never intend to have my hand in a silver mine and he will understand as well as you what I mean.

We have some in this neighborhood who have a little land and few slaves and cattle to give their children that never think of making a will till they come upon a sick bed and find it too expensive to send to town for a lawyer. If you will not laugh too immoderately at me, I'll trust you with a secret. I have made two wills already. I know I have done no harm, for I [learned] my lesson very perfect and know how to convey by will estates real and personal and never forget in its proper place, him and his heirs forever, nor that 'tis to be signed by 3 witnesses in presence of one another.

A widow hereabouts with a pretty little fortune teased me intolerable to draw her a marriage settlement, but it was out of my depth and I absolutely refused it, so she got an abler hand to do it. Indeed she could afford it. But I could not get off from being one of her trustees to her settlement and an old gentleman the other. I shall begin to think myself an old woman before I am well a young one, having these weighty affairs upon my hands.

Deborah Sampson Gannet (1760–1812)[20]

Deborah Sampson Gannet was another exceptional woman. She dressed in soldier's uniform and served in the Continental Army during most of the Revolutionary War without detection, long enough at any rate to receive a pension from the United States government. Although the facts of her life are fascinating, equally interesting is this account and explanation of her behavior by a male author who was clearly trying to fit Gannet into his preconceptions about femininity.

My first business with the public is to inform them, that the FEMALE, who is the subject of the following memoirs, does not only exist in theory and imagination, but in reality. And were she not already known to the public, I might take pride in being the first to divulge a distinguished character. Columbia has given her birth, and I estimate her natural source too highly to presume she is dishonoured in the acknowledgement of such an offspring.

She was born and educated in humble obscurity—distinguished during her minority only by unusual propensities for learning, and few opportunities to obtain the inestimable prize. At the age of eighteen she stepped forward upon a more exalted stage of action. She found Columbia, her common parent, enveloped and distracted with confusion, anguish, and war. She commiserated as well as participated [in] her suffering. And as proof of her fidelity and filial attachments, she voluntarily offered her services in the character of a Continental soldier, in defense of her cause; by which she seemed resolved to rescue the rest of her brothers and sisters from the flagrant destruction, which every instant seemed ready to bury them in one general ruin.

After delineating the life of a person it seems natural to recapitulate in a closing assemblage, the leading features of [this] character.

Perhaps a spirit of enterprise, perseverance, and competition was never more distinguished in a female than in Miss Sampson. And whilst we are surprised she left her own tranquil sphere for the most perilous, the field of war, we must acknowledge a circumstantial link in the chain of our illustrious revolution. She would never accept a promotion while in the army, though she was urged to take a lieutenant's commission. Let this be a memento to Columbia's daughters; that they may beware of too vicious scuffles with our sex. We are athletic, haughty, and unconquerable.

Jemima Hunt, 1811[21]

This black free woman had the opportunity to make a very significant and unusual contribution to her family's welfare. It would be interesting to know how Hunt was able to earn this sum of money. Note that her petition stressed the economic necessity of a two-parent family.

JEMIMA HUNT

Petition number 5870, Southampton County, December 9, 1811 Petition To the Honorable, the Speaker and House of Delegates of the General Assembly of Virginia.

"The petition of Jemima Hunt (a free woman of color) of the County of Southampton, humbly sheweth that some time in the month of November, in the year 1805, your petitioner entered into a contract with a certain Benjamin Barrett of said County for the purchase of Stephen, a Negro man slave, the property of said Barrett, and husband to your petitioner, for the sum of ten pounds annually for ten years, and the said Barrett farther bound himself to take the sum of ninety pounds if paid within five years and at the expiration of that time to make a complete bill of sale for the said Negro Stephen, which will appear by reference being made to the obligation entered into between the said Barrett and your petitioner. Your petitioner further states that she has paid the full amount of the purchase money and has obtained a bill of sale for the said Negro Stephen; who (being her husband) she intended to emancipate after she had complied with her contract. But in some short time after, as your petitioner has been informed, an act of Assembly was passed, prohibiting slaves, being emancipated after the law went into operation, from residing in the state. Your petitioner farther states that she has a numerous family of children by the said Stephen, who are dependent upon the daily labor of herself and husband for a support, and without the assistance of her husband Stephen, they must suffer or become burthensome to their county.

Therefore, your petitioner humbly prays that the legislature would take her case into consideration and pass a law to permit the said negro Stephen to reside in the State after emancipation, and to enjoy all the privileges that other free people of colour are entitled to and as in dutybound your petitioner will ever pray, etc."

Seventy persons signed the above petition.

NOTES

1. Karl J. R. Arndt, *Harmony on the Connoquenessing: George Rapp's First American Harmony, 1803–1815* (Worcester, Mass., 1980), pp. 103–4.

2. Margaret Van Horn Dwight (Bell), *A Journey to Ohio in 1810*, ed. Max Farrand (New Haven, 1920), pp. 5, 16, 40, 56, 62–64.

3. John C. Fitzpatrick, ed., *Diaries of George Washington, 1748–1799*, vol. III (Boston, 1925), pp. 293–95.

4. Kirtland and Morse Family Papers, 1779–1909, MS. 1463, Western Reserve Historical Society, Cleveland, Ohio. Reprinted with permission of the Western Reserve Historical Society.

5. Elizabeth Donnan, ed., *Documents Illustrative of the History of the Slave Trade in America*, vol. III (Washington, D.C., 1932, 1931), pp. 30–31.

6. *New England Courant*, April 2–April 9, 1722; May 14–21, 1722.

7. *Pennsylvania Gazette*, May 13, 1742; July 22, 1742.

8. *Virginia Gazette*, October 6, 1768.

9. *The Norfolk Herald*, February 8, 1814.

10. John C. Fitzpatrick, ed., *Diaries of George Washington, 1748–1799*, vol. IV (Boston, 1925), pp. 37–38.

11. [Sarah Savage], *The Factory Girl* (Boston, 1814), pp. 1–7, 9–10.

12. F. B. Dexter, ed., *Extracts from the Itineraries and Other Miscellanies of Ezra Stiles, 1748–1794* (New Haven, 1916), p. 29.

13. Laws, Rules, and Regulations for the Government of the Lying-in Hospital of the City of New York (New York, 1799), n.p.

14. *Historical Collections of the Essex Institute*, Vol. 2 (Salem, 1860), pp. 85–87.

15. C. C. Chamberlayne, ed., *Vestry Book of Kingston Parish* (Richmond, Va., 1929), pp. 88–89.

16. Ethel Armes, ed., *Nancy Shippen: Her Journal Book* (Philadelphia, 1935), pp. 139–44.

17. Constitution of the Ladies Society Established in New York for the Relief of Poor Widows with Small Children (New York, 1799), pp. 1–9.

18. *Minutes of the Proceedings of the Fourth Convention of Delegates from the Abolitionist Societies Established in Different Parts of the United States, Assembled at Philadelphia, May 3, 1797* (Philadelphia, 1797), pp. 31–34.

19. Elise Pinckney, ed., *The Letterbook of Eliza Lucas Pinckney, 1739–1762* (Chapel Hill, N.C., 1972), pp. 34–35, 40, 41. Reprinted with permission of the University of North Carolina Press.

20. Herman Mann, *The Female Review, or Memoirs of an American Young Lady, Whose Life and Character are Peculiarly Distinguished, Being a Continental Soldier, For Nearly Three Years, in the late American War, During Which Time She Was Called, with Punctual Exactness, Fidelity, and Honor, and Preserved her Chastity Inviolate, By the Most Artful Concealment of Her Sex* (Dedham, Mass., 1797), pp. v–viii; 239–240.

21. *Journal of Negro History* 13 (January 1928): 88–89.

BIBLIOGRAPHY

Jeffries, Julia Roy. *Frontier Women: The Transmississippi West, 1840–1880.* New York, 1979.

Kerber, Linda and Mathews, Linda DeHart, eds. *Women's America: Refocusing the Past.* New York, 1982.

Kessler-Harris, Alice. *Out to Work: A History of Wage-Earning Women in the United States.* Oxford, 1982.

Norton, Mary Beth. "Eighteenth-Century Women in Peace and War: The Case of the Loyalists." In Nancy F. Cott and Elizabeth Pleck, eds., *A Heritage of Her Own: Toward a New Social History of Women.* New York, 1979, 136–51.

———. *Liberty's Daughters: The Revolutionary Experience of American Women, 1750–1800.* Boston, 1980.

Ryan, Mary. *Womanhood in America from Colonial Times to the Present.* New York, London, 1979.

Spruill, Julia Cherry. *Women's Life and Work in the Southern Colonies.* New York, 1972.

7   WOMEN AND RELIGION, 1700–1815

The transformations which took place in the religious lives of Americans in this period were as dramatic as the accompanying economic changes. The powerful established churches, Congregational and Anglican, gave way to a proliferation of Protestant churches and organizations, both native and immigrant, and fresh waves of Protestant evangelicalism recalled the missionizing fervor of the seventeenth century. Religious diversity was stimulated also by the immigration of non-Protestants—Catholics and Jews. Simultaneously, rationalism attracted middle-class and educated Americans. This was reflected most clearly in the ideals of the Enlightenment, espoused by the political and intellectual leadership which directed the American Revolution and shaped the first American political institutions. Rationalism also left its mark on some Protestant denominations such as Unitarianism.

In the seventeenth century, only a few very exceptional women, such as Anne Bradstreet and Elizabeth White, wrote of their religious experiences, allowing male ministers to give literary definition to female religiosity. But in the eighteenth century, women increasingly became authors as well as subjects of religious literature. The purpose of these later writings was the conversion of their large and probably female readership. Equally significant were the scores of female missionary societies which financed male missionaries and also proselytized families and neighbors. Since churches also supplemented the meager charities and services to the poor provided by public officials, women became active in church-based benevolent activities, forming their separate organizations and using their presumed piety to move into the public arena.

Women also joined Protestant sects which allowed them unorthodox roles of leadership or quasi-equality. The theological justification for this lay in the Protestant belief in the spiritual equality of the sexes, but the male dominance of the established churches in the seventeenth century allowed for little practice of this belief, except in the case of Quakers. The fragmentation of these older churches opened the way for women to put the doctrine of equal sanctity into practice.

The experience of women within the Roman Catholic church was in some ways different, but in other ways similar. Except for the Virgin Mary, women had little status or power within the Church; its rigid religious hierarchy maintained the power of the male clergy. Still, this time period did produce Mother Elizabeth Seton, the first American saint and founder of the first American female religious order, which pursued the same benevolent tasks as did Protestant lay women.

There is little argument among historians over the increased numbers and roles of women in Protestant churches and growing female influence over clergy. Barbara Welter has called this the "feminization" of American Protestantism; although she describes this primarily as a nineteenth-century phenomenon, feminization clearly has its origins in the eighteenth century, if not earlier.

However, as in the case of eighteenth-century changes in women's work lives, historians disagree whether this feminization represents gain or loss for American women. Keith Melder, for example, has located the "beginnings of sisterhood," which would later culminate in the women's rights movement, in the religious and benevolent activities growing out of the Second Great Awakening. Mary P. Ryan, however, has concluded from her study of Utica, New York, that evangelical activities may have brought a short-term expansion of female roles but a long-term contraction as maternal evangelism diminished into maternal associations narrowly concerned with children and family.

Anne Douglas has described the alliance between women and Protestant clergymen as damaging to both and argues that the feminization of Protestant theology contributed to the conservatism and sentimentalization of American thought and culture. Welter's more recent analysis of women missionaries in the nineteenth century concedes that although these women played more important roles in a less important institution, the church, missionary work nevertheless gave them a sense of satisfaction and pride which might have had broader social implications in the future.

Whether women gained or lost, the eighteenth and early nineteenth centuries offered them new roles as writers, revivalists, missionaries, and benevolent ladies which helped to shape their own lives and the direction of American churches.

VARIETIES OF THE PROTESTANT EXPERIENCE

The conversion experience, a powerful inner-emotional awareness of sinfulness and the desire for salvation, was central to seventeenth-century Protestantism and a prerequisite for Puritan church membership. The converted often sought to bring the blessings of salvation to others. In the seventeenth century this missionary impulse had provided strong impetus for the settlements in New England particularly.

For Indians, regardless of the time period, conversion meant espousal not only of Christianity but of white culture and values, and for Indian women, this meant the adoption of white definitions of femininity, including monogamy; missionaries hoped this would also help to civilize Indian men. To this purpose, missionary societies were founded, preachers sent forth, and schools established, although mostly for male Indians.

This emotional pietism and evangelicalism surfaced throughout the eighteenth and nineteenth centuries. The best known early example is the Great Awakening, which began with Jonathan Edwards' scores of conversions in Northampton, Massachusetts, in 1733–1734, and nearby towns in the Connecticut River valley, and then flourished and spread under the direction of the great British evangelist George Whitefield during his journeys around the country in 1740–1743. The Second Great Awakening began in the 1790s and continued through the first decade of the nineteenth century, having its most significant impact on small towns and villages in northern New England and New York, which became known as the "burned over district" because of the flames of religious revivalism which swept over it.

Both awakenings split the established churches and created new ones, providing men and women with a widening variety of religious experiences and roles. The awakenings also encouraged the growth of missionary societies in which white women, still barred from the ministry by most Protestant denominations, could act as spiritual leaders.

Awakenings and Conversions

David Brainerd, Indian Conversions, 1746[1]

Brainerd was a missionary to the Indians of New Jersey and Pennsylvania for the Society for Propagating Christian Knowledge. He was apparently a powerful preacher in the evangelical style associated with the frontier, but even so, his description of the successful conversion of a young woman should be analyzed cautiously. With some few exceptions, Protestant missionaries had little luck at converting the Indians. The reader ought to be skeptical also of the alleged motives of the Indian couple, who might have had reasons for their behavior other than the desire for salvation.

There was one remarkable instance of awakening this day, that I can't but take particular notice of here. A young Indian woman who, I believe, never knew before she had a soul, nor ever thought of any such things, hearing that there was something strange among the Indians came to see what was the matter. She called at my lodgings, and when I told her I designed presently to preach to the Indians, laughed and seemed to mock, but went however to them. I had not proceeded far in my public discourse before she felt effectually she had a soul, and before I had concluded my discourse, was so convinced of her sin and misery, and so distressed with concern for her soul's salvation, that she seemed like one pierced through with a dart, and cried out incessantly. She could neither go nor stand, nor sit on her seat without being held up. After the public service was over, she lay flat on the ground praying earnestly, and would take no notice of, nor give any answer to any that spoke to her. I hearkened to hear what she said, and perceived the burden of her prayer to be [in Indian language] i.e. have mercy on me, and help me to give you my heart. And thus she continued praying incessantly for many hours together.

This was indeed a surprising day of God's power, and seemed enough to convince an atheist of the truth, importance, and power of God's word.

There was one of [the Indians] who had some time since put away his wife (as is common among them) and taken another woman, and being now brought under some serious impressions, was much concerned about that affair in particular, and seemed fully convinced of the wickedness of that practice, and earnestly desirous to know what God would have him do in his present circumstances. When the law of God respecting marriage had been opened to them, and the cause of his leaving his wife inquired into, and when it appeared she had given him no just occasion by unchastity to desert her, and that she was willing to forgive his past misconduct, and to live peaceably with him for the future, and that she moreover insisted on it as her right to enjoy him, he was then told, that it was his indispensable duty to renounce the woman he had last taken, and receive the other who was his proper wife, with which he readily and cheerfully complied, and thereupon publicly renounced the woman he had last taken, and publicly promised to live with and be kind to his wife during his life, she also promising the same to him.

And here appeared a clear demonstration of the power of God's word upon their hearts.

Hannah Hill's "Legacy," 1718[2]

This description of the death of an eleven-year-old Quaker girl reminds us of the strength which seventeenth-century women like Anne Bradstreet and Mary Rowlandson drew from their deep religious faith. The "Legacy" was published to inspire the conversion of others, especially women. The death of young women, particularly when accompanied by the appropriate signs of spiritual salvation, became a popular subject of both religious and secular literature.

Tender Reader,

As the ardent desires of the deceased were for the general good and welfare of all the sons and daughters of men, under what denomination soever, so 'tis hoped the effect of that same love, which filled her heart will redound [in] this little book which is published as her last bequest to the world, that God over all may be glorified in his own works and thy heart with hers, may lovingly say, so be it, now and for evermore.

AMEN

On the twenty-third day of the fifth month, this dear Child was seized with a violent fever and flux which so increased upon her by the third day of the week following that both herself and others present expect she would have departed. But the Lord was pleased to continue her a little longer, to testify of his goodness for the encouragement of the living. At this time she was in a deep travail of spirit concerning her future state, and diverse times crying out, Am I prepared! Am I prepared! Oh, that I might die the death of the Righteous and be numbered with them at Thy right hand, O Almighty God! Prepare me, prepare me for thy Kingdom of Glory.

Then she earnestly entreated those that stood around her to help with their prayers, that her passage might be easy.

A friend present (being moved thereto and sympathizing with her afflictions) kneeled down to prayer, during which (notwithstanding her extreme pain) she lay still, with great attention, and lifting up of hands and eye; a little after she said, Father, I shall die, and am now very willing, and [was] admonished (without fear or doubting to rely on God's mercy, whose love to innocent children was so exceeding great that Christ had bid them come unto him).

Doctor Owens (after all hopes to her recovery failed) came to visit her. She prayed him to sit down beside her, and said, My dear Doctor, all the town knoweth thou art a good doctor, but I knew from the beginning I should die, and that all your endeavors would signify nothing. But Doctor (added she with a pleasant air), the Lord has hitherto given me patience, and I shall pray to him for more, that I may be enabled to hold out to the end, for my extremity of body is very great.

When any would seem to encourage her, with hopes of recovery, she made light of it, saying, Why is there so much to do about me? Who am but dust and ashes? We are all but clay and must die.

She would diverse times say to her dear mother, Art thou sorry I am going to see dear brother? And to others about her, Why are you troubled and weep, seeing I am going to a better place. Adding, O that the messenger would come!

At a certain time, near the medium of her six days, in a most violent extremity of pain with a sorrowful countenance and a very mournful voice, she said, O my dear mother, I fear the Lord is displeased with me again because I am continued thus long, to endure this extremity of body which none knows but myself, nor can any think how great my pains are.

About an hour before her decease, being in a slumber, she said, The fire would not cease burning, until the chaff was all consumed, though men strive never so much in vain to quench it. Then took drink from her mother's hand, and said, Now my dear mother, pray lay thy head close to mine, and pressed hers toward her mother's bosom.

Then she recommended her spirit to God, saying, Glory! Glory! Glory! And so as with the sound of a hymn, this innocent lamb closed her eyes and expired as one fallen into a sweet sleep, without groan or sigh.

Phillis Wheatley, 1773[3]

Wheatley (1753–1784) was born in Africa and brought to this country as a slave. Her Boston owners allowed her to learn to read and write, and she was manumitted in1773. Her poetry often had religious themes, such as this one from her book *Poems on Various Subjects, Religious and Moral.* She was hardly typical of black women, but her religious faith was important to her as it was to so many other women of this period. Compare this expression of faith with the others you have read.

> On Being Brought From Africa to America
> T'was mercy brought me from my pagan land
> Taught my benighted soul to understand
> That there's a God, that there's a Saviour too:
> Once I redemption neither sought nor knew,
> Some view our sable race with scornful eye,
> "Their colour is a diabolic die."
> Remember, Christians, Negroes, black as Cain,
> May be refin'd and join th'angelic train.

The Second Great Awakening: Mrs. Clarinda Preston, 1805[4]

Like Hill's "Legacy," this narrative appeared after the subject's death as a memoir in a religious journal; this document is also autobiographical, as were Elizabeth White's and Anne Bradstreet's writings. Compare this experience with those of the seventeenth century. What other changes in women's lives are suggested by Preston's recollections?

[My family] practically said unto the Most High, depart from us, for we desire not the knowledge of thy ways. But glory to God, whose tender mercies are over all this works! God manifested strange designs of mercy toward myself, the degenerate plant of a strange vine. I began to be seriously impressed about the age of eighteen. I could find no rest day or night. I flew to secret prayer. Having long been inclined to think and speak lightly of awakenings, and of the concerns of the soul, I resolved to conceal my feelings as much as possible, and though I imagined I had a new taste for public worship, and experienced a sort of pleasure in reading the Bible, yet my ideas were very confused and indistinct respecting the way of salvation through Jesus Christ, having received but little instruction in doctrinal points.

At times I felt my heart much opposed to what are commonly denominated the doctrines of grace; but hearing a sermon which so clearly exhibited the propriety of God's being a sovereign, and finding my reason in such a good measure convinced, I resolved never more openly to oppose the doctrine. Being in the habit of disputing with a near relative upon religious subjects, I often advocated the doctrine of divine decrees. I was not, however, so firmly on the side of God and of religion, as to be willing to risk my reputation in the gay circle, by refusing to comply with solicitations to youthful amusements. Accordingly, when a ball was appointed, and I invited, among others, I interrogated myself as follows—shall I go and hazard the loss of my soul, and expose myself to the pains of eternal damnation? Or shall I stay at home, and lose the friendship of the world, which has hitherto been dearer to me than life? After I had endeavored to implore the divine blessing, I went to the ball and was as gay as the gayest.

But an abused conscience will not always sleep. Instead of rest and the siren song of festivity and joy, I felt an unsupportable weight of guilt. Still I was in pursuit of happiness; and my ardor did not abate but took fresh courage at disappointment. I resolved upon more steady and useful line of conduct, and became very economical of my time, improving as much of it in reading and writing as possible. That I might lay a better foundation for improvement, I spent several months at a respectable boarding school in a neighboring parish, where I endeavored to be fashionably religious, which is in effect to possess no religion at all. After this I was engaged in school-keeping and domestic duties, not fully persuaded of the truth of the divine declaration, that "the friendship of the world is enmity with God." But hearing of awakenings in a number of towns adjacent, I became solicitous with regard to myself, while I found I was trifling upon the brink of ruin.

On a certain occasion while conversing with a woman who was much of the same stamp with myself, as it respected certain serious impressions, I told her that I had been for a considerable time unusually hardened; that I had much reason to fear I had so slighted the invitations of the Gospel and grieved the Spirit of God that the Lord had said, let her alone. Upon this, she said she had a book which would suit my case which was Doddridge's *Rise and Progress of Religion in the Soul*. It was indeed a welcome messenger. It spoke directly to my conscience and left me wholly without excuse.

Although I had found that my sins had made a separating wall between God and my soul, and I could neither pray nor weep, yet now I found the partition broken down, and that I could enter in by the door, saying, whose joy is like unto my joy, for it is the joy of penitence. I resolved, by the assisting grace of God, let others do what they would, I would serve the Lord.

Church Builders and Missionaries

Presbyterian Church of Christ, Canfield, Ohio, 1804[5]

Like the early Puritan churches, this small church was formed by an assembly of like-minded men and women who covenanted together.

It was supported by funds from the Connecticut Missionary Society, which also sent occasional clergymen to conduct services in the homes of church members. The records show how significant a role women played in this new and relatively informal church.

FORMATION OF THE CHURCH

Canfield, April 25, 1804

Several persons, inhabitants of this town, met together to confer upon the subject of uniting together in Christian Church. The Rev. Mr. Joseph Badger and Thomas Robbins, missionaries from the Connecticut Missionary Society, were present and attended with them. After a sermon delivered by Mr. Badger, the persons offering themselves produced recommendatory letters from the churches with which they had been connected, which were deemed satisfactory. The confessions of Faith and Covenant adopted by the churches in this vicinity were then read and approved. The persons presenting themselves, on being asked, then unanimously desired to be embodied in a church state. Adjourned to meet tomorrow.

Concluded with prayer

Thursday, April 26

John Everett, Sarah his wife, Nathaniel Chapman and Hepzibah his wife, Jonathan Sprague, Lidia Doud, and Mary Gillson, being examined in their experimental doctrinal acquaintance with Christianity, with their views in uniting together, were approved, and considered as worthy to be members in the Church of Christ. Adjourned till tomorrow.

Concluded with prayer

Friday, April 27

After a religious exercise, a sermon delivered by Mr. Robbins, Mary Brainard, and Lavinia Collar, were examined as candidates for membership in the Church and approved of. After which, the following persons, John Everett, Sarah Everett, Nathaniel Chapman, Hepzibah Chapman, Jonathan Sprague, Mary Gillson, Lidia Doud, Lavinia Collar, Mary Brainard, were solemnly organized in church state, entered into covenant with each other, and were solemnly charged to keep covenant with one another, and with God. They were then solemnly commanded to the care and protection of the Great Head of the church, by whose mercy and grace, may this tender vine planted in this wilderness, flourish and grow till it become a mighty and glorious tree.

Joseph Badger,
Moderator

Female Missionary Society, Massachusetts, 1804[6]

Missionary societies were important in the evangelization of the American frontier and later in the spread of the Protestant gospel around the globe. The Missionary Society of Connecticut, publisher of the journal in which this address appeared, was organized in 1797 to take the gospel to the heathen in Ohio and other parts of the western wilderness and, as noted, was the sponsor of the Presbyterian Church of Christ in Canfield, Ohio. Although phrased in spiritual language, this address was actually meant to raise funds to distribute Bibles and ministers. Church work was generally regarded as suitable for women, but note the female author's slightly defensive tone.

Worthy and respectable friends,

Are we not engaged in a glorious cause, and may we not hope for the divine presence of our God, and expect his blessing to rest upon us? What can be more animating to a heaven-born soul, than to be striving to advance the interest of the dear Redeemer, and doing everything in its power (the grace of God attending) to build up his kingdom in this world? Methinks that every child of God must and will say when he reflects upon the late happy meeting of the Female Society: how transporting and soul-refreshing was that precious season!

And when we contemplate upon that wise and judicious plan, which was proposed by our worthy and reverend pastor, that of forming ourselves into a society for the purpose of contributing for the relief of our poor heathen brethen who are perishing in the native darkness, can we be destitute of gratitude to him? What can more sensibly touch the feelings of a tender, pious heart, than this consideration: that one soul should perish for the want of knowledge? Can anyone feel the power of religion and not wish others feel the same? If we have ever tasted that the Lord is gracious, we shall long to have others partake with us. And if so, we shall be ready to improve every opportunity that God gives us, to manifest our love for our dear Lord and Master. How thankful ought we to be, to the Supeme Being, that we are indulged this precious opportunity, which we now enjoy? Is it not animating to think of being used as instruments in the hand of the great God, of bringing some poor, ignorant souls to the knowledge of truth as it is in Christ Jesus? It surely is.

Then what calm serenity and heavenly peace will set upon every countenance if Jesus deigns to converse with us. But it may be, that some will be filled with doubts and fearful apprehensions. We must look out for trials, that will perhaps sift the true Christian as wheat. Many reproaches have already and will still be cast upon the Female Society. This is no sure evidence that the cause is not good, or that the work is not the Lord's.

Christ says, if they have persecuted me, they will also persecute you. We will have enemies without, and perhaps some within, who will not be friendly to the cause, and they may bring up an evil report of this good work. But, my friends, let us not fear, neither be cast down. But rather obey Jesus, and stretch forth the hand of faith and lay hold of those promises of God, which are applicable in such a case.

The last words which our dear Lord spoke to his disciples were, observe all things whatsoever I have commanded you, and lo, I am with you always, even to the end of the world.

Address to the Female Bible Society of Philadelphia, 1814[7]

This society was formed to distribute free Bibles to the poor of Philadelphia. The Reverend Bishop White's address reveals the close connections between this missionary activity and benevolent or charitable undertakings, as the society distributed relief to the poor as well as the Gospel. Although women had traditionally engaged in both kinds of activities, White, as he defends the appropriateness of such undertakings for women, suggests that male and female spheres of activity have already been clearly delineated. White's important role in support of the society also suggests, as does the preceding document, the growing alliance between women and male ministers, symptomatic of the feminization of religion in this period. Note also the typically eighteenth-century explanation of poverty.

Having been present in this respectable company of ladies about a week ago when the proposal was made to them for the forming of themselves into a Society for the distribution of the Bible, I took the liberty of delivering my opinion in favor of the measure. Since that meeting, the subject has been frequently in my mind, and I take this opportunity, at the request of the Parent [Bible] Society, of renewing the expression of my opinion.

The question was asked (and by the ladies determined to contribute at least their money to the object) whether their donations might, with equal utility, be thrown into the treasury of the Society already instituted, and conducted by the other sex. It was answered, and is now repeated, in order to show perseverance in the sentiments 1st. That there will be a greater number of persons, not merely contributing but taking such an interest in the work, as to induce others also to contribute and opportunities may occur, and 2nd. That in the line of distribution, there come under your notice many cases of judges, and especially as to the question, how far the pecuniary relief of poverty would be enhanced by the additional gift of a Bible, with the prospect of its being both acceptable and profitable.

If there should press upon the minds of any of you, the apprehension of exceeding the bounds which the modesty of your sex prescribes, it does not appear to me, that there is the least ground for such reproach, so long as the association is within yourselves. As to the circumstance that some of you will be called upon to act in certain official characters necessary for the conducting of business, if we look beyond names, there is nothing in the subject itself, but what would apply with equal force against the presiding at a dinner, or at a tea table, unless indeed it could be alleged, that this is less alien from the female character than the gathering and dispensing of alms. But this is a sentiment which, it is supposed, will hardly be hazarded by the most jealous asserters of the prerogatives of men.

It is one of the most conspicuous of the many beneficent properties of the scriptures, that they are the charter of the female sex against degradation and oppression. Look at the condition of women, in the countries where the religion of the Gospel is unknown; and all the arrangements of a domestic life will be found a comment on the position. Can it then be out of the sphere of your sex, to be actively engaged in disseminating a system of truth and morals which has so excellent a bearing immediately on your interest and through you or whatever contributes to the rectitude, to the decorum, and to all the rational enjoyments of social life?

You have also this especial interest in the same sacred treasure, that of our sex as well as your own, you are the earliest instructors of morality and in religion, and what is there deserving the commendation of the moral or religious, if detached from the lessons which speak so immediately from the Oracles of God, to the best sensibilities of the human heart? Under so loud a call as this to the estimation of the Bible, surely you can not be stepping out of your proper sphere, by being prominent in measures for the depositing of it in such needy families, as would otherwise be without the means which you enjoy, of rendering it salutary to their rising hopes.

It there were nothing more than the undeniable property of the human condition, that under all states of society the women sustain the greatest sorrows, it must give them an essential interest in the best source of countervailing consolation. That source is the word of truth, and this being the case, can it be out of character, where pecuniary means are within the power, to add their personal attention and exertion for the extending of so estimable a benefit?

Memoir of Rebecca Hubbs, 1814[8]

Rebecca Hubbs was a Quaker missionary and preacher in the tradition of the Quaker women of the seventeenth century. This account of her travels suggests the informality of Quaker religious services and the evangelical fervor characteristic of the other Protestant sects of this period. Compare the response of non-Quakers here with the response of Puritans to Quakers in the seventeenth century. What might account for the change?

Third-day, 16th
Came to St. Clairsville very much fatigued, and as I sat in the Friend's house where we put up, I said in my heart, How glad should I be if I could enjoy the privilege of working in my own house, lying down under my own roof and in my own bed, without looking out for new quarters every night. But I am a stranger in a strange land, as a poor pilgrim in this world. Then the prayer arose in my soul, O my dear Redeemer, for whose sake I have been made willing to leave all and to bear all that may be permitted to come upon me, suffer me not, I pray thee, to murmur or repine, but grant me ability to perform all thy will.

Third-day, 3d of Eighth month
Attended Stillwater meeting where was also our friend, Charity Cook. The case of Zaccheus, the publican, came before my mind and ability being afforded, I labored to encourage all who felt themselves little and low to come unto

Christ just as they are—for our dear Saviour condescended to be the guest of Zaccheus, and his visit had a glorious and blessed effect.

We stopped at New Lancaster to stay all night, and having a pain in my head, and being much fatigued, I laid myself down for a little rest. On rising, I saw nearly opposite the tavern a camp of soldiers, and found that the exercise which had been weighing upon my spirit, was for meeting with these soldiers. My concern increased so that I found I dare not omit making the effort, and accordingly gave up to it. I requested the men Friends who were with us to mention it to the tavern-keeper, and for some of them to go to the head officer, and inquire if he was willing his men should receive a visit from us next morning. Although I thought it my duty to make the effort, yet, as it was their review day, I concluded it would be in vain to expect to see them together in any stillness, as it was a time of so much noise and excitement, and they were preparing to go out to battle. On the return of the men Friends, they said they had seen the commanding officer on the subject, and he was very willing and proposed that we should meet next morning at the court house.

On seventh-day morning, near the time appointed, the officer came to the inn and asked if we had a choice in having the townspeople invited; for if we had, by ringing the court house bell, they would soon collect. I told him I had no desire to see any but the soldiers and officers, and such as he might choose to sit with him. He accompanied us to the court house, and then went to bring his troops, and pretty soon returned with them. Several officers came with the soldiers, and many of the townspeople, the meeting being made up of high and low, rich and poor, the lame and the blind. I may say with truth that they behaved with much solidity, and though on my first sitting down I felt so poor, and under such a sense of my own weakness, that I said in my heart, why am I thus left, and was ready to query whether I had ever known any good, yet blessed be the name of Israel's God He was pleased to grant a spring of Divine life, and to manifest his tender compassion and the redeeming love of his dear Son, and sent comfort into some poor souls. He was pleased to own the meeting with his living presence to the humbling and tendering of many, in particular, some of the poor soldiers, as well as some of the officers in their shining apparel. It was affecting to see their tenderness.

We left New Lancashire feeling the reward of sweet peace, and some tears of rejoicing fell from my eyes as I rode on my way, in contemplating the many favors and mercies I have received from the bountiful hands of Israel's God.

OUT OF THE PROTESTANT MAINSTREAM

The series of awakenings and the stirrings of abolitionist sentiment prompted by the Revolution spurred missionizing efforts in the North directed at free blacks, especially by the less orthodox Protestant churches. In the South, on the other hand, slaves were forbidden to assemble for religious or other purposes, which hindered—but did not prevent—the establishment of black churches and clergy. Protestantism left its mark on black leadership and the black people for generations to come.

A handful of white women sought alternative roles in religious institutions or alternative uses for theology outside of mainstream Protestantism. These women were beneficiaries of the toleration born of the religious pluralism and secularization of the period. A century earlier, they would perhaps have been banished, excommunicated, or whipped through the streets. Some of these women were in fact direct and indirect descendants of Protestant dissenters and Quaker heretics.

An even smaller number of Roman Catholic women found unusual positions for themselves in separate institutions within the church, then just on the verge of its own dramatic expansion of the nineteenth century. The Enlightenment belief in man's reason and a reasoning deity found female adherents, for whom these ideas provided justification for greater educational opportunities for women. The period was more tolerant of religious heterodoxy, however, than of divergence from conventional ideas about appropriate female conduct.

Protestantism

Slaves in the Moravian Church, 1766[9]

The Moravians were a German Pietist sect which first arrived in the New World in the 1730s with the conversion of the heathen Indians as their primary goal. They established several communities in the South and in Pennsylvania, their missionaries ranging the eastern seaboard, and won black as well as Indian converts. This is a partial list of black slaves and servants of a Moravian congregation in Philadelphia.

John Rebo, b. 1721, in Angola, Guinea, Africa. In 1733 taken to Jamaica, W.I. [West Indies], and in 1737 to New York. Baptized Oct. 19, 1747, by Bishop J. C. F. Cammerhoff.
Silpa Fortune (baptized 1761, Anna Elizabeth), b. Jan. 1, 1730.
Tobias, b. 1721, in Ibo Nation, Africa, brought to America in 1763.
Woodridge, b. 1748, in Guinea, Africa, taken to Barbados, W.I., 1756, and to Philadelphia in 1764.
Dinah, b. 1740, in Guinea, Africa, brought to Philadelphia in 1756.
Flora, b. 1725, in Ibo Nation, Guinea, Africa, brought to Pennsylvania in 1735.
Rose, b. 1726, in Guinea, Africa, brought here in 1736.

The Shaker Ministry, 1791–1809[10]

Mother Ann Lee (1736–1784), the founder of the Shakers, or the United Society of Believers in Christ's Second Coming, taught that God embodied both masculine and feminine elements, and as these records show, the ministry of the Shaker community was shared by both men and women. The Shakers practiced celibacy in their several communities, strictly segregating the sexes in their daily activities. Despite this—or because of it—the Shakers gained many female followers. Their communities had a membership of about 6,000 at their peak between 1830 and 1850, sending their own missionaries into the West to found Shaker communities. The first document illustrates the careful lines of male and female succession in these religious communes. The second document, however, shows that women's secular work was conventionally defined despite the rigors of frontier life.

[RECORD OF THE SUCCESSION IN THE MINISTRY]

1791
  The forepart of this year Father Eleasar Rand and Mother Hannah Kendall were sent from New Lebanon to gather the people at Harvard and Shirley.

1792
  Brother Daniel Tiffany was sent from Hancock to live with Father Eleaser, and deceases of consumption, September 24, 1793. Sister Unice Wilds went to live with Mother Hannah the season that Br. Daniel came to live with Father.

1794
  In Autumn Brother John Warner went to live with Father, and Sister Unice Wilds, released and moves into the family because of ill health, and sister Mehitabel Keep went to live with Mother. The order standing now thus—Father Eleasar, Mother Hannah, Brother John, and Sister Mehitabel.

1808, November 9th
  Father Eleasar, deceased, age 45 years. [Then] the first gift fell upon Mother Hannah, Brother John, and Sister Mehitabel remaining with her as helpers.

1816, August 16th
  Mother Hannah, deceased, age 55 years. [Then] the first gift fell upon Elder John with Sister Mehitabel, who has received a change in name from Mehitabel to Hannah and then to Rachael, and on the 17th instant Sister Hannah Bridges having been appointed went to live with Eldress Rachael in the Ministry. She has been for several years the Elder Sister in the 2d family, and the order now stands Elder John Warner, Eldress Rachael Keep and Sister Hannah Bridges.

1818, November 9th
  Grove B. Blanchard having been previously appointed to the ministry went to live with Elder John Warner and now the ministry stands thus—Elder John Warner, Eldress Rachael Keep, Brother Grove B. Blanchard, and Sister Hannah Bridges.

1822, March 3
  Eldress Rachael Keep—deceased, age 48 years, and on the 17th, Sister Caroline King being previously appointed went to live with Sister Hannah Bridges

in the Ministry, who now received the title Eldress Hannah. Thus, E. John, E. Hannah, Br. Grove, and Sister Caroline.

[DAILY RECORD OF EVENTS]

1790

Saturday [July] 24th

Father Joseph, Henry Clough, Mother Lucy, Thankful Hamlin, and Desire Turner started for Watervliet [another Shaker community].

Wednesday [August] 18th

Nathan Slosson went to Watervliet to carry Roswell Goodrich, Rhoda Chase, Susannah Cole, Hannah Benedict, and Patty (Martha) Cunningham, who have gone to live there.

Wednesday [September] 15th

Some time near the middle of the month, Calvin Harlow, Reuben Harrison, and Jeremiah Goodrich were sent over to Hancock to labor for a gift, and establish church order in that Society. Sarah Harrison was also sent from the church here.

Saturday [December] 11th

The little girls moved into the little brick shop.

1791

Monday [January] 12th

Mother, Elizur, Eleasar, and Hannah K. started for Harvard. Returned Friday 21st.

Saturday [February] 22

Four hands went to make a beginning at making sugar.

Wednesday [April] 28th

The brethren finished making sugar, and returned home this evening. They made 7 barrels, and caked nearly 200 lbs., and made one barrel of molasses.

1805

Tuesday [January] 1st

John Meacham, Benjamin S. Young, and Yoachar Bates, having been appointed by the ministry in union with the Church to make a journey to the Western States, and preach the gospel to the subjects of the great revival in that country, took their departure this day from New Lebanon for Kentucky and Ohio.

June

About the middle of this month the Church received a second letter from the missionaries in the Western States, giving information of their wearisome journey, their toil and labours, and requesting that new laborers be sent. Accordingly, the ministry concluded on sending Elder David Darrow, Daniel Mosley, and Solomon King.

November 12th

It [was] decided and agreed by the ministry and Elders for the Elder Ruth Farrington to go to the State of Ohio next spring. She is now to be called Eldress. Molly Goodrich is with her. She and other sisters are to go with her to Ohio.

Monday, April 21st

All things being in readiness for the journey to Ohio, the company consisting of Peter Pease, Samuel Turner, Eldress Ruth Farrington, Prudence Smith (now called Lucy Smith), Martha Sanford, Prudence Farrington, Molly Goodrich, and Ruth Darrows, all from the Church, and Constant Mosely, from the family on the hill, and John Wright from Hancock, in three wagons well loaded with all things necessary for the journey started off at 4 o'clock in the morning.

Saturday, July 5th

We received a packet of letters from our brethren and sisters in Ohio, dated June 5th, the company who started from hence on the 21st of April, arrived safely after a journey of 41 days.

1807
September 21

Today the hands commence working at the dam of our first saw mill.

September 30

Finish plastering the upper loft of the Elders' frame dwelling.

October 10

Elder David, Elder John, Daniel Joseley, Solomon K. and Saul Turner are at work framing the saw mill dam.

November 6

Sisters husk corn today; cold weather.

1808
October 26

Elder John Meacham, Samuel Turner, and Constant Moseley set out for Shawnee Run, Kentucky (now Pleasant Hill) to make it their home, and take charge of the Society there.

November 10
Our first school commences; male teacher John Woods, female teacher, Malinda Watts.

1809
January 4
Elder John Meacham and Samuel Turner, accompanied by Eldress Lucy Smith and Anna Cole, set out for Shawnee Run, Kentucky; the ministerial lot being now fully made up for the Society in that place.

Jemima Wilkinson, the Publick Universal Friend, 1799[11]

The experiences of Jemima Wilkinson (1752–1819) resembled those of the Shakers in several ways: the charismatic female leadership, the millennialism, the founding of a religious commune, the preaching of celibacy. Wilkinson assumed the role of prophetess within her community and surrounded herself with an entourage of young women. The author of this account clearly regarded her as an unpleasant anomaly, but Wilkinson's preachings and sometimes her practices were typical of the period's evangelical and communal impulses, as well as the important religious roles of women. The document also provides us with a later view of the Quakers, by this time an established church.

Friendsmill is a place, consisting of several houses, which takes its name from its being settled or founded by the Friends or Quakers. It lies in the center of the district, which is called the Friends' settlement.

One JEMIMA WILKINSON, a Quaker, and a native of Rhode Island, manifested so fervent a zeal in her religion, that at the age of twenty, she was admitted to all the meetings of the Society, which were held weekly, monthly, and quarterly, for settling the general concerns and watching over the conduct of the brethren. She at length fancied, that she was called to act some great and extraordinary part, and in this persuasion formed the project of becoming the leader of a sect. In the course of a long and dangerous illness, she was suddenly seized, or gave it out that she was seized with a lethargy, so that to her friends she appeared as really dead. She continued, several hours, in this situation; and preparations were actually making for her internment, when she suddenly started up, called for her clothes, declaring "that she had risen from the dead, and that she had cast off all her material substance, and retained only the spiritual." She went, accordingly, to the next meeting, as if with the authority of some celestial being, spoke there as one inspired, and gained some followers. She ere long, expressed her displeasure at some religious observances of the Quakers; and was, on this account, reprimanded by the meeting; which appears to have been precisely the thing she wished for and expected. Being now a persecuted person, at least by her own account, she began to gain some partisans. She preached publicly on the necessity of the abolition of all meetings convened to censure, of a reform of the church-establishment, of granting to the Friends universal liberty to preach what they pleased, without first asking leave to do so, etc. She soon made some proselytes, and at the same time drew on herself the displeasure of all, who adhered to the old forms of the religion of the Quakers. She experienced, therefore, a very unfavorable reception for herself and her doctrines, both in Philadelphia and New York. Wherever she came, every Quaker turned away from her with abhorrence, as the enemy of his religion; and all other persons deemed her a fool or an enthusiast. This disposition of the public she again called a persecution, it being favorable to her ultimate views. The number of her followers was now daily increasing; and as she confidently trusted it would become more considerable, she thought they might perhaps be willing to follow her. Accordingly, she proposed to a number of them, to flee from these regions of intolerance, and to settle in a place where they might worship God undisturbed, and free from that bitter spirit of persecution, which men had introduced in opposition to the divine will.

Soon after the country about Lake Seneca and Crooked Lake was fixed upon as the place of their settlement. The company of New York, which had purchased this land from the Indians, entered into a treaty for the sale of it with these reformed Quakers. They were promised three tracts of land, containing each six thousand square acres, which were to form three districts, and to which Jemima instantly gave the name of Jerusalem. Thirty families removed hither with her; but she had confidently expected three or four hundred more, of whom, however, not above twenty at least arrived.

We saw Jemima, and attended her meeting, which is held in her own house. We found there about thirty persons, men, women, and children. Jemima stood at the door of her bedchamber on a carpet, with an arm-chair behind her. She had on a white morning gown, and waistcoat, such as men wear, and a petticoat of the same color. Her black hair was cut short, carefully combed, and divided behind into three ringlets; she wore a stock, and a white silk cravat, which was tied about her neck with affected negligence. In point of delivery, she preached with more ease, than any other Quaker I have yet heard; but the subject matter of her discourse was an eternal repetition of the same topics, death, sin, and repentance. She is said to be about forty years of age, but she did not appear to be more than thirty. She is of middle stature, well made, of a florid countenance, and has fine teeth, and beautiful eyes. Her action is studied; she aims at simplicity, but there is somewhat of pedantic in her manner.

Roman Catholicism: Mother Elizabeth Seton, 1808–1812[12]

Mother Elizabeth Seton (1774–1821), the widow of a wealthy New York manufacturer, converted to Catholicism after his death in 1803. She founded first a school and then a teaching order of nuns, the Sisters of Charity. She was beatified in 1963 and canonized in 1975. These letters describing her daughter's religious faith and the collection of religious maxims written for her students provide a useful comparison of Catholic female piety with its Protestant counterpart, described elsewhere in this volume.

It is true: the dear, lovely, and excellent child of my heart is on the point of departure. The last week (second in February) she has been every moment on the watch, expecting every coughing-fit would be the last; but, with a peace, resignation, and contentment of soul truly consoling—not suffering a tear to be shed round her—she has something comforting to say to all, telling all her many companions who come occasionally to her bedside, "See how soon you may die! think how you would wish to be, if you were on this bed of death with me!"—always calculating with me, "If I was to live, dearest mother," and drawing all her conclusions that she is not only willing but happy to go, before she passes the dangers and trials of future years. When the last change took place, and cold sweat, gasping breathing, and agonizing pain, indicated immediate dissolution, the pain of her eyes so great she could no longer fix them, she said, "I can no longer look at you my dear crucifix, but I enter my agony with my Savior. I drink the cup with him. Yes, adorable Lord, your will, and yours alone, be done! I will it too. I leave my dearest mother because you will it—my dearest, dearest mother." Poor mother, you will say, and yet happy mother! You can well understand this. For me, dear friend, to see her receive the last sacraments with my sentiments of them, her precious soul stretching out toward heaven, the singular purity of her life, of which I could give you the most amiable proofs, my calculations of this world,—all dear friend, combine to silence poor nature.

The spring is come, and the voice of the turtle is heard in our grove. Arise, my love, and come away! Hasten to the arms of your Jesus, and fear nothing.

[MOTHER SETON'S ADVICE TO HER STUDENTS]

Do you love? Have no other will but that of your Beloved. Abandon yourself to him, and cast all your care upon him. He has said it; he will never leave you or forsake you. Trust and love.

"I have loved you with eternal love," says your Beloved, "and laid down my life for your sake. Come, then, follow me." Answer him, "Yes, dear Lord, even unto death." Courage and Love.

Be not grieved and afflicted if your good intentions fail you. Know your kind Master accepts even your desires, and what you would do if you could. Confidence and Peace.

Finish the work your Father had given you to do, and remember, after putting your hand to the plough, you must not turn back. Fidelity.

The light affliction of a moment will obtain for you a weight of eternal glory. Suffer, then, with love, and rejoice to be counted worthy to share with your Beloved. Love your Cross.

Do not try to get down from the cross, for the cross and your Jesus are inseparable. The way you walk in is covered with thorns, but it leads you direct to his throne. Courage and Faith.

Rationalism and the Enlightenment: Mary Wollstonecraft, 1790[13]

In her *Vindication of the Rights of Woman*, from which this excerpt is taken, the English feminist pled for equal education for women, blaming the male culture for shaping women into useless and virtueless ladies. Wollstonecraft's works were read by American women of this period—and later periods—who sought equality for women in all areas of life. She was much influenced by the thought of the Enlightenment. This is seen here in her humanist approach to deity, which she viewed as knowable and rational although omnipotent. Compare her statements with those of the more orthodox Protestant and Catholic women.

Probably the prevailing opinion, that woman was created for man, may have taken its rise from Moses's poetical story. Yet as very few, it is presumed, who have bestowed any serious thought on the subject, ever supposed that Eve was, literally speaking, one of Adam's ribs, the deduction must be allowed to fall to the ground; or, only be so far admitted as it proves that man, from the remotest antiquity, found it convenient to exert his strength to subjugate his companion, and his invention to show that she ought to have her neck bent under the yoke, because the whole creation was only created for his convenience or pleasure.

Let it not be concluded that I wish to invert the order of things; I have already granted, that, from the constitution of their bodies, men seem to be designed by Providence to attain a greater degree of virtue. I speak collectively of the whole sex; but I see not the shadow of a reason to conclude that their virtues should differ in respect to their nature. In fact, how can they, if virtue has only one eternal standard? I must therefore, if I reason consequentially, as strenuously maintain that they have the same simple direction, as that there is a God.

I know that many devout people boast of submitting to the will of God blindly, as to an arbitrary sceptre or rod, on the same principle as the Indians worship the devil. In other words, like people in the common concerns of life, they do homage to power and cringe under the foot that can crush them. Rational religion, on the contrary, is a submission to the will of a being so perfectly wise, that all he wills must be directed by the proper motive—must be reasonable.

NOTES

1. David Brainerd, *Mirabilia Dei inter Indicas* (Philadelphia, 1746), pp. 24–25.

2. *Legacy for Children, Being Some of the Last Expressions from and Dying Sayings of Hannah Hill* (Philadelphia, 1718), pp. 1–21.

3. Phillis Wheatley, *Memoir and Poems of Phillis Wheatley* (Boston, 1835), p. 48.

4. "Memoir of Mrs. Clarinda Preston," *Connecticut Evangelical Magazine* (November 1805): 185–87.

5. Presbyterian Church of Christ, Canfield, Ohio, Records, 1804–1807, MS. 1303, Western Reserve Historical Society, Cleveland, Ohio. Reprinted with permission of the Western Reserve Historical Society.

6. "An Address, Written by a Female, to the Female Missionary Society, Massachusetts," *Connecticut Evangelical Magazine* (August 1804): 72–76.

7. The Constitution of the Female Bible Society of Philadelphia (Philadelphia, 1814).

8. *A Memoir of Rebecca Hubbs, Minister of the Gospel in the Society of Friends, Late of Woodtown, N.J.* (Philadelphia, n.d.), pp. 32–38.

9. Elizabeth Donnan, ed., *Documents Illustrative of the History of the Slave Trade to America*, vol. III (Washington, D.C., 1932), p. 459.

10. Record of the Succession in the Ministry at both Harvard and Shirley, Mass., Reel 32 and Reel 40. Domestic Journal of Important Occurrences Kept for the Elder Sisters at New Lebanon, Reel 60, and Daily Record of Events of the Church Family in Union Village, Ohio, Reel 40, Shaker Manuscript Collection, Western Reserve Historical Society, Cleveland, Ohio. Reprinted with permission of the Western Reserve Historical Society.

11. Francois Alexandre Frederick, Duc de La Fochefoucauld-Liancourt, *Travels throughout the United States of North America* (London, 1799), pp. 110–12.

12. Charles L. White, *Life of Mrs. Eliza A. Seton, Foundress and First Superior of the Sisters and Daughters of Charity in the United States* (Baltimore, 1879), pp. 308–9, 479–80.

13. Mary Wollstonecraft, *Vindication of the Rights of Woman* (New York, 1845), pp. 26–27, 201.

BIBLIOGRAPHY

Douglas, Anne. *The Feminization of American Culture.* New York, 1977.

Kolmer, Sr. Elizabeth, A.S.D. "Catholic Women Religious and Women's History: A Survey of the Literature." *American Quarterly* 30 (Winter 1978): 639–51.

Melder, Keith. *The Beginnings of Sisterhood: The American Woman's Rights Movement, 1800–1850.* New York, 1977.

Ryan, Mary. "A Women's Awakening: Evangelical Religion and the Families of Utica, N.Y., 1800–1860." *American Quarterly* 30 (Winter 1978): 602–23.

Welter, Barbara. "The Feminization of American Religion, 1800–1860." In William O'Neill, ed., *Insights and Parallels: Problems and Issues in American Social History.* Minneapolis, Minn., 1973, 305–55.

———. "She Hath Done What She Could: Protestant Women's Missionary Careers in Nineteenth-Century America." *American Quarterly* 30 (Winter 1978): 624–38.

8 WOMEN AND THE LAW, 1700–1815

Under the inexorable pressures of a changing society, the American legal system underwent sweeping change during the course of the eighteenth century. The legal doctrines formulated by and for an agrarian society and the simple, informal systems of law derived from common-law rules and religious ideas had served well the needs of the small, geographically isolated rural communities that dotted the Atlantic coast in the seventeenth century. But the development in the eighteenth century of secular, competitive commercial centers, linked by roads and intracoastal shipping, necessitated fundamentally different rules and practices of law. Pressed by the needs of the times, American jurists turned instinctively to England.

Beginning around 1750, a rapid legal Anglicization was apparent throughout the thirteen colonies. One of the major developments was the professionalization of the American bar. Community prejudice, particularly in Puritan New England, against making profits from personal disputes, had contributed to the domination of the practice of law by amateurs, or pettifoggers, in the colonial period. But the growing secularization of American life and the increasingly conspicuous connection between law and political preferment made legal practice more attractive to many young men and traditional professions, such as the ministry, less so. The growth in the size of the legal profession by 1750 was matched by a corresponding rise in its prestige as male members of leading provincial families began to study for the bar. Large numbers of them, particularly from the plantation colonies, were trained at the English Inns of Court.

The professionalization of the American bar was accompanied by the gradual reception of English common law and procedures in the colonies. Although no substantial body of case law was in print until after the Revolution, the publication in 1765 of Sir William Blackstone's *Commentaries on the Laws of England* provided colonial lawyers with a concise discussion of English legal principles and statute law. As a result of the influence of great English text writers like Blackstone, English law, which had sent out wide if not deep roots in the seventeenth century, became so strongly implanted that by the time of the American Revolution the colonists looked on it as their birthright and their inheritance. In their struggle for independence, Americans tended to rely on the common law as the embodiment of their rights. To that extent the legal struggle was as much a cause of the American Revolution as politics or taxes.

The Revolutionary War itself produced a crisis in legal history, centering on the issue of whether to abolish common-law principles and institutions completely or to retain them. Despite a temporary rise of Anglophobia and a corresponding surge of Francophilia, the common-law tradition proved too deeply entrenched to be displaced by the civil law, which was, in any case, too technical to be read in Latin or French. Ultimately, through the so-called reception statutes, most states formally adopted the common-law tradition that was their heritage, although they continually adapted it to suit the requirements of the new republic. As the legal system evolved, far-reaching changes occurred in American law. For one thing, the subjects of the law were radically different from those prevailing in the seventeenth century. In keeping with their aim of establishing the kingdom of God on Earth, seventeenth-century communities had tried to secure conformity to Scripture through the regulation of personal conduct and behavior. The acquisitive societies that emerged in the post-Revolutionary period were more concerned with their members' economic well-being than with their spiritual health. The revolution in society and in the economy, and the decline of established churches during and after the Revolution, produced an equivalent decline in the legal enforcement of morality and a relative rise of economic crime. The new market economy also produced drastic changes in the law of property as feudal tenures, such as primogeniture and entail, which had long outlived their social usefulness, disappeared from the statute books and new laws, such as copyright and patent laws, which encouraged economic growth, appeared in their place.

The extent to which the reception of English law and the debates over it generated by the Revolution affected the legal status of women is not clear. On the one hand, the wholesale importation of common-law doctrine resulted in a vigorous reaffirmation of the laws of coverture in the new republic. Guided by Blackstone's chapters on husbands and wives, American jurists tried to make local practices conform to those of England, producing in some cases a regressive effect on the legal rights of women. On the other hand, the transplantation of equity jurisprudence acted to relieve some of the financial constraints by which women were bound under the common law. Certain legal mutations that had developed in response to the peculiar social and economic conditions in America survived the legal transformation, enabling married women from the propertied classes to enjoy a measure of economic power.

The Revolution itself produced other beneficial effects on women. An emerging market economy, together with the social and ideological forces unleashed by the Revolution, gave, at least to white women, a new civic visibility and a degree of economic autonomy they had never enjoyed before. Women's participation in the war effort politicized many women, prompting some of them to think better of themselves and to claim greater independence. Although the laws of coverture were reaffirmed in the young republic and in some cases became even more constraining, the debate over women's political status produced what one scholar has called the ideology of Republican Motherhood. A compromise between the continued exclusion of women from politics and their full integration into citizenship, the new ideology called upon women to serve the republic by instilling in their sons republican virtue. Thus were women for the first time given an explicit political role that anticipated later political and legal advances.

Although the common law continued to be preponderant through most of settled America, the colonization by France and Spain of the vast region known as *Louisiane* established the legal ideas of the Romano-Germanic system of law formed in continental Europe in the thirteenth century. Both the common-law system of marital rights and the community property system had a common conceptual origin. Firmly rooted in the hierarchal ideology that prevailed through most of the eighteenth century, both systems aimed to preserve the stability of the family by resting broad marital powers in the husband, deemed to be gifted by providence with the attributes requisite to strong family government. Wide differences, however, existed between the two systems, particularly in the area of property rights.

The law of community recognized two types of property of married persons: separate property and property held in a common fund. Either spouse might own separate property, so called because it is separated from the common fund in which both spouses have certain defined legal rights. According to the civil-law tradition, all antenuptial acquisitions by either spouse are separate as are all property and pecuniary rights acquired by either spouse during marriage by gift, devise, or descent. Although under the law the husband and wife share ownership in the common property or property acquired after marriage, the husband as *seul seigneur* enjoys full power of management and disposition of its profits. Should he, however, prove profligate, she may by law seize her portion or secure it out of his reach. Moreover, on the death of either spouse the common property is divided, with half going to the survivor, the other half to the heirs of the deceased.

In addition to a claim to half of the community property, the *Coutume de Paris*, which formed the basis of the law in Louisiana, prescribed dower rights. The *douaire* was the property claim of the wife to a share in her husband's personal property. Defined by customary law as half the inheritance held by the husband the day of marriage and half of what he might inherit during the marriage, the *douaire* assured the French woman a measure of economic security should she survive her husband.

Although the former Spanish possessions of Florida, California, New Mexico, Arizona, and Texas, among others, have become common-law jurisdictions, what is now the present state of Louisiana has successfully maintained the tradition of Romano-Germanic law to the present time. What is more, the community property system of marital property as it exists in California, Louisiana, and Texas, and with modifications in New Mexico, was derived either mediately or intermediately from the civil law, and persists in some form today.

DOMESTIC RELATIONS

Although there is some disagreement among scholars over the historical appearance of the modern family, most historians of the American family agree that the transformation occurred during the eighteenth century. To the new emotional and psychological dimension that the family had come to assume, the American Revolutionary War experience added a novel political purpose: preservation of the young republic. Convinced that the future of the republic would depend upon the public virtue of its citizens, the Revolutionary generation defined a new obligation of parenthood, and especially of motherhood: rearing virtuous sons and daughters for the republic. Inevitably the transformation of the concept of the family involved a reformulation of husband-wife and parent-child relationships. Characterized by mutual affection and companionship, the new concept of domestic relations qualified somewhat the power of the husband while expanding the authority of the wife, at least in family affairs and particularly where childrearing was concerned.

Although some scholars see this redistribution of authority as an important step in the modernization of family relations, the laws regulating such relations were slow to change. For the most part, the legal preeminence of the husband endured unaltered. Indeed the preachments of theologians, clergymen, and moralists on woman's historic subjection to man were vitalized by the publication in America of Sir William Blackstone's *Commentaries on the Laws of England.* A standard textbook for training American lawyers, Blackstone became the authority on women's status in law. Overlooking the corroding effects of equity jurisprudence on the common-law restrictions on women, Blackstone declared his famous dictum: "By marriage, the husband and wife are one person in law; that is, the very being or legal existence of the woman is suspended during the marriage, or at least is incorporated and consolidated into that of the husband, under whose wing, protection, and *cover,* she performs everything." The effort of Blackstone lawyers to make colonial laws conform to English practice eliminated some of the local variations that had previously operated in favor of women. Blackstone's doctrine was not, however, undisputed in America. The reformulation of interpersonal relations and the new concept of the family which followed from it operated as an ideological wedge which opened the way for the growth and development of the personal rights of women, particularly in the areas of divorce law and custody rights. The gains made by middle- and upper-middle-class women over their persons and property did not immediately extend to slave women or to poor women, whose lives were regulated by different sets of legal rules: the slave codes and the poor laws.

The Persistence of Patriarchy

Eliza Wilkinson, "On Seeing a Man Beat His Wife," 1781[1]

Despite the new status of the wife within the home, patriarchy persisted in American law. For example, the common-law doctrine of the dominion of the husband over the person of his wife, which assumed that his proprietary interest also extended to his right to reasonable chastisement, was undisturbed. In theory, if not always in practice, this permitted the possibility of wife-abuse. Although courts ordinarily protected a wife from random physical violence at the hands of her husband, scenes such as the one witnessed by a young South Carolina woman, Eliza Wilkinson, were perhaps not unusual. The poem inspired by the incident reveals something about the legal power that husbands held over their wives; at the same time it suggests a reason why marriage held out not only promise but anxiety as well for many young women.

> Poor Wives are made to Honour and obey.
> Must yield unto a husband's lordly sway.
> Whether you live in Peace, or horrid strife,
> You must stay with him, aye, and that for life.
> If he proves kind, then happy you will be,

If otherways——O! dreadful misery!——
Kind husbands now-adays you scarcely find
The lover's seldom in the husband's mind.
The imperious Mortal makes his wife his slave,
He *will*, he *won't*, yet knows not what he'd have.
While she—poor trembling Soul! in vain doth try
To please him: marks the motion of his eye;
He still storms on, while from his eyes flash fire.
She trembles more—is ready to expire.
Wou'd any stander by but hand a glass
He'd start! amaz'd! to see his frightfull face.
O shamefull sight, he cou'd not then dispute.
But that he made himself a very brute.
Guard me good Heaven whene'er I change my state!
That this may never be my wretched fate.——

French Law on Adultery, 1783[2]

In both common-law and civil-law jurisdictions, adultery was still regarded as a serious threat to domestic harmony and family stability. Both the common law and the civil law prescribed harsh punishments for adultery, which was still defined by reference to a married or betrothed woman and thus perpetuated the dual system of morality which had existed from colonial times. Although common-law courts tended to punish both offenders equally, French law in colonial Louisiana dealt more severely with the woman. For example, though the husband's adultery was not legal grounds for separation, the wife's was. Furthermore, a wife convicted of adultery lost all of her dower rights, as the following document shows.

Adultery is considered in France as a private wrong so that revenge is exclusively reserved to the husband, supervisor of the morals of his wife, in which he is the most interested party. And when the husband has no complaints about the conduct of his wife, no one else is permitted to complain against her. Otherwise it would be to surrender the family to a terrible inquisition filled with problems.

The separation of the domicile, when it is legally obtained by the wife, by no means deprives the husband of the right to oversee her conduct, nor does it deprive him of the right to accuse her of adultery, if she gives him cause. Since the separation does not give the wife justification or authority to alienate her property, still less does it have the effect of removing conjugal respect, which subsists as long as the marriage itself, and which can only be destroyed by the death of the husband.

Now is the time to ask if a husband who is convicted of an offense which results in civil death, has lost the right to charge his wife with adultery. One can say for the husband that civil death, not having the effect of destroying the marriage, it must not have that of destroying the rights that are attached;

that conjugal fidelity is an essential and necessary part of the contract entered into by both parties, under the seal of religion and the guaranties of the civil law. It would be inconsistent to admit that the condemnation of the husband results in surrendering him without defense to the insults of his wife and to give the latter (the wife) the hope of abandoning herself with impunity to disorder. Just as civil death does not open the douaire [the dower rights] (because according to the law, the husband although dead civilly is nevertheless considered living by his wife, who can only obtain widow's rights by his natural death), for the same reason the husband, until his natural death should have the exclusive use and possession of his spouse's (dower rights) and the legitimate means of maintaining it.

Challenges to the Patriarchy

An Act to Dissolve the Marriage of Peter Summers and Catherine, His Wife, 1782[3]

The growing importance of the family in American society ironically resulted in the liberalization of divorce laws and in the subsequent rise of divorce. As a result of the new conception of the family as companionate, grounds for divorce were significantly expanded, although they varied from state to state. New York's law, for example, permitted absolute divorce for the single ground of adultery, a result of the demise of Romano-Dutch law and the reception of common law; Rhode Island's law by contrast allowed divorce for "gross misbehavior" by either party. The size of the demand led generally to the rise of courtroom, or modern judicial divorce, although legislative divorce was still granted in some states (in Connecticut both forms were available). Recent studies show that men still filed for divorce more frequently than did women but the number of female petitioners increased during the eighteenth century. The expanded ability of women to gain divorces, and concomitant changes in the law of child custody, suggest some of the legal implications of the concept of moral motherhood.

Whereas Catherine Summers of the city of Philadelphia, wife of Peter Summers of the said city, victualler, has represented to the general assembly of this state that her husband, Peter Summers, has separated himself from her bed and her board, and has, since his intermarriage with her frequently beat her in a most cruel and inhuman manner and has estranged his affections from her and placed them on other women and has within the period aforesaid frequently committed the heinous sin of adultery and has boasted of such his crime, and has prayed the general assembly aforesaid to grant her leave to bring in a bill to dissolve her from her marriage with the said Peter Summers and the said general assembly willing to ascertain the truth of the said facts that justice may be done in the premises, and being thoroughly convinced of the truth of the said facts on a proper and legal examination having taken place in the presence of the said parties before a committee of this general assembly who have reported the testimony before them:

Be it therefore enacted and it is hereby enacted by the Representatives of the Freemen of the Commonwealth of Pennsylvania in General Assembly met, and by the authority of the same, That the marriage of the said Catherine Summers with the said Peter Summers be and is hereby declared to be dissolved and annulled to all intents and purposes whatsoever; and the said Catherine Summers and Peter Summers shall be and they are hereby henceforth respectively declared to be separated, set free and totally discharged from their matrimonial contract and from all duties and obligations to each other as wife and husband as fully, effectually and absolutely to all intents and purposes as if they had never been joined in matrimony or by any other contract whatsoever, any law, usage or custom to the contrary notwithstanding.

Rachel Teakle, Petition to the South Carolina Senate, 1802[4]

In the South, where adherence to English practice persisted from colonial times, divorce remained uncommon. Moreover, most southern states did not immediately adopt courtroom divorce, but continued the costly practice of private bills. Known as legislative divorce, these were private acts passed in response to individual petitions, such as the action being taken by Rachel Teakle against her husband, Richard Teakle. The legislature's response to Mrs. Teakle's petition is not known, but given the fact that as late as 1817 the South Carolina jurist Henry William Desaussure maintained that South Carolina had never granted a single divorce, it is highly probable that her request was denied, although she might have been granted a legal separation. The fact that southern legislatures retained jurisdiction over divorce after it had been granted to the judiciary elsewhere, suggests the endurance of patriarchy and of a social order that tended to cater to the interests of the upper classes.

15 November 1802
To the Honorable the Senate of the State of South Carolina the petition of Rachel Teakle formerly Rachel Darby Humbly shew that your petitioner a few months past was married to a person by the name of Richard Teakle. Your Petitioner asserts that she never knew the above named Richard Teakle as a man and he absented his self from me in a short time as may more fully appear by a Probate accompanying a petition laid before the House of Representatives your petitioner prays that your Honors will take her case into consideration and exonerate her from being called the wife of the above named Richard Teakle and to prohibit him from making use of any part of her property as his and your petitioner as in duty bound will ever pray

her mark
Rachel Teakle

Nickols v. Giles, Connecticut, 1796[5]

One of the most important components in the preservation of patriarchal power was paternal custody rights. Although the new notion of Republican Motherhood assigned to the woman primary responsibility for childbearing and home management, common-law guardianship rights, created in a feudal society for essentially economic reasons, survived long after the society that gave it birth, especially in the South, where the patriarchy remained more or less intact. The development of the child-centered family and the growth of the notion of moral motherhood led to the slow erosion of those old attitudes, however, and is reflected in the tendency of the courts to exercise judicial discretion rather than adhere strictly to common law in custody disputes. Although the courts were still far from turning custody over to women, this 1796 decision by a Connecticut appellate court to allow the mother to retain custody rights of her child is an important step in the history of modern child custody law and in the development of the wife's right of guardianship.

NEW LONDON COUNTY, SEPT. TERM, A.D. 1796
WILLIAM NICKOLS VERS. THOMAS GILES

William Nickols exhibited his motion for a habeas corpus to take a daughter of his, about three years old, from one Thomas Giles, who as he said, unjustly detained and withheld her from him, and unlawfully imprisoned her; and also to bring said Giles, before this court to show reason why he thus detained and imprisoned his daughter, &c.—Upon inquiry it appeared that the child was with its mother, who lived with her father the said Thomas Giles; that the child was well provided for; and said Nickols having no house and very little property, and very irregular in his temper and life, his wife had left him and went and lived with her father, where both she and her child were well provided for. Upon which the court refused to grant said writ.

Family Law of the Poor

The Overseers of the Poor of the Town of Vernon against the Overseers of the Poor of the Town of Smithville, 1819[6]

Balanced against the general improvement in domestic relations enjoyed by women of the middle- and upper-middle classes was the apparent degeneration of family life among the poor, owing, some scholars think, to the regressive effects of the poor laws. A primitive welfare system whose roots are traceable to the Elizabethan Poor Law, the family law of the poor obliged each community to support its indigent members through a system of tax levies. In response to the growing problem of indigency in the eighteenth century, settlement and removal provisions, which required candidates for poor relief to remain in the place ascertained to be their legal residence, were added to poor law regulations. In order to avoid adding welfare recipients to their relief rolls, many towns, like Vernon, New York, sued other towns under the settlement laws. The separation of families, like that of the Crittenden family, approved by the New York Supreme Court, occurred with increasing frequency in the nineteenth century. Such separation is evidence of what Maxwell Bloomfield has called "a dual system of family law," which on the one hand supported the institution of marriage and the family as a matter of public policy, and on the other hand unhesitatingly disrupted family life among the poor.

THE OVERSEERS OF THE POOR OF THE TOWN OF VERNON AGAINST THE OVERSEERS OF THE POOR OF THE TOWN OF SMITHVILLE

IN ERROR, on certiorari to the Court of General Sessions of the Peace of the county of Chenango.

On the 9th of November, 1816, two justices of Smithville, in the county of Chenango made an order for the removal of William Chittenden, a pauper, of the age of eleven years and five months, from Smithville to Vernon, and adjudged that his legal settlement was in Vernon. (Revised Statutes, 621, & c) There was an appeal from this order to the Court of General Sessions of the Peace of the county of Chenango, which affirmed the order. At the hearing, the appellants excepted to the order, 1. Because the justices had not adjudicated that the last legal settlement of the pauper was in Vernon; and 2. Because it did not appear, by the order, that the pauper was ordered or directed to remove to his former place of settlement, before the justices issued their warrant for removal.

It appeared in evidence, that about twelve years ago, Truman Chittenden, and Lois, his wife, came to Vernon, and remained there a few months, were warned out of the town, and departed, not having gained a settlement in that town. During their residence in Vernon, W. Chittenden, the pauper, was born. In 1800, and the two succeeding years, T. Chittenden resided in Lisle, in the county of Broome. Seymour, who was collector of Lisle, in 1801 testified, that he could not positively say whether he collected a tax of T. Chittenden, but he thought it likely that he did. Lois Chittenden, the mother of the pauper, testified that her husband paid one year a tax of six shillings, and she thought that he paid it to Seymour. Beach, who was collector in 1802, testified, that T. Chittenden was on his tax list; that he went to his house for the tax, and believed that he received it, though he did not recollect clearly, but he knew that he paid over the full amount of his tax bill to the treasurer.

About 1813, Lois Chittenden, with her family, of which the pauper was one, was removed from the town of Cincinnatus to the town of Lisle, by an order of two justices. The overseers of the poor of Lisle appealed from that order, and gave notice of the appeal to the overseers of Cincinnatus, who, thereupon, sent for her and her family, and brought them back to Cincinnatus. In consequence of this, the appeal was not prosecuted, nor the order reversed. It also appeared that, previous to making the order of removal by the justices of Smithville, L. Chittenden and her family, including the pauper, had been warned to depart.

The case, on the return to the certiorari, with the exceptions taken, was submitted to the court with argument.

Woodworth, J., delivered the opinion of the court. I will first consider the exceptions taken by the appellants to the form of the order. The justices "adjudge that the legal settlement of the pauper is in Vernon." This is sufficient; legal settlement, and last legal settlement, are the same thing, because, by every new settlement, the preceding one is discharged. (2 Salk. 473.)

The second exception is not tenable; for whatever might be the construction given to the statute, in a case where it is stated that the pauper was likely to become a charge, there is no ground for the objection, when it is alleged, that the pauper had actually become chargeable; in this latter case, the justices need not order the pauper to remove to his former settlement previous to issuing a warrant; for the statute only requires such previous order in cases where the pauper is likely to become a charge, not where he is actually chargeable.

The pauper was born in Vernon, which is, prima facie, his place of settlement, and remains so until the settlement to which he is entitled, by parentage, is discovered, (14 Johns. Rep. 334. Delavergne v. Noxen.)

The settlement of a child is where the father was last settled; if the father has none, the child must go to its mother's settlement. It is not pretended that the father or the mother of the pauper ever gained a settlement in Vernon; yet that town is chargeable, by reason of the birth of the pauper, unless it can be shown, that the parents gained a settlement elsewhere. This has been attempted in two ways; the appellants contend, that the order of removal made by the justices of Cincinnatus has not been reversed, and that this is conclusive, that the pauper was settled in the town of Lisle. It will be admitted, that an order not appealed from, is conclusive as to the place of settlement; but that is not this case; an appeal was made by the town of Lisle and notice given thereof. The overseers of Cincinnatus sent to Lisle, and brought back the pauper, preferring that course to a trial on the question of settlement; for this cause the appeal was not further prosecuted. The order made by the justices of Cincinnatus must be considered as abandoned, and at an end, and that by the consent of both parties. It was the same as if it never had existed, and consequently, Lisle was not concluded by it. The case of The King v. The Inhabitants of Lanchydd (Burrow's Settlement Cases, 658.) is in point.

It is lastly contended, that Truman Chittenden, the father of the pauper, paid taxes for two years in the town of Lisle by which he gained a settlement; the testimony on this point is satisfactory as to the payment of taxes for one year, but doubtful and uncertain as to the other. A settlement by payment of taxes, is gained by being charged with, and paying such taxes. (14 Johns. Rep. 88.)

Ira Seymour, the collector, has no distinct recollection that Truman Chittenden ever paid a tax to him, although he thinks it likely: he has no knowledge that he was charged with the payment. Lois Chittenden recollects that her husband paid a tax of six shillings one year, and thinks it was to Ira Seymour; but whether her husband had even been assessed, or whether the six shillings paid, if paid to Seymour, was a part of the public taxes of the town, we are left to conjecture. It would be manifestly unjust, from such uncertain testimony, to draw the conclusion, that Truman Chittenden ever gained a settlement in the town of Lisle.

The order of Sessions must, therefore, be affirmed.

Order of Sessions affirmed

PROPERTY RELATIONS

In the area of property rights, as in domestic relations, the record of the eighteenth century is ambiguous. Although the transformation of American society and of the economy argued for the abandonment of the old procedures and arrangements that had characterized family property law throughout the colonial period, lawmakers were reluctant to tamper with existing legislation for fear of the destabilizing effects on family relationships. As a result, changes in property law were slow to come about. In the meantime, however, women from the affluent classes of society took advantage of the remedies available to them through equity jurisprudence to protect themselves against the legal presumptions embodied in marriage. By resorting to equitable remedies such as the trust, the bequest, and the antenuptial or postnuptial contract, some women from the upper classes won limited economic concessions, which led eventually to a broadening of the wife's right to property and, in a more limited sense, to contract.

There were, to be sure, important shortcomings. Although the southern states generally had courts of chancery, Massachusetts and Pennsylvania, except briefly, had no separate courts of chancery, so that questions of equity had to be handled on a piecemeal basis by common-law courts. In other states where courts of chancery existed, they often had limited jurisdiction. Most importantly, however, equitable relief benefitted principally educated women from the wealthy classes, whose families were interested in protecting the family inheritance from profligate husbands. Finally, even though equitable relief led to a relaxation of certain restrictions, many constraints on women remained in force and, in the late eighteenth century, new ones were added. Nevertheless, in time the use of equitable remedies did erode some of the legal limitations on women. After the passage in the nineteenth century of married women's property acts, the protective devices that had once benefitted privileged women became available to all women.

Marriage Contracts

Marriage Contract between William Moody of Newbury and
Abigail Fryer of Berwick, 1714[7]

The principal device used to extend the property rights of married women was the institution of the wife's separate equitable estate, which could arise by trust, gift, bequest, or agreement between prospective marriage partners, as is the case in the prenuptial agreement between William Moody and Abigail Fryer shown below. Such an agreement could be used by both parties, but women like Abigail Fryer used it to assert rights in a legal system which accorded them no rights. By this agreement Moody relinquished his right to his future wife's estate and gave to her full managerial control, thus allowing her a degree of economic power denied to women under the common law. Like most women who made marriage settlements, Abigail Fryer was a widow whose experience in marriage probably influenced her desire to manage her own property.

This Indenture tripartite made and concluded this Ninth day of December 1714 Annoq... R[t]R[s] Georgi Magn Brittan. & c. Primo Between William Moody of Newbury in the County of Essex and Province of the Massachusetts Bay in New England Gent. of the first part, Abigail Fryer of Berwick in the County of York and Province aforesaid Widow of the second part and Stephen Sewall of Salem in the County of Essex Esquire & Jeremiah Wise of Berwick in the County of York on the third part witnesseth that whereas a Treaty of Marriage has been had and agreed on and intended by God's Grace shortly to be solemnized and consummated between the said William Moody and Abigail Fryer. It is covenanted and granted by and between the said parties as follows that is to say, in case the said marriage take effect, the said Abigail on her part doth grant and consent and agree that the said William shall be entitled to have and receive to his own proper use and behoove for ever, the sum of one hundred pounds in money of her estate of her former Husband Joshua Fryer and the full and free disposition and bestowment thereof according to her own good pleasure at her decease, by her last Will and Testament or otherwise, her coverture notwithstanding always securing and fully discharging the said William Moody his Executors and Administrators of and from all debts of her said former husband Fryer and her own debts contract in her widowhood if any appear or shall be demanded.

And the said William Moody for himself does accept the hundred pounds aforementioned in lieu of all pretension right title claim or demand to be had or made by him his Heirs' Executors or Administrators of in or to the further estate of the said Abigail or her said former husband, he his heirs & tc. being always secured and defended against all debts as aforesaid and does further covenant grant and agree to and with the said Stephen Sewall and Jeremiah Wise Trustees for and in behalf of the said Abigail their Executors and Administrators that she the said Abigail shall have full Power and Authority at any time or times during her Coverture and that notwithstanding, in and by her last Will and Testament or other instrument in writing to be by her executed in the presence of two or more credible witnesses to give bestow and imploy according to her good pleasure, at her decease all and singular her own, and remaining goods and estate of her said former husband and that such will or other writing by her executed shall be of the same force and effort as if she had been sole and unmarried.

And the said William does further covenant grant and agree to and with the said Trustees their Executors and Administrators that if it happen the said Abigail, to survive and outlive him the said William, she shall have and enjoy to her own use and behoove the best lower room in his the said Williams present dwelling house in Newbury aforesaid with the chamber over it and that part of the cellar underneath those rooms and that his heirs' Executors and Administrators shall provide and supply her with ten cords of good fire wood yearly to be laid down at the door and a good milk cow to be well kept winter and summer and also pay to her the sum of eight pounds in money or good lawful bills of public credit per annum during her widowhood bearing the name of Moody, but if she said Abigail shall intermarry, then to pay to her or her order, at the new dwelling House of the said William Moody, the sum of ten pounds per annum in money or good and lawful bills of credit as aforesaid during her natural life in lieu of all the provision made for her as aforesaid which is accepted by her and on her behalf accordingly.

In witness whereof the parties to these present have interchangeably set their hands and seals the day and year first within written. Mem. It is agreed and so to be understood that the provision made for the said Abigail as above, is in full of all her dower or thirds in your estate of your said William Moody.

Signed Sealed and Delivered
   in presence of us—
   the words (in the country of
   York Clerk) first interlined,   Abigail Fryer
   as also the word (Heirs) was   William Moody
   Interlined, between the seventh
   and eighth line, from the bottom
   in your second page—John Croade.

Humphrey Chadbourn

Marriage Agreement between John Custis and Frances Custis, 1714[8]

Because of the state's interest in preserving the institution of marriage, courts were reluctant to recognize prenuptial agreements, which by their very nature admitted the possiblity of the dissolution of the marriage. Contracts between married couples were even less widely recognized in law, both because of their presumed destabilizing effects on marital relations and because creditors opposed them on the grounds that they could be used to evade lawful debts. Nonetheless, as a result perhaps of the more egalitarian nature of marital relations in the post-Revolutionary War period, postnuptial agreements such as the one shown below became increasingly common during the late eighteenth and early nineteenth centuries. Although their importance should not be exaggerated, the growing popularity of postnuptial agreements suggests a tendency to view marriage as more of an economic partnership.

ORIGINAL DRAFT OF AN AGREEMENT ON FILE AT EASTVILLE, NORTHAMPTON COUNTY, VIRGINIA

Articles of Agreement between Mr. John Custis and his wife—

Whereas some differences and quarrels have arisen between Mr. John Custis of York County and Frances his wife concerning some money, plate and other things taken from him by the said Frances and a more plentiful maintenance for her. Now to the end and all animosities and unkindness may cease and a perfect love and friendship may be renewed between them they have mutually agreed upon the following articles this_____day of June anno Domi 1714:

1st. First it is agreed that the said Frances shall return to the said John all the money, plate and other things whatsoever that she had taken from him or removed out of the house upon oath and be obliged never to take away by herself or any other, anything of value from him again or run him in debt without his consent, nor sell, give away or dispose of anything of value out of the family without his consent, upon the condition that the plate and damask linen shall not be given or disposed of by the aforesaid John from the said during her life and the said John doth covenant said plate and linen to be delivered by the said Frances to the said John shall be given to the children of the said John by the said Frances immediately after her decease.

2d. That Frances shall henceforth forbear to call him the said John any vile names or give any ill language, neither shall he give her any but to live lovingly together and to behave themselves to each other as a good husband and good wife ought to do. And that she shall not intermeddle with his affairs but that all business belonging to the husband's management shall be solely transacted by him, neither shall he intermeddle in her domestic affairs but that all business properly belonging to the management of the wife shall be solely transacted by her.

3d. That the said John shall pay all the debts he has already contracted out of the debts now due to the estate and the money he has received if there will be sufficient to pay them; and that he shall enter into bond to Philip Ludwell in the sum of one thousand pounds that from hence forward he shall keep true and perfect accounts of all the profits and disbursements of his whole estate in any part of Virginia that he is now possessed of and also of all the estate he shall at any time hereafter by her means be possessed of in any part of the world, and shall produce the same accounts yearly if it be required upon oath. And that after all debts hereafter necessarily accrueing for buying clothes, tools and all the necessary for the servants and plantations, paying levies and

Quit-rents & making necessary repairs of his whole estate and also all other necessary charges accruing for the use & benefit of the estate which is to descend to the child of the said Frances are deducted and paid he shall freely & without grudging allow one full moity or half of all the clear produce of his whole estate as aforesaid anually to the said Frances for clothing herself and the children with a reasonable proportion thereof and the remainder to be all laid out in the education of the children & for furnishing and providing all things that are necessary for house keeping (that are to be brought from England) and Phisick so long as the said Frances shall live peace quietly with him, and that he shall allow for the maintenance and family one bushel of wheat for every week and a sufficient quantity of indian corn and as much flesh of all kinds as the stocks of cattle, sheep and hogs of his whole estate will afford without impairing them if so much shall be necessary, and sufficient quantity of cider and brandy if so much be made on the plantations: Provided that nothing herein contained shall be construed to debar the said John of the free command and use of anything that shall be provided for house keeping so as he does not sell any of it without her consent. Provided also that the condition of this bond be that if the said Frances do exceed the allowance herein expressed in these articles, run him in debt or break any of them the bond to be void and the allowance to cease.

4th. That the said John shall allow the said Frances to keep in the house to do the necessary work in and about the same servants she now hath vizt: Jenny, Queen, Pompy or such others in their stead and also Billy Boy or little Roger and Anthony or such another in his stead to tend the garden, go of errands or with the coach, catch horses and do all other necessary works about the house, and if any of them die your said John shall put others in their stead.

5th. That the said John shall allow the said Frances fifteen pounds of wool and fifteen pounds of fine dressed flax or fifteen pounds of wool in lieu thereof every year to spin for any use in the family she shall think fit.

6th. That the said Frances shall have free liberty to give away twenty yards of Virginia cloth every year to charitable uses *if so much remain after the servants are clothed.*

7th. That the said Frances shall have free liberty to keep a white servant if she shall think fit out of the above allowance so as the said servant be also subject to your said John.

8th. And foreasmuch as the one half of the clear produce of the tobacco being to be taken upon the sale of it and the clothing and other necessaries to be bought in England and that it will generally be at least twelve months before an account of sales can be had from thence and an invoice sent thither, therefore for the supplying the present wants of the said Frances the children and house in manner and for the use aforesaid, the said John shall allow to the said Frances fifty pounds in money if there shall be so much left remaining of the debts now due to the estate and money now on hand after all the debts already contracted by him or her shall be paid as aforesaid.

9th. That your said Frances shall render a true account under oath to your said John if he shall require it how your said fifty pounds and also your clear profits yearly are expended and laid out.

I do not remember Mr. Custis mentioned any sum for the bond. Mrs. Custis named 1,000£ but I do not know what he said to it.

French Marriage Contract, 1776[9]

In keeping with French family law, most parties contemplating matrimony signed standardized marriage contracts, such as the one between Jean Baptiste Boucher de Monbrun and Francoise Petit de Coulange. Typically all eighteenth-century French marriage contracts contained a clause declaring that the antenuptial debts and mortgage obligations of the respective spouses were their separate obligations, to be satisfied out of their separate property. The provisions dealing with *dot*, or dowry contributed by parents or others, usually stipulated both dower and the right of the spouse to a specific amount in the event of the dissolution of the community. The standard contract also included a donation clause, which generally stipulated a reciprocal gift to the survivor of all or part of the predeceasing spouse's estate.

A FRENCH MARRIAGE CONTRACT, 1776

Before Royal Notary of the Province of Louisiana, residing in New Orleans, in the presence of the undersigned witnesses were personally present themselves M. Jean Baptiste Boucher de Monbrun, Sieur de St. Lorent, son of the late Jean Etienne Boucher de Monbrun and Lady Francoise Charet with her father and mother, and Lady Francoise Petit de Coulange, and the late Francoise Gallard Chamelly, her grandfather and tutor, on presenting and stipulating conjointly with Mariane Herieux, his spouse, grandmother of the said minor, stipulating consent as well.

The above said parties in the presence and with the consent of their parents and friends be it known on the part of the said Monbrun of the great and powerful lord Pierre de Rigaud, Marquis of Vaudreüil Knight of the Military Order of St. Louis, governor in this province, of Madame a Marquis de Vaudreüil, his wife, of Monsieur Sebastian Francois Ange Lettormant commander general of La Marine Ordonnateur, of the said province, Monsieur Pierre de Benac, Knight of the Military Order of St. Louis, major of New Orleans, Monsieur de Membre, Captain of a Company attached to the navy of this colony, in the absence of parents and for the part of the said Demoiselle de Coulange with Chamilly, her maternal grandfather and grandmother, of Monsieur de Grandpré and Madame, (Grandpré), his spouse, her uncle and aunt, of Madame Le Saffier, also her aunt, of Monsieur Raquet, Superior Commander of this province and of Monsieur Fleurian Drocureur, general, her friends in the absence of parents have voluntarily recognized and confessed to [illegible] the agreements and the conventions of marriage which follow. It is known that the said Monsieur Monbrun and the said Demoiselle de Coulange have promised to take in the name and laws of marriage to celebrate and to solemnify their union before our mother Holy Church as soon as it can be done as it will be perceived by [unclear] the said parents.

To be done in effect by the two future spouses and the community of moveable effects and acquired immoveables pursuant to and according to the Customs of Paris.

Will not restitute past debts and newly created ones before the celebration of the future marriage but if any have been made, they will be paid and discharged by and from the effects on the part of the one from which they proceeded without the other's effects being enjoined.

The said future husband acknowledging before these present that the said Demoiselle Petit de Coulange brings to the marriage the contents of the statement signed by him, just as he recognizes this statement which is all the effects which remain coming from M. and Madame Petit de Coulange, father and mother of the said future wife, which are negroes, effects and money that the said Gaillard Chamelly, grandfather of the said future wife and her tutor will remit to the said future husband when he will judge it appropriate.

Recognizing in addition the said Monbrun, future husband that the said Gaillard Chamilly has rendered an account in the presence of Monsieur Grandpre, uncle and surrogate guardian of the said Demoiselle Coulange, future wife, of all which he has charged as tutor, approving and ratifying the said account with the articles contained therein, the contents of which form the dowry of the said future wife as of now he will have ownership in the community and the other two will remain that of the said future wife and from her lineage and line all that can fall to her by the succession of her grandfather or grandmother or otherwise.

In favor of this marriage the said future husband has endowed and endows his future wife with the sum of 10,000 livres from the settled jointure paid at one time, to have over and above the present and future effects. If the occasion should arise, this jointure will remain and will belong to her without return, in the case she has no children born of the said future marriage, and in the case of children, most of which will be theirs.

The donation will be reciprocal on behalf of the survivor for the sum of 5,000 livres which will be taken from the remaining money or moveables, linen apparel, moveables according to the inventory, which will be then done and without thought or choice and option of the survivor.

On the dissolution of the community occurring, it will be permissible for the said future wife and her children who will be born from the marriage to accept it [the community] or to renounce it, and in case of renunciation, to retake all which she will have brought to it, with all which will have fallen to her during it [the community] by succession, donation, legacy or otherwise to the said community and for which neither she nor her children will be held liable for debts charged to the said community. Yet if she had a share in them or was obliged or responsible for them, she will be relieved by the effects of her said future husband, that is why there will be a mortgage from this day.

All the above has been agreed upon and reconciled between the parties; on passing the present acts for execution of them and their attachments the said Monbrun and the said M. and Madame Chamilly stipulate for the said Demoiselle Coulange, future wife, having their domicile in this city of New Orleans and to which place they promise in addition to render and pay all costs, expenses, damages and interests which are and will be sustained according to the execution of the present acts under obligation of both. And each or their present and future effects they will [illegible] to each other by law [according] to justice, jurisdiction and constraint, which will appertain, renouncing all things to the contrary. Done and passed in New Orleans in the home of Monsieur and Madame Chamilly the year 1776, November 19 in the presence of Augustin Chantalou and Jacques Contrelle, witnesses. . . .

Wills

Will of Ann Fuller, 1794[10]

Among the most commonly used arrangements to allow married women to own and control property separately from their husbands were bequests with stipulations against the interference of husbands. In writing her will, Ann Fuller, a widow, expressly removed familial property from any control of her sister Elizabeth's husband. Her purpose was probably to give to her sister a measure of financial security and independence and to protect the family inheritance from possible business mismanagement by the husband.

I do by this my Will give devise and bequeath unto my beloved Sister Elizabeth Wife of Alexander McQueen Esquire My Wench Judy with her two Children by name Hagar and Tom with their future Issue for ever. I also will devise and bequeath to my above mentioned sister Elizabeth my Gold Watch with all and Singular my Wearing apparel, Item I give devise and bequeath to my aforementioned Sister Elizabeth That my Portion in part of a Certain house Situated in Trade Street in the City of Charleston which said House was left me and the rest of my Brothers and Sisters by our deceased Father Thomas Fuller of St. Andrews Parish Esquire to have and to hold the above bequeaths for ever, exclusive from any Right that her present or any future husband may claim thereto. A true Extract from the Will of Mrs. Ann Fuller.

CH Lining
February 4, 1794

Will of Thomas Jefferson, 1826[11]

Another device used to protect the economic interests of married women and to guard family property was the trust. Because property left to a woman might pass out of the family or fall prey to creditors, landed property was usually settled on women or left in trust as an estate during widowhood or as a life interest for daughters. To avoid passing his property on to his son-in-law, Thomas M. Randolph, Thomas Jefferson set up a caretaker trust. Through it the property that would otherwise devolve upon his son-in-law was left to his grandson, Thomas J. Randolph, and two friends in trust for Jefferson's daughter. By this circuitous scheme Jefferson's estate would vest in his daughter and her heirs.

I, Thomas Jefferson, of Monticello, in Albemarle, being of sound mind and in my ordinary state of health, make my last will and testament in manner and form as follows:

I give to my grandson Francis Eppes, son of my dear deceased daughter Mary Eppes, in fee simple, all that part of my lands at Poplar Forest lying west of the following lines, to wit: beginning at Radford's upper corner near the double branches of Bear Creek and the public road, and running thence in a straight line to the form of my private road, near the barn: thence along that private road (as it was changed in 1817), to its crossing of the main branch of North Tomahawk Creek; and from that crossing, in a direct line over the main ridge which divides the North and South Tomahawk, to the South Tomahawk, at the confluence of two branches where the old road to the Waterlick crossed it, and from that confluence up the northermost branch (which separate M'Daniels' and Perry's fields) to its source: and thence by the shortest line to my western boundary. And having, in a former correspondence with my deceased son-in-law, John W. Eppes, contemplated laying off for him, with remainder to my grandson Francis, a certain portion in the southern part of my lands in Bedford and Campbell, which I afterwards found to be generally more indifferent than I had supposed, and therefore determined to change its location for the better; now to remove all doubt, if any could arise on a purpose merely voluntary and unexecuted. I hereby declare that what I have herein given to my said grandson, Francis, is instead of, and not additional to, what I had formerly contemplated. I subject all my other property to the payment of my debts in the first place. Considering the insolvent state of the affairs of my friend and son-in-law, Thomas Mann Randolph, and that what will remain of my property will be the only resource against the want in which his family would otherwise be left, it must be his wish, as it is my duty, to guard that resource against all liability for his debts, engagements or purposes whatsoever, and to preclude the rights, powers, and authorities over it, which might result to him by operation of law, and which might, independently of his will, bring it within the power of his creditors, I do hereby devise and bequeath all the residue of my property, real and personal, in possession or in action, whether held in my own right, or in that of my dear deceased wife, according to the powers vested in me by deed of settlement for that purpose, to my grandson, Thomas J. Randolph, and my friends Nicholas P. Trist and Alexander Garrett, and their heirs, during the life of my said son-in-law, Thomas M. Randolph, to be held and administered by them, in trust, for the sole and separate use and behoof of my dear daughter, Martha Randolph, and her heirs; and aware of the nice and difficult distinction of the law in these cases, I will further explain by saying, that I understand and intend the effect of these limitations to be, that the legal estate and actual occupation shall be vested in my said trustees, and held by them in base fee, determinable on the death of my said son-in-law, and the remainder during the same time be vested in my said daughter and her heirs and of course disposable by her last will, and that at the death of my said son-in-law the particular estate of the trustees shall be determined, and the remainder in legal estate, possession, and use, become vested in my said daughter and her heirs, in absolute property forever. In consequence of the variety and indescribableness of the articles of property within the house at Monticello, and the difficulty of inventorying and appraising them separately and specifically, and its inutility, I dispense with having them inventoried and appraised; and it is my will that my executors be not held to give any security for the administration of my estate. I appoint my grandson Thomas Jefferson Randolph, my sole executor during his life, and after his death, I constitute executors my friends Nicholas P. Trist and Alexander Garrett, joining to them my daughter Martha Randolph, after the death of my said son-in-law Thomas M. Randolph. Lastly, I revoke all former wills by me heretofore made; and in witness that this is my will. I have written the whole with my own hand on two pages, and have subscribed my name to each of them this sixteenth day of March, one thousand eight hundred and twenty-six.

"Thomas Jefferson"

Will of William Sanders, 1775[12]

By common law as well as American legal practice, widows were entitled to a life interest in their husband's estate, which meant that they could not sell or significantly alter the property, but must pass it on intact to their husband's designated heirs. In order to guarantee greater economic security and autonomy for their wives, or perhaps to relieve them of the responsibility of managing a large estate, some husbands, like William Sanders of Charleston, provided a set income in lieu of the life interest, a practice which was not uncommon among large southern plantation owners.

In the Name of God Amen I Wm. Sanders of St. George's Parish Dorchester, planter being weak in body but of perfect mind and memory to dispose of my worldly goods it has pleased God to bestow on me in the following manner. . . .

1st, I desire my funeral may be conducted in the Most Simple and plain manner to be made planed of cedar and cypress and that six of my negro men be my bearers. . . .

2d, It is my Will that my just debts be paid as soon as possible and to enable my Executors the sooner to accomplish it, it is my desire that the place I now live on which I purchased of Jon [unclear] be sold as soon as they can get a good purchaser for it. . . .

3rd, I give and bequeath to my beloved wife Ann Sanders all my household furniture and what liquors I possess at the time of my death, also the four following negroes wenches Tellesaw and Dinah, & the boy Ned who now waits in the house, also a young fellow called Caesar son of Hagar—fourthly, I also give and bequeath to my beloved Wife the Sum of Two Thousand pounds Sterling to be paid her as soon as my Executors can conveniently raise so large a sum of money, but if it should be her choice to take the amount in negroes or any part, provided she take them in families and at their full value, and that the value of negroes be equal with what they are or was twelve months since, It is my desire that my Executors (with the exceptions mentioned above) shall divide the said negroes to the amount of the aforesaid legacy or any part thereof. It is my desire further that my Executors do pay to my Wife Ann Sanders the sum of one thousand pounds yearly till the legacy be paid off, which shall be in lieu of the interest on the legacy and that ... she be supplied with provisions, butter, poultry, etc. from my plantations during her widowhood. My full interest and meaning is that the two thousand pounds sterling I have bequeathed to my beloved Wife is entirely her own disposal and which is in consideration and in lieu of all dowers, jointers, etc. and every other consideration....

I do hereby disallow revoke and disannual all and every other former will signed, sealed pronounced and declared by the said William Sanders as his last Will and Testament in the presence of us on the 4th day of August 1775.

Thomas Waring
Rich Broughton
William Sanders

Dower Rights

An Act to Regulate the Descent of Real Estate, 1784[13]

Although the resort to equitable remedies materially improved the economic condition of some married women, their limited gains must be balanced against the gradual erosion of certain protective rights traditionally enjoyed by women. The most important regressive action affecting such rights was the weakening in some jurisdictions of the ancient right of dower. Although American jurists eagerly embraced those parts of the common-law tradition that suited American needs, they tended to abandon inherited doctrines that did not. Such was the case with dower rights. Because the wife's dower rights took precedence over the claims of her husband's creditors, dower could, and in some cases did, inhibit business transactions. The growth of the free-market economy in the years after independence produced a drive to remove such impediments to the land market and to commercial development. This North Carolina act, which reflects that trend, revised dower rights by declaring that if there were more than two children to inherit, the widow would, instead of receiving the traditional third, share equally with the children. Court decisions in other states produced similar results.

An act to regulate the descent of real estates, to do away entails, to make provision for widows, and to prevent frauds in the execution of last wills and testaments.

WHEREAS it will tend to promote that equality of property which is of the spirit and principle of a genuine republic, that the real estates of persons dying intestate should under a more general and equal distribution than has hitherto prevailed in this state:

And whereas the dower allotted by law in lands for widows in the present unimproved state of this country, is a very inadequate provision for the support of such widows, and it is highly just and reasonable that those who by their prudence, economy and industry, have contributed to raise up an estate to their husbands, should be entitled to share in it; Be it therefore enacted, that if any person shall die intestate, or shall make his last will and testament, and not therein make any express provision for his wife, (a) by giving and devising unto her such part or parcel of his real or personal estate, or to some other for her use, as shall be fully satisfactory to her, such widow may signify her dissent thereto, before the judges of the superior court, or in the court of the county wherein she resides, in open court, within six months after the probate of the said will, and then and in that case, she shall be entitled to dower in the following manner, to wit, one-third part of all the lands, and tenements and hereditaments, of which her husband died, seized or possessed. Provided always, That any conveyances made fraudulently to children or otherwise, with an intention to defeat the widow of the dower hereby alloted, shall be held and deemed to be void, and such widow shall be entitled to dower in such land so fraudulently conveyed, as if no conveyance had been made, which said third part shall be and enure to her own proper use, benefit and behoof, for and during the term of her natural life; in which said third part shall be comprehended the dwelling-house in which the said husband shall have been accustomed most generally to dwell next before his death, and commonly called the mansion-house, together with the offices, out-houses, buildings and other improvements thereunto belonging or appertaining. Provided always, That in case it should appear to the said judges or justices that the whole of the said dwelling-house, out-houses, offices and appurtenances, cannot be applied to the use of the wife, without manifest injustice to the children or other relations, then and in that case such widow shall be entitled to such part or portions of said dwelling-house, out-houses, offices and improvements thereunto belonging, as they shall conceive will be sufficient to afford her a decent residence, due regard being had to her rank, condition and past manner of life; which dwelling-house, out-houses, offices and improvements, or such part thereof so allotted the said widow shall be and enure to her during the term of her natural life; and furthermore, if such husband shall die leaving no child, or not more than two, then and in that case she shall be entitled to one-third part of the personal estate; but if such husband shall die leaving more than two children, then and in that case such widow shall share equally with all the children, she being entitled to a child's part.

Renunciation of Dower, 1778[14]

Still another right whose protective features were apparently weakened in the eighteenth century was the separate examination. In recognition that married women contributed significantly to the family property, the common law prohibited a husband from disposing of dowry property without the consent of his wife. To free her from the power of her husband to force her to surrender her rights, the paternalistic device of the separate examination was developed. By it a wife was required to appear privately before a judge to swear her consent to the alienation of the property, as Mary Elliott Savage's renunciation of dower shown below illustrates. Theoretically a wife could prevent the sale of any property she had brought to the marriage, in which case the separate examination could operate as a protective device. Because the process came to be treated very informally during the eighteenth century, its protective function was considerably impaired, however.

MRS. MARY ELLIOTT SAVAGE TO JOSEPH ATKINSON.
RENUN. OF DOWER

By the Honorable Thomas Bee Esquire, one of the justices of the Court of Common Pleas in the State of South Carolina. To all to whom these presents shall come be seen or made known greeting. Know you that on the seventeenth day of February in the year of Our Lord 1778 before me personally appeared Mary Elliott the wife of Thomas Savage of Charleston in the state aforesaid esquire who being by me privately and separately examined did acknowledge and declare that she did freely and voluntarily without any manner of compulsion dread or fear of from her said husband the said Thomas Savage or any other person or persons whomsoever consent to and join with her said husband in conveying and assuring by a certain indenture of release bearing date the 14th day of this instant month of February unto Joseph Atkinson of Charleston in the state aforesaid Merchant and to his heirs and assigns forever all that piece part or parcel of a town lot of Land situated lying and being near Broughton's Battery on White Point in Charleston.... Together with all and singular the houses, outhouses, and appurtenances whatsoever to the said lot or piece of land belonging or in any wise appertaining and the reversion and reversions remainder and remainders rents issues and profits thereof and of every [unclear] parcel thereof and also all the Estate Right Title Interest use Trust Dower and Thirds Possession both in Law and Equity of them the said Thomas Savage and Mary Elliott his Wife or either of them of into or out of the same and the said Mary Elliott being now before me privately and separately examined as aforesaid freely and voluntarily without any manner of compulsion dread or fear of her said husband or of any other person or persons for herself and her heirs doth remise release and forever quit claim unto the said Joseph Atkinson his heirs and assigns all and all manner of Estate Right Title Interest and Trust Dower and Thirds Possession Property claim and demand whatsoever and also all manner of Dower either in law and equity which she the said Mary Elliott now has or which she or her heirs hereafter may or of right ought to have or claim of in and to the said premises and appurtenances before mentioned and all manner of Writs of Dower and Real Actions and all Rights of Entry or Right whatsoever so as neither she the said Mary Elliott nor any other person or persons whosoever for her or in her name any manner of Action of Dower or any other real action or Writ or any other right Title or claim whatsoever of or in the said premises above mentioned or any part thereof at any time hereafter shall or may prosecute against the said Joseph Atkinson his heirs or assigns but of and from the same shall be utterly debarred and forever excluded———— In Testimony whereof I the said Thomas Bee have here unto set my hand and caused the Seal of Office to be affixed the Day and Year first above written————

PUBLIC RELATIONS

Despite its transforming effects on the private lives of most women, the American Revolution produced ambiguous results so far as their public status in the new republic was concerned. Although their unprecedented contributions to the patriot war effort proved conclusively that women were capable of political behavior, the full rights and privileges of citizenship were nowhere extended to them. Excluded from the franchise on the basis of their supposedly limited judgment in public matters, women were still barred from public office and they rarely engaged in direct political action. They frequently appeared before the courts as litigants, but they never sat on the bench, they continued to be absent from juries, and they disappeared from the courtroom as attorneys-in-fact.

Nonetheless, by exposing the contradictions between the roles women played in the war effort and in the reality of their lives, the American Revolution helped to change the way women thought about themselves and about what their role in the political culture of the new republic should be. In searching for a political context that would reconcile domesticity and politics, they developed the ideology of Republican Motherhood.

Abigail Adams to John Adams, 1776[15]

Although women remained outside the select circle of full citizenship, in the post-Revolutionary period they began to object to the law as never before, seeking recognition in the form of political rights. Many women, particularly those from the educated upper classes, began to openly engage in political discourse, which led a few of them to begin to demand political and legal rights. One of the strongest demands for political rights was made by Abigail Adams. The wife of a diplomat actively involved in the Revolution, she displayed in her correspondence with her husband John a keen understanding of politics. Despite her call for a code of laws that would "remember the ladies," she did not believe that women should express their political views publicly.

ABIGAIL ADAMS TO JOHN ADAMS, 31 MARCH 1776

Though we felicitate ourselves, we sympathize with those who are trembling least the lot of Boston should be theirs. But they cannot be in similar circumstances unless pusilanimity and cowardice should take possession of them. They have time and warning given them to see the evil and shun it—I long to hear that you have declared an independancy—and by the way in the new code of laws which I suppose it will be necessary for you to make I desire you would remember the ladies, and be more generous and favorable to them than your ancestors. Do not put such unlimited power into the hands of the husbands. Remember all men would be tyrants if they could. If particular care and attention is not paid to the ladies we are determined to foment a rebellion, and will not hold ourselves bound by any laws in which we have no voice, or representation.

That your sex are naturally tyrannical is a truth so thoroughly established as to admit of no dispute, but such of you as wish to be happy willingly give up the harsh title of master for the more tender and endearing one of friend. Why then, not put it out of the power of the vicious and the lawless to use us with cruelty and indignity with impunity. Men of sense in all ages abhor these customs which treat us only as the vassals of your sex. Regard us then as beings placed by providence under your protection and in imitation of the Supreme Being make use of that power.

JOHN ADAMS TO ABIGAIL ADAMS, 14 APRIL 1776

As to your extraordinary code of laws, I cannot but laugh. We have been told that our struggle has loosened the bands of government everywhere. That children and apprentices were disobedient—that schools and colleges were grown turbulent—that Indians slighted their guardians and Negroes grew insolent to their masters. But your letter was the first intimation that another tribe more numerous and powerful than all the rest were grown discontented.— This is rather too coarse a compliment but you are so saucy, I wont blot it out.

Depend upon it, we know better than to repeal our masculine systems. Although they are in full force, you know they are little more than theory. We dare not exert our power in its full latitude. We are obliged to go fair, and softly, and in practice you know we are the subjects. We have only the name of masters, and rather than give up this, which would completely subject us to the despotism of the petticoat, I hope General Washington, and all our brave heroes would fight. I am sure every good politician would plot, as long as he would against despotism, empire, monarchy, aristocracy, oligarchy, or ochlocracy—A fine story indeed. I begin to think the ministry as deep as they are wicked. After stirring up tories, landjobbers, trimmers, bigots, Canadians, Indians, Negroes, Hanoverians, Hessians, Russians, Irish Roman Catholics, Scotch renegades, at last they have stimulated the [blank] to demand new privileges and threaten to rebel.

ABIGAIL ADAMS TO JOHN ADAMS, MAY 7, 1776

I believe tis near ten days since I wrote you a line. I have not felt in a humor to entertain you. If I had taken up my pen perhaps some unbecoming invective might have fallen from it; the eyes of our rulers have been closed and a lethargy has seized almost every member. I fear a fatal security has taken possession of them. While the building is on flame they tremble at the expense of water to quench it, in short two months has elapsed since the evacuation of Boston, and very little has been done in that time to secure it, or the Harbor from future invasion till the people are all in a flame; and no one among us that I have heard of even mentions expense, they think universally that there has been an amazing neglect somewhere. Many have turned out as volunteers to work upon Nodles Island, and many more would go upon Nantaskit if it was once set on foot. "Tis a maxim of state that power and liberty are like heat and moisture; where they are well mixed everything prospers, where they are single, they are destructive."

A Government of more stability is much wanted in this colony, and they are ready to receive it from the hands of the Congress, and since I have begun with maxims of state I will add another viz. that a people may let a king fall, yet still remain a people, but if a king let his people slip from him, he is no longer a king. And as this is most certainly our case, why not proclaim to the world in decisive terms your own importance?

Shall we not be despised by foreign powers for hesitating so long at a word?

I cannot say that I think you very generous to the ladies, for while you are proclaiming peace and good will to men, emancipating all nations, you insist upon retaining an absolute power over wives. But you must remember that Arbitrary power is like most other things which are very hard, very liable to be broken—and notwithstanding all your wise laws and maxims we have it in our power not only to free ourselves but to subdue our masters, and without violence throw both your natural and legal authority at our feet—

"Charm by accepting, by submitting sway
Yet have our Humor most when we obey."

Richard Henry Lee to Hannah Lee Corbin, 1778[16]

Except for New Jersey, whose state constitution, adopted in 1776, unintentionally confirmed the right of property-owning widows and spinsters to vote in state elections until the election reform of 1807 again disfranchised them, the American Revolution did not affect the right of women to vote. Although the Revolutionary War had been fought to protect the right of consent to taxation, the full implications of the principle were denied to women, a fact that did not escape Hannah Lee Corbin. A contemporary of Abigail Adams and sister to two signers of the Declaration of Independence, Richard Henry Lee and Francis Lightfoot Lee, Hannah Lee Corbin not only defied social conventions by living with Richard Lingan Hall without benefit of marriage, she also became a strong advocate of women's suffrage. Her indignant letter of March 1778, complaining against male domination in law and politics, provoked this response from her brother, Richard Henry Lee, a prominent member of the Continental Congress.

My Dear Sister,   Chantilly, March 17, 1778

Distressed as my mind is and has been by a variety of attentions, I am illy able by letter to give you the satisfaction I could wish on the several subjects of your letter. Reasonable as you are and friendly to the freedom and happiness of your country, I should have no doubt giving you perfect content in a few hours' conversation. You complain that widows are not represented, and that being temporary possessors of their estates ought not to be liable to the tax. The doctrine of representation is a large subject, and it is certain that it ought to be extended as far as wisdom and policy can allow; nor do I see that either of these forbid widows having property from voting, notwithstanding it has never been the practice either here or in England. Perhaps 'twas thought rather out of character for women to press into those tumultuous assemblages of men where the business of choosing representatives is conducted. And it might also have been considered as not so necessary, seeing that the representatives themselves, as their immediate constituents, must suffer the tax imposed in exact proportion as does all other property taxed, and that, therefore, it could not be supposed that taxes would be laid where the public good did not demand it. This, then, is the widow's security as well as that of the never married women, who have lands in their own right, for both of whom I have the highest respect, and would at any time give my consent to establish their right of voting. I am persuaded that it would not give them greater security, nor alter the mode of taxation you complain of; because the tax idea does not go to the consideration of perpetual property, but is accommodated to the high prices given for the annual profits. Thus no more than ½ per cent is laid on the assessed value, although produce sells now 3 and 400 per cent above what it formerly did. Tobacco sold 5 or 6 years ago for 15s and 2d—now 'tis 50 and 55. A very considerable part of the property I hold is, like yours, temporary for my life only; yet I see the propriety of paying my proportion of the tax laid for the protection of property so long as that property remains in my possession and I derive use and profit from it. When we complained of British taxation we did so with much reason, and there is great difference between our case and that of the unrepresented in this country. The English Parliament not their representatives would pay a farthing of the tax they imposed on us but quite otherwise. Their property would have been exonerated in exact proportion to the burthens they laid on ours. Oppressions, therefore, without end and taxes without reason or public necessity would have been our fate had we submitted to British usurpation. For my part I had much rather leave my children free than in possession of great nominal wealth, which would infallibly have been the case with all American possessions had our property been subject to the arbitrary taxation of a British Parliament. With respect to Mr. Fauntleroy, if he spoke as you say, it is a very good reason why he ought not to be assessor. But if he should be the law has wisely provided a remedy against the mistakes or the injustice of assessors by giving the injured party appeal to the commissioners of the tax, which commissioners are annually chosen by the freeholders and housekeepers, and in the choice of whom you have as legal a right to vote as any other person. I believe there is no instance in our new government of any unnecessary placemen, and I know the rule is to make their salaries moderate as possible, and even these moderate salaries are to pay tax. But should Great Britain gain her point, where we have one placeman we should have a thousand and pay pounds where we pay pence; nor should we dare to murmur under pain of military execution. This, with the other horrid concomitants of slavery, may well persuade the American to lose blood and pay taxes also rather than submit to them.

My extensive engagements have prevented from adverting to yours and Dr. Hall's subscription for Lord Camden's pictures not having been refunded, as the rest have long since been, but the money is ready for your call.

   I am, My dear Sister,
     Most sincerely and affectionately yours.

Judith Sargent Murray, "On the Equality of the Sexes," 1790[17]

Women's experience in the war as petitioners and fundraisers, and their crucial role in the success of the economic boycott, helped to develop in them a new awareness of their own political capacities, which some historians see as the intellectual antecedent of the suffrage movement of the nineteenth century. In the years immediately following the Revolution, women succeeded in defining for themselves a new political role as republican mothers. Convinced that education for women must precede their political involvement, women like Judith Sargent Murray, one of the principal architects of the new female ideology, vigorously demanded the creation of educational opportunities for women as the key to their advancement in all areas. By developing the ideology of the republican mother, which stressed the central role of mothers in shaping the characters of their sons and husbands for responsible independence, the role of the mother was transformed, with far-reaching consequences for the women's movement of the nineteenth century.

Is it upon mature consideration we adopt the idea, that nature is thus partial in her distributions? Is it indeed a fact that she hath yielded to one half of the human species so unquestionable a mental superiority? I know that to both sexes elevated understandings, and the reverse, are common. But, suffer me to ask; in what the minds of females are so notoriously deficient, or unequal. May not the intellectual powers be ranged under their four heads—imagination, reason, memory and judgement. The province of imagination has long since been surrendered up to us, and we have been crowned undoubted sovereigns of the regions of fancy. Invention is perhaps the most arduous effort of the mind; this branch of imagination has been particularly ceded to us, and we have been time out of mind invested with that creative faculty. Observe the variety of fashions (here I bar the contemptuous smile) which distinguish and adorn the female world; how continually are they changing, insomuch that they almost render the whole man's assertion problematical, and we are ready to say, *there is something new under the sun.* Now, what a playfulness, what an exuberance of fancy, what strength of inventive imagination, does this continual variation discover? Again, it has been observed, that if the turpitude of the conduct of our sex, has been ever so enormous so extremely ready are we that the very first thought presents us with an apology so plausible, as to produce our actions even in an amiable light. Another instance of our creative powers, is our talent for slander; how ingenious are we at inventive scandal? What a formidable story can we in a moment fabricate merely from the force of a prolific imagination? How many reputations, in the fertile brain of a female, have been utterly despoiled? How industrious are we at improving a hint? Suspicion how easily do we convert into conviction, and conviction, embellished by the power of eloquence, stalks abroad to the surprise and confusion of unsuspecting innocence. Perhaps it will be asked if I furnish these facts as instances of excellency in our sex. Certainly not; but as proofs of a creative faculty, of a lively imagination. Assuredly great activity of mind is thereby discovered, and was this activity properly directed, what beneficial effects would follow. Is the needle and kitchen sufficient to employ the operations of a soul thus organized? I should conceive not. Nay, it is a truth that those very departments leave the intelligent principle vacant, and at liberty for speculation. Are we deficient in reason? We can only reason from what we know, and if opportunity of acquiring knowledge has been denied us, the inferiority of our sex cannot fairly be deduced from thence. Memory, I believe, will be allowed us in common, since every one's experience must testify, that a loquacious old woman is as frequently met with, as a communicative old man; their subjects are alike drawn from the fund of other times, and the transactions of their youth, or of maturer life, entertain, or perhaps fatigue you, in the evening of their lives. "But our judgment is not so strong—we do not distinguish so well." Yet it may be questioned, from what does this superiority, in this discriminating faculty of the soul, proceed. May we not trace its source in the difference of education, and continued advantages? Will it be said that the judgment of a male of two years old, is more sage than that of a female's of the same age? I believe the reverse is generally observed to be true. But from that period what partiality! How is the one exalted and the other depressed, by the contrary modes of education which are adopted! The one is taught to aspire, and the other is early confined and limited. As their years increase, the sister must be wholly domesticated, while the brother is led by the hand through all the flowery paths of science. Grant that their minds are by nature equal, yet who shall wonder at the *apparent* superiority, if indeed custom becomes *second nature*; no if it takes the place of nature, and that it does the experience of each day will evince. At length arrived at womanhood, the uncultivated fair one feels a void, which the employments allotted her are by no means capable of filling. What can she do? To books, she may not apply; or if she does, to *those only of the novel kind* lest she merit the appellation of a *learned lady*; and what ideas have been affixed to this term, the observation of many can testify. Fashion, scandal and sometimes what is still more reprehensible, are then called in to her relief; and who can say to what lengths the liberties she takes may proceed. Meantime she herself is most unhappy; she feels the want of a cultivated mind. Is she single, she in vain seeks to fill up time from sexual employments or amusements. Is she united to a person whose soul nature made equal to her own, education has set him so far above her, that in those entertainments which are productive of such rational felicity, she is not qualified to accompany him. She experiences a mortifying consciousness of inferiority, which embitters every enjoyment. Does the person to whom her adverse fate has consigned her, possess a mind incapable of improvement, she is equally wretched, in being so closely connected with an individual whom she cannot but despise. Now, was she permitted the same instructors as her brother, (with an eye however to their particular departments) for the employment of a rational mind an ample field would be opened. In astronomy she might catch a glimpse of the immensity of the Deity, and thence she would form amazing conceptions of the august and supreme Intelligence. In geography she would admire Jehova in the midst of his benevolence; thus adapting this globe to the various wants and amusements of its inhabitants. In natural philosophy she would adore the infinite majesty of heaven, clothed in condescension; and as she traversed the reptile world, she would hail the goodness of a creating God. A mind, thus filled, would have little room for the trifles with which our sex are, with too much justice, accused of amusing themselves, and they would thus be rendered fit companions for those, who should one day wear them as their crown. Fashions, in their variety, would then give place to conjectures, which might perhaps conduce to the improvement of the literary world; and there would be no leisure for slander or detraction. Reputation would not then be blasted, but serious speculations would occupy the lively imaginations of the sex. Unnecessary visits would be precluded, and that custom would only be indulged by way of relaxation, or to answer the demands of consanguinity and friendship. Females would become discreet, their judgments would be invigorated, and their partners for life being circumspectly chosen, an unhappy Hyman would then be as rare, as is now the reverse.

Will it be urged that those acquirements would supersede our domestic duties, I answer that every requisite in female economy is easily attained; and, with truth I can add, that when once attained, they require no further *mental attention*. No, while we are pursuing the needle, or the superintendency of the family, I repeat, that our minds are at full liberty for reflection; that imagination early laid, our ideas will then be worthy of rational beings. If we were industrious we might easily find time for such an indulgence, the hours allotted for conversation would at least become more refined and rational. Should it still be vociferated, "Your domestic employments are sufficient"—I would calmly ask, is it reasonable, that a candidate for immortality, for the joys of heaven, an intelligent being, who is to spend an eternity in contemplating the works of Deity, should at present be so degraded, as to be allowed no other ideas, than those which are suggested by the mechanism of a pudding, or the sewing of the seams of a garment? Pity that all such censurers of female improvement do not go one step further, and deny their future existence; to be consistent they surely ought.

Yes, you lordly, you haughty sex, our souls are by nature *equal* to yours; the same breath of God animates, enlivens, and invigorates us; and that we are not fallen lower than yourselves, let those witness who have greatly towered above the various discouragements by which they have been so heavily oppressed; and though I am unacquainted with the list of celebrated characters on either side, yet from the observations I have made in the contracted circle in which I have moved, I dare confidently believe, that from the commencement of time to the present day, there has been as many females, as males, who, by the *mere force of natural powers*, have merited the crown of applause; who *thus unassisted*, have seized the wreath of fame. I know there are who assert, that as the animal powers of the one sex are superior, of course their mental faculties also must be stronger; thus attributing strength of mind to the transient organization of this earth born tenement. But if this reasoning is just, man must be content to yield the palm to many of the brute creation, since by not a few of his brethren of the field, he is far surpassed in bodily strength. Moreover, was this argument admitted, it would prove too much, for ocular demonstration evinceth, that there are many robust masculine ladies, and effeminate gentlemen. Yet I fancy that Mr. Pope, though clogged with an enervated body, and distinguished by a diminutive stature, could nevertheless lay claim to greatness of soul; and perhaps there are many other instances which might be adduced to combat so unphilosophical an opinion. Do we not often see, that when the clay built tabernacle is well nigh dissolved, when it is just ready to mingle with the parent soil, the immortal inhabitant aspires to, and even attains heights the most sublime, and which were before wholly unexplored. Besides, were we to grant that animal strength proved anything, taking into consideration the accustomed impartiality of nature, we should be induced to imagine, that she had invested the female mind with superior strength as an equivalent for the bodily powers of man. But waving this however palpable advantage, for *equality* only, we wish to contend.

CONSTANTIA

NOTES

1. Eliza Wilkinson, 1781, South Caroliniana Library, University of South Carolina, Columbia, South Carolina.

2. M. Fournel, *Traité de L'Adultere*, 2d ed. (Paris, 1783).

3. J. T. Mitchell and Henry Flanders, eds. *Statutes at Large of Pennsylvania from 1682 to 1801*, 17 vols. (Harrisburg, 1896–1915), XI, pp. 174–75.

4. Petitions to the General Assembly, 1802, No. 15, South Carolina State Archives, Columbia, South Carolina. Reprinted with permission of the South Carolina State Archives.

5. *Reports of Cases Adjudged in the Superior Court and in the Supreme Court of Errors, in the State of Connecticut*, 2 vols. (Hartford, 1802), II, pp. 461–62.

6. New York (State) Supreme Court, *Reports of Cases Argued and Determined in the Supreme Court of Judicature. William Johnson Reports*, 17 (1819), pp. 89–92.

7. Essex Institute, *Essex Institute Historical Collection* (Salem, Massachusetts, 1859), 81, pp. 385–87.

8. *Virginia Magazine of History and Biography* 4 (1897), pp. 64–66.

9. Kuntz Collection, French Colonial Period, 1746/11/19, Howard Tilton Library, Tulane University, New Orleans, Louisiana.

10. De Saussure Family Papers, 1740–1930, MS. 11 121/125, South Carolina Historical Society, Charleston, S.C.

11. Virgil McClure Harris, ed., *Ancient, Curious and Famous Wills* (London, 1912), pp. 397–99.

12. Broughton Family Papers, MS. 11 98/8, South Carolina Historical Society, Charleston, S.C.

13. Henry Potter et. al., eds., *Laws of the State of North Carolina* (Raleigh, 1821), I, pp. 465–72.

14. Renunciation of Dower, vol. 1775–1787, pp. 104–5, South Carolina State Archives, Columbia, S.C.

15. L. H. Butterfield et. al., eds., *The Book of Abigail and John. Selected Letters of the Adams Family 1762–1784* (Cambridge, Mass., 1975), pp. 121, 123, 126–27. Reprinted by permission of Harvard University Press.

16. James Curtis Ballagh, ed., *The Letters of Richard Henry Lee*, 2 vols. (New York, 1911–1914), vol. I, pp. 392–94.

17. Judith Sargent Murray, "On the Equality of the Sexes," *The Massachusetts Magazine* (March 1790): 132–35 and (April 1790): 223–26.

BIBLIOGRAPHY

Bloomfield, Maxwell. *American Lawyers in a Changing Society, 1776–1876.* Cambridge, Mass., 1976.

Botein, Stephen. "The Legal Profession in Colonial North America." In *Lawyers in Early Modern Europe and America*, Wilfred Prest, ed. London, 1981, 129–46.

Censer, Jane Turner. " 'Smiling Through Her Tears': Antebellum Southern Women and Divorce." *American Journal of Legal History* 25, (1981):24–47.

Cohen, Henry S. "Connecticut's Divorce Mechanism, 1636–1969." *American Journal of Legal History* 14, (1970):35–54.

Cott, Nancy F. "Divorce and the Changing Status of Women in Eighteenth-Century Massachusetts." *William and Mary Quarterly*, 3d ser., 33 (1976):586–614.

———. "Eighteenth-Century Family and Social Life Revealed in Massachusetts Divorce Records." *Journal of Social History* X (1976):20–43.

Gundersen, Joan R. and Gwen Victor Gampel. "Married Women's Legal Status in Eighteenth-Century New York and Virginia." *William and Mary Quarterly*, 3d ser., 39 (1982):114–34.

Horwitz, Morton J. *The Transformation of American Law, 1780–1860.* Cambridge, Mass., 1977.

Murrin, John M. "The Legal Transformation: The Bench and Bar of Eighteenth-Century Massachusetts." In Stanley N. Katz, ed., *Colonial America: Essays in Politics and Social Development.* Boston, 1971, 415–49.

Nelson, William E. *Americanization of the Common Law: The Impact of Legal Change in Massachusetts Society, 1760–1830.* Cambridge, Mass., 1975.

Reid, John. *"In a Defiant Stance": The Conditions of Law in Massachusetts Bay, the Irish Comparison, and the Coming of the American Revolution.* University Park, Pa., 1977.

Salmon, Marylynn. "Women of Property in South Carolina: The Evidence from Marriage Settlements, 1730–1830." *William and Mary Quarterly*, 3d ser., 39 (1982):655–85.

Zainaldin, Jamil S. "The Emergence of a Modern Family Law: Child Custody, Adoption, and the Courts, 1796–1851," *Northwestern University Law Review* 73 (1978–1979):1038–89.

SUGGESTED READINGS

Axtell, James. *School Upon a Hill: Education and Society in Colonial New England.* New Haven, 1974.

——, ed. *The Indian Peoples of Eastern America: A Documentary History of the Sexes.* New York, 1981.

Battis, Emory. *Saints and Sectaries: Anne Hutchinson and The Antinomian Controversy in the Massachusetts Bay Colony.* Williamsburg, Va., 1962.

Baxandall, Rosalyn, Linda Gordon and Susan Reverby, eds. *America's Working Women: A Documentary History, 1600 to the Present.* New York, 1976.

Berkin, Carol R. and Mary Beth Norton, eds. *Women of America: A History.* Boston, 1979.

Billias, George A., ed. *Law and Authority in Colonial Massachusetts.* Barre, Mass., 1965.

Botein, Stephen. "The Legal Profession in Colonial North America." In Wilfred Prest, ed., *Lawyers in Early Modern Europe and America.* London, 1981, 129–46.

——. *Early American Law and Society.* New York, 1983.

Boyer, Paul and Stephen Nissenbaum. *Salem Possessed: The Social Origins of Witchcraft.* Cambridge, Mass., 1974.

Carr, Lois Green and Lorena S. Walsh. "The Planter's Wife: The Experience of White Women in Seventeenth-Century Maryland," *William and Mary Quarterly,* 3d. ser., 34 (1977):542–71.

Censer, Jane Turner. " 'Smiling through Her Tears': Antebellum Southern Women and Divorce." *American Journal of Legal History* 25 (1981):24–47.

Clark, Alice. *The Working Life of Women in the Seventeenth Century.* London, 1968.

Cohen, Henry S. "Connecticut's Divorce Mechanism, 1636–1969." *American Journal of Legal History* 14 (1970):35–54.

Cott, Nancy F. "Divorce and the Changing Status of Women in Eighteenth-Century Massachusetts." *William and Mary Quarterly,* 3d. ser., 33 (1976):586–614.

———. "Eighteenth-Century Family and Social Life Revealed in Massachusetts Divorce Records." *Journal of Social History* 10 (1976):20–43.

———. *The Bonds of Womanhood: "Woman's Sphere" in New England, 1780–
1835*. New Haven, 1977.

Demos, John. *A Little Commonwealth: Family Life in Plymouth Colony*. New
York, 1970.

DePauw, Linda Grant. *Founding Mothers*. Boston, 1975.

Dexter, Elisabeth A. *Colonial Women of Affairs: Women in Business and
Professions in America Before 1776*. Boston, 1931.

———. *Career Women of America, 1776–1840*. Tracestown, N.H., 1950.

Donegan, Jane B. *Women and Men Midwives: Medicine, Morality, and Misogyny
in Early America*. Westport, Conn., 1978.

Douglas, Anne. *The Feminization of American Culture*. New York, 1977.

Dublin, Thomas. *Women at Work: The Transformation of Work and Community
in Lowell, Massachusetts, 1826–1869*. New York, 1979.

Dunn, Mary Maples. "Saints and Sisters: Congregational and Quaker Women
in the Early Colonial Period." *American Quarterly* 30 (Winter, 1978): 582–
601.

———. "Women of Light." In Carol R. Berkin and Mary Beth Norton, eds.,
Women of America: A History. Boston, 1979, 114–36.

Erikson, Kai. *Wayward Puritans: A Study in the Sociology of Deviance*. New
York, 1966.

Flaherty, David H., ed. *Essays in the History of Early American Law*. Chapel
Hill, N.C., 1969.

———. "Law and the Enforcement of Morals in Early America." *Perspectives
in American History* 5 (1971):201–53.

Flexner, Eleanor. *Century of Struggle: The Woman's Rights Movement in the
United States*. Cambridge, Mass., 1959.

Friedman, Jean E. and William O. Shade, eds. *Our American Sisters: Women
in American Life and Thought*. Lexington, Mass., 1982.

Friedman, Lawrence M. *A History of American Law*. New York, 1973.

Frost, William J. *The Quaker Family in Colonial America: A Portrait of the
Society of Friends*. New York, 1973.

Gordon, Michael, ed. *The American Family in Social-Historical Perspective*.
New York, 1978.

Greven, Philip. *Four Generations: Population, Land, and Family in Colonial
Andover, Massachusetts*. Ithaca, N.Y., 1970.

———. *The Protestant Temperament: Patterns of Child-Rearing, Religious Experience and the Self in Early America*. New York, 1970.

Gundersen, Joan R. and Gwen Victor Gampel, "Married Women's Legal Status
in Eighteenth-Century New York and Virginia," *William and Mary Quarterly*, 3d ser., 39 (1982):114–34.

Gutman, Herbert G. *The Black Family in Slavery and Freedom, 1750–1925*.
New York, 1978.

Haskins, George L. *Law and Authority in Early Massachusetts: A Study in
Transition and Design*. New York, 1960.

Hemphill, C. Dallett. "Women in Court: Sex-Role Differentiation in Salem,

Massachusetts, 1636–1683." *William and Mary Quarterly*, 3d. ser., 39 (1982):164–75.

Horwitz, Morton J. *The Transformation of American Law, 1780–1860*. Cambridge, Mass., 1977.

Jeffries, Julia Roy. *Frontier Women: The Transmississippi West, 1840–1880*. New York, 1979.

Jones, Ann. *Women Who Kill*. New York, 1980.

Jordan, Winthrop D. "Familial Politics: Thomas Paine and the Killing of the King." *Journal of American History* 60 (1973):294–308.

Kerber, Linda. "Daughters of Columbia: Educating Women for the Republic, 1787–1805." In Stanley Elkins and Erick McKitrick, eds., *The Hofstadter Aegis: A Memorial*. New York, 1974, 36–59.

————. *Women of the Republic: Intellect and Ideology in Revolutionary America*. Chapel Hill, N.C., 1980.

Kessler-Harris, Alice. *Out to Work: A History of Wage-Earning Women in the United States*. Oxford, 1982.

Keyssar, Alexander. "Widowhood in Eighteenth-Century Massachusetts." In *Perspectives in American History* 8 (1974):83–119.

Koehler, Lyle. *A Search for Power: The "Weaker Sex" in Seventeenth-Century New England*. Urbana, Chicago, London, 1980.

————. "The Case of the American Jezebels: Anne Hutchinson and Female Agitation during the Years of the Antinomian Turmoil, 1636–1640." In Linda K. Kerber and Jane deHart Mathews, eds., *Women's America: Refocusing the Past*. New York, 1982, 36–50.

Kolmer, Sr. Elizabeth, A.S.D. "Catholic Women Religious and Women's History: A Survey of the Literature." *American Quarterly* 30 (Winter, 1978):639–51.

Kulikoff, Allan. "A 'Prolifick People': Black Population in the Chesapeake Colonies, 1700–1790." *Southern Studies* 16 (1977):391–414.

————. "The Origins of Afro-American Society in Tidewater Maryland and Virginia, 1700–1790." *William and Mary Quarterly*, 3d. ser., 35 (1978):226–59.

Lerner, Gerda, ed. *The Female Experience: An American Documentary*. Indianapolis, 1977.

————. *The Majority Finds Its Past: Placing Women in History*. New York, 1979.

————. "The Lady and the Mill Girl: Changes in the Status of Women in the Age of Jackson." In Jean E. Friedman and William G. Shade, eds., *Our American Sisters: Women in American Life and Thought*. Lexington, Mass., 1982, 183–95.

Melder, Keith. *The Beginnings of Sisterhood: The American Woman's Rights Movement, 1800–1850*. New York, 1977.

Menard, Russell. *Virginians at Home: Family Life in the Eighteenth Century*. Williamsburg, Va., 1952.

————. "The Maryland Slave Population, 1658–1730: A Demographic Profile of Blacks in Four Counties." *William and Mary Quarterly*, 3d. ser., 32 (1975):29–54.

Morgan, Edmund S. *The Puritan Family: Religion and Domestic Relations in Seventeenth-Century New England*. Rev. ed. New York, 1966.

Morris, Richard B. *Studies in the History of American Law*. Philadelphia, 1959.

Murrin, John M. "The Legal Transformation: The Bench and Bar of Eighteenth-Century Massachusetts." In Stanley Katz, ed., *Colonial America: Essays in Politics and Social Development*. Boston, 1971, 540–71.

Nelson, William E. *Americanization of the Common Law: The Impact of Legal Change in Massachusetts Society, 1760–1830*. Cambridge, Mass., 1975.

Norton, Mary Beth. "Eighteenth-Century Women in Peace and War: The Case of the Loyalists." In Nancy F. Cott and Elizabeth Pleck, eds., *A Heritage of Her Own: Toward a New Social History of Women*. New York, 1979, 136–51.

———. *Liberty's Daughters: The Revolutionary Experience of American Women, 1750–1800*. Boston, 1980.

Reid, John. *"In a Defiant Stance": The Conditions of Law in Massachusetts Bay, the Irish Comparison, and the Coming of the American Revolution*. University Park, Pa., 1977.

Reinier, Jacquelyn S. "Rearing the Republican Child: Attitudes and Practices in Post-Revolutionary Philadelphia." *William and Mary Quarterly*, 3d. ser., 39 (1982):150–63.

Rutman, Darrett B. and Anita H. Rutman. "Of Agues and Fevers: Malaria in the Early Chesapeake." *William and Mary Quarterly*, 3d. ser., 33 (1976):31–60.

———. " 'Now-Wives and Sons-in-Law': Parental Death in a Seventeenth-Century Virginia County." In Thad W. Tate and David L. Ammerman, eds., *The Chesapeake in the Seventeenth Century: Essays on Anglo-American Society*. Chapel Hill, N.C., 1979, 153–79.

Ryan, Mary P. *Womanhood in America from Colonial Times to the Present*. New York, 1975.

———. "A Women's Awakening: Evangelical Religion and the Families of Utica, N.Y." *American Quarterly* 30 (Winter, 1978):602–23.

Salmon, Marylynn. "Equality or Submersion? Feme Covert Status in Early Pennsylvania." In Carol R. Berkin and Mary Beth Norton, eds., *Women of America: A History*. Boston, 1979, 92–111.

Sirmans, M. Eugene. "The Legal Status of the Slave in South Carolina, 1670–1740." *Journal of Southern History* 28 (1962):462–73.

Smith, Daniel B. *Inside the Great House: Family Life in the Eighteenth-Century Chesapeake*. Ithaca, N.Y., 1980.

Smith, Daniel Scott and Michael Hindus. "Premarital Pregnancy in America, 1640–1871: An Overview and Interpretation." *Journal of Interdisciplinary History* V (Spring, 1975):537–70.

Smith, Page. *Daughters of the Promised Land*. Boston and Toronto, 1970.

Spruill, Julia Cherry. *Women's Life and Work in the Southern Colonies*. Chapel Hill, N.C., 1938.

Tate, Thad and David Ammerman, eds. *The Chesapeake in the Seventeenth Century: Essays on Anglo-American Society*. Chapel Hill, N.C., 1970.

Ulrich, Laurel Thatcher. *Good Wives: Images and Reality in the Lives of Women in Northern New England, 1650–1750.* New York, 1982.

Wells, Robert V. "Demographic Change and the Life Cycle of American Families." *Journal of Interdisciplinary History* 2 (1971):273–82.

———. "Family Size and Fertility Control in Eighteenth-Century America: A Study of Quaker Families." *Population Studies* 25 (1971):73–82.

Welter, Barbara. "The Feminization of American Religion, 1800–1860." In William O'Neill, ed., *Insights and Parallels: Problems and Issues in American Social History.* Minneapolis, 1973, 305–55.

———. "She Hath Done What She Could: Protestant Women's Missionary Careers in Nineteenth-Century America." *American Quarterly* 30 (Winter, 1978):624–38.

Wilson, Joan Hoff. "The Illusion of Change: Women in the American Revolution." In Alfred F. Young, ed., *The American Revolution: Explorations in the History of American Radicalism.* DeKalb, Ill., 1976, 383–445.

Wolf, Stephanie Grauman. *Urban Village: Population, Community, and Family Structure in Germantown, Pennsylvania, 1683–1800.* Princeton, N.J., 1976.

Wolloch, Nancy. *Women and the American Experience.* New York, 1984.

Zainaldin, Jamil S. "The Emergence of Modern Family Law: Child Custody, Adoption, and the Courts, 1796–1851." *Northwestern University Law Review* 73 (1978–1979):1038–89.

INDEX

About the Authors

SYLVIA R. FREY, Professor of History, Tulane University, is author of *The British Soldier in America: A Social History of Military Life in the Revolutionary Period.*

MARIAN J. MORTON, Professor of History, John Carroll University, is author of *The Terrors of Ideological Politics: Liberal Historians in a Conservative Mood.* Her most recent articles were published in the *Journal of Urban History* and *Ohio History.*